Murder by Numbers

The 100 Most Prolific

Serial Killers Worldwide

Robert Keller

Please Leave Your Review of This Book At
http://bit.ly/kellerbooks

ISBN-13: 978-1535212595
ISBN-10: 1535212594

© 2016 by Robert Keller

robertkellerauthor.com

Table of Contents

The 100 Most Prolific Serial Killers Worldwide

Depending on which definition you read, a serial killer is someone who commits at least two (some say three) murders, in separate incidents, with a cooling off period in between.

Some killers, of course, go way beyond that, evading capture long enough to amass quite staggering victim counts. This volume documents 100 such cases. Like Dr. Harold Shipman, convicted of 15 murders but connected to at least 250; or Luis Garavito, suspected of butchering a barely believable 400 victims; or Javed Iqbal, slayer of 100 young boys over a period of just five months.

And they are by no means the only ones. Further down the list you'll find Ahmad Suradji, an Indonesian "witchdoctor" who slaughtered at least 40 women in an effort to increase his magical powers; David Simelane, a horrific rape slayer who terrorized the tiny kingdom of Swaziland, brutally strangling as many as 45 women; Irina Gaidamachuk, a unique female serial killer who bludgeoned 18 elderly victims to death to fund her boozing binges; Zhang Yongming, a gruesome Chinese cannibal who kept a jarful of human eyeballs in his home. The list goes on.

America has, of course, birthed more serial killers than any other nation on earth. So it is no surprise that 43 of the 100 cases listed here are from the United States. These include infamous names like Bundy, Gacy, and Dahmer, as well as lesser-known psychopaths like Ronald Dominique, Anthony Sowell, and Vaughn Greenwood. Elsewhere, there are cases from 27 different nations, proving that serial murder is truly a global phenomenon.

This is a book about killers. But lest we forget, the victim numbers beside each entry are not just numbers. They represent real people. People whose lives were cruelly snatched away in the most horrific fashion by the monsters listed here. The intention of this volume is not to celebrate the nefarious deeds of these reprobates but rather to grasp the magnitude of their evil.

100. Anthony Sowell

Country: United States

Confirmed Victims: 11

Suspected Victims: 11+

Anthony Sowell was born in Cleveland, Ohio, on August 19, 1959. His father having departed the scene before his birth, he was raised by his mother, a strict disciplinarian who often meted out beatings with a length of electrical cord. Anthony however, seemed unaffected by his dysfunctional childhood. Neighbors remember him as a respectful, if introverted, boy.

At the end of 1977, Sowell dropped out of school to join the Marines. He'd spend eight years in the military, serving a spell in Japan and marrying a fellow soldier, Kim Yvette Lawson. The marriage eventually fell apart in 1985 due to Sowell's drinking. That same year, he left the Corps and moved back to East Cleveland.

But the neighborhood he returned to was very different to the one he'd grown up in. Once it had been middle-class. Now, it was plagued by crack addicts, drug dealers, petty criminals, and prostitutes. And Sowell was soon contributing to the neighborhood's sky-high crime rate, acquiring a string of arrests for disorderly conduct, DUI, public drunkenness, and possession of narcotics.

It was also during this time that the strangled bodies of young women began turning up in East Cleveland, three of them in the space of just under a year. Sowell was a suspect, but the police had no evidence to link him to the crimes.

They could, however, connect Sowell to the rape of a 21-year-old woman. Indicted on that charge, Sowell skipped out on bail and went on the run. He reappeared months later to commit a near identical crime, raping his victim orally, vaginally and anally. Having finished the assault, Sowell passed out, and the woman escaped. When she returned with the police, he was still asleep.

Sowell faced trial for both this rape and the one he had run out on, eventually entering a guilty plea and earning a 15-year sentence. Despite good behavior on the inside, he'd serve every year of that time.

Emerging from prison in June 2005, the 45-year-old Sowell appeared to be a changed man. He rented a room at 12205 Imperial Avenue, got a job as a rubber-molder at Custom Rubber Corp, and was apparently clean and sober. He also started helping the crack-addicted prostitutes of the area. At least four women would later testify that he had provided them with shelter and protection.

It was also around this time that Sowell began dating Lori Frazier, a self-confessed crack addict who was the niece of Cleveland mayor, Frank Jackson. Frazier moved into Sowell's Imperial Avenue home and the two had a steady relationship from 2005 until 2007.

But then things started to go wrong in Sowell's life. First, he was fired from his job. Then Frazier ended their relationship, leaving him devastated. Not long after, women began to disappear from East Cleveland.

In May 2007, a woman named Crystal Dozier went missing. Twelve months later, Tishana Culver, a 31-year-old beautician who lived a few blocks from Sowell, disappeared. Twenty-five-year-old Leshanda Long vanished in August 2008. In October of that year, Michelle Mason, a 45-year-old who lived nearby on East 121st Street, went missing. Her family put up flyers asking for information, but no one came forward, certainly not Anthony Sowell, who knew exactly where Michelle was.

Tonia Carmichael, 52, disappeared in the fall of 2008, her car later found abandoned near East 115th Street. April 2009 brought two disappearances. First, mother-of-three Nancy Cobbs, then Amelda Hunter, 47, a regular visitor to Sowell's Imperial Avenue home. In June, Telacia Fortson, 31, and Janice Webb, 48, were gone. Kim Yvette Smith, a 44-year-old singer who had worked with Gerald

Levert, vanished in September 2009. Like most of the other victims, she was a drug addict.

The police were baffled by this spate of disappearances, but it was not as though they were without clues. Sowell had in fact been brought to their attention on several occasions. In December 2008, a woman named Gladys Wade claimed that he'd raped her and tried to kill her. Sowell said that the sex had been consensual and that he'd only beaten Wade after she tried to rob him. The police declined to take the matter further.

In September 2009, Fawcett Bess, a local restaurant owner, saw Sowell standing naked in the bushes bordering his house, beating a woman who was also naked. Bess called 911 but the police didn't arrive until hours later. When they did, they didn't even bother questioning Sowell.

Later that month, on September 22, Sowell dragged a woman into his house and choked her with an extension cord, before raping her. The woman later persuaded him to let her go and went directly to the police. It took them 36 days to follow up on the complaint. During that time, a neighbor saw a naked woman jump from a second floor window at Sowell's house.

On October 29, police officers eventually arrived at the Imperial Avenue house to question Sowell about the rape. Finding no one at home, they left, returning a few hours later. When knocking at the door again brought no response, they entered the residence.

The first thing that struck them was the stench. Almost immediately, they found its source, the decomposing corpses of two women lying on the floor in plain view. The officers immediately stepped away and called in a crime scene unit. Soon the Imperial Avenue residence was crawling with forensics officers.

The following day, while the police continued their search for Anthony Sowell, three more bodies were uncovered. By the time Sowell was taken into custody, the remains of ten women had been discovered in his house.

Anthony Sowell went on trial in June 2011 and was convicted on 82 charges including aggravated murder, kidnapping, and abuse of a corpse. Judge Dick Ambrose pronounced sentence of death on August 12.

Sowell currently resides on death row at Chillicothe Correctional Institution.

99. Clifford Olson

Country: Canada

Confirmed Victims: 11

Suspected Victims: 11+

Clifford Robert Olson was born on New Year's Day 1940, the eldest of Clifford and Leona Olson's four children. He grew up in Vancouver and Richmond, and was an intelligent boy, although he failed to apply himself to his studies, eventually quitting school in the eighth grade and falling straight into a life of crime.

Sentenced to his first jail term in July 1957, Olson was in and out of prison over the next 24 years, on a catalog of offenses ranging from forgery, through breaking and entering, to sexual assault. He escaped from prison on seven occasions.

After being released from yet another jail term in January 1980, Olson hooked up with divorcee Joan Hale, who he'd later marry. The union would produce a son, Stephen, in April 1981. By that time Olson was already engaged in a horrendous killing spree.

The first murder attributed to this callous killer occurred on November 19, 1980, when 12-year-old Christine Weller was abducted from her home in Richmond, British Columbia. Her body turned up over a month later, on Christmas Day. She'd suffered 10 deep stab wounds to her chest and abdomen, including wounds that had sliced through her heart and liver.

Less than four months later, on April 15, 1981, 13-year-old Colleen Daignault was snatched off a street in South Surrey. Olson drove her to a remote area where he beat her to death with a hammer. Less than a week later, he lured Daryn Johnsrude from a shopping mall in New Westminster and drove him to Deroche. The 16-year-old was sodomized and then bludgeoned repeatedly with a hammer.

The disappearance of three children from the same general area in such a short space of time caused alarm. Yet the police were unperturbed, insisting that the youngsters had run away from home.

They were still sticking to that line when Sandra Lynn Wolfsteiner, 16, went missing on May 19, 1981. Olson had picked Sandra up from a bus stop in Surrey and driven to a remote area near Chilliwack Lake. When Sandra's body was eventually found, an autopsy revealed that she'd died from severe blunt force trauma, most likely caused by a hammer.

Ada Anita Court, 13, was reported missing on June 21, 1981, after she failed to return from a babysitting job. Olson had picked her up on North Road in Coquitlam. He had driven her to Weaver Lake and there, raped her, before bludgeoning her to death.

The next victim, Simon Patrick Partington, was Olson's youngest, just nine years old when he was abducted from a Richmond street, driven to an isolated area and strangled. That was on July 2nd. Just one week later, Olson talked 14-year-old Judy Kozma into his car and took her to Weaver Lake, where he raped and then stabbed her to death.

By now the police's "runaway" theory lay in tatters and with the media and concerned citizens demanding action, the RCMP drew up a list of potential suspects. One of the names on the list was Clifford Olson and he was placed under intermittent surveillance. Yet even now, with over 200 officers working the case, the police were unable to stop his murderous rampage.

Fifteen-year-old Raymond Lawrence King Jr. died on July 23, 1981, near Weaver Lake. Olson had picked him up at the bus depot in Westminster, luring him with the offer of construction work. Once in the car, Olson offered the youth a soft drink drugged with chloral hydrate. After Raymond passed out, he was sodomized and then thrown down an embankment and beaten to death with a rock.

On July 24, German student Sigrun Arnd was hitchhiking in Coquitlam when Olson stopped to offer her a ride. He drove her to his favorite killing ground in Richmond and bludgeoned her to death. Two days later, he raped and strangled 15-year-old Terry Lyn Carson near Chilliwack.

Finally, on July 30, 1981, Olson picked up 17-year-old Louise Chartrand as she walked to work in Maple Ridge, B.C. He drove her to Whistler where he raped her and beat her to death.

Olson was accelerating, killing his last three victims over the space of just a week. It is frightening to consider the additional damage he might have caused had he remained at large. Fortunately, the police decided to bring him in on July 31, arresting him as he picked up two female hitchhikers on Vancouver Island.

But even with their prime suspect in custody, the police had very little evidence to go on. Olson might well have walked had he not offered investigators a deal. He'd give up the location of the bodies, as well as a confession to each of the murders, in exchange for $100,000, to be paid to his wife.

Placed in an impossible position, Attorney General Allan Williams agreed to the deal. Olson's response was to phone his wife Joan and tell her, "Honey, you're going to be rich."

With the money held in trust, Olson directed a convoy of police vehicles, including dog teams and forensic specialists, to the forest-cloaked hills of British Columbia. Over the next few days, he led them to one decomposed corpse after the other, describing with relish what he'd done to his victims. One child had had a six-inch spike nailed into his skull. In another instance, Olson had injected an air bubble into the victim's vein, in order to induce an embolism.

Clifford Olson went on trial in January 1982. He entered guilty pleas to all counts and was sentenced to eleven concurrent life terms.

But the case was far from over. A furor soon followed the media revelations that Olson had been paid for his confession. In its wake, Attorney General Williams was forced to resign, while legal action to force Joan Olson to return the $100,000 failed. Appeals to her conscience also fell on deaf years. She insisted that she was as much of a victim as any of the murdered children and was therefore entitled to the money.

Olson, meanwhile, refused to go quietly. He continued to correspond with the press and to phone radio talk shows. He sent letters to the parents of his victims boasting of what he'd done to their children. He also claimed more murders, anything between 30 and 134, depending on his mood.

Whether those claims are true or not we will never know. Clifford Olson died of cancer on October 2, 2011, at the age of 71.

98. Vaughn Greenwood

Country: United States

Confirmed Victims: 11

Suspected Victims: over 11+

Criminal profilers, such as those employed by the FBI's Behavioral Sciences Unit, have attained near mythic status in the public perception, and with good reason too. Their criminal profiles have helped bring countless dangerous criminals to book, no doubt saving many lives in the process. There are, however, cases where the profile hinders rather than helps the situation. Once such instance was the hunt for the "Skid Row Slasher."

The Slasher's first known victim was David Russell, a transient found stabbed to death on the steps of the Los Angeles public library on November 13, 1964. The following day, the killer struck again, slashing and stabbing 67-year-old Benjamin Hornberg, in the restroom of a seedy hotel.

The police were sure that the two murders were connected, but with no concrete leads, the trail soon went cold and detectives moved on to more pressing cases. Then, more than a decade later, the Slasher was back, emerging on December 1, 1974, to kill 46-year-old Charles Jackson. The alcoholic drifter was slain on the exact spot where David Russell had died 10 years earlier.

A week later he struck again, knifing 47-year-old Moses Yakanac to death in a Skid Row alley on December 8. Arthur Dahlstedt, 54, was killed in an abandoned building three days later, and on December 22, 42-year-old David Perez was found stabbed to death in shrubbery adjacent to the LA public library, a favorite dumping ground for the killer.

The police barely had time to open a case file when another down-and-out, 58-year-old Casimir Strawinski, was found dead in his hotel room on January 9. The next to die was 46-year-old Robert Shannahan, found dead by a hotel maid with a bayonet protruding from his chest. The final Skid Row victim was 49-year-old Samuel Suarez, discovered in a seedy hotel room on January 17.

With the police swarming all over his favored hunting ground, the killer switched his attention to Hollywood. On January 29, 1975, he stabbed 45-year-old George Frias to death in his own apartment. Two days later, he struck again, killing and mutilating 34-year-old Clyde Hays in his Hollywood home.

Criminal profiling at this time was not commonly in use as an investigative technique. However, with a brutal series of mutilation murders on their hands and not much to go on, the

LAPD decided to commission a psychiatric profile. They also took the ill-advised step of publishing their findings, something that would come back to embarrass them before long.

The profile described the Slasher as a white male in his late twenties or early thirties, six feet tall, 190 pounds, with shoulder-length blond hair. He was further described as sexually impotent with feelings of inadequacy, a friendless, poorly educated loner, who was probably homosexual and had an unspecified physical deformity.

On February 2, William Graham was attacked in his Hollywood home by a hatchet-wielding prowler. Fortunately for Graham, his houseguest, Kenneth Richer, came to the rescue. In the struggle that ensued, both men crashed through a plate-glass window, at which the attacker fled. His escape route led him past the home of actor Burt Reynolds, where he carelessly dropped a letter bearing his name, in the driveway.

Police made an arrest soon after. The suspect was 32-year-old Vaughn Orrin Greenwood and contrary to their profile he was a black man with no obvious deformities. Greenwood was a loner and a homosexual, but there was no evidence that he was impotent.

Originally from Pennsylvania, Greenwood had spent most of his adult life drifting between Chicago and the West Coast. He'd pulled a five-year jail term for aggravated battery in Chicago in 1966, which partially explained the decade-long gap between murders two and three.

Greenwood was convicted on nine counts of first-degree murder on December 30, 1976. He was sentenced to life in prison, with the recommendation that he should never be released.

97. Zhang Yongming

Country: China

Confirmed Victims: 11

Suspected Victims: 12+

China has a long history of cannibalism dating back to the Tang Dynasty of the 7th and 8th centuries when it was common practice for soldiers to eat fallen enemies. More recently, when the ill-planed "Great Leap Forward" left tens of millions of Chinese on the brink of starvation in the 1950s, millions of ordinary citizens resorted to eating human flesh in order to survive.

China has also had its fair share of cannibalistic killers, most notably Zhang Yongming, the so-called "Cannibal Monster." Over a period of four years, from 2008 to 2012, Yongming strangled and dismembered at least 12 youths in the tiny village of Nanmen, later selling their dried flesh as ostrich meat in the local market.

Little is known about Zhang's early life. He first appears on the radar in 1979, when he was arrested for killing a man and mutilating his corpse. A conviction in that case saw him sentenced to death, but the punishment was subsequently reduced to life imprisonment. Paroled in September 1997, after serving just 16 years, Yongming was relocated to Nanmen, in southwest China's Yunnan province. There, he was given a tract of land and a meager government stipend and promptly forgotten about.

That was until teenaged boys started going missing from the village.

At first, the distraught parents thought that their sons had been kidnapped to work as slave labor in the brick quarries. However, their appeals to local authorities brought a tepid response at best and self-funded inquiries fared no better. Not a single one of the missing boys was found. They seemed simply to have vanished.

There were rumors, of course, clues even. Like the mysterious green garbage bags seen hanging outside Yongming's shack. Someone said they'd seen bones protruding from the bags, but no one seriously suspected the dim-witted farmer or the suspicious looking dried meat he sold at market.

Had any of the villagers known about Yongming's murderous past, they might have taken it more seriously when he looped a leather belt around a youth's neck and tried to strangle him. The boy escaped and reported the matter to the police, but Yongming claimed it had been a prank and the police believed him.

Eventually, reports of over a dozen boys and young men missing from an area that spanned just two square miles, leaked to the media and the Ministry of Public Security sent a team of investigators to Nanmen. They immediately picked up a pattern to the disappearances. All of the boys had gone missing along a particular stretch of road, a path that led directly past Yongming's house.

When the investigators heard the stories about the mysterious garbage bags hanging outside Yongming's home, they decided to call on him. They were in for a shock. The bags really did contain human bones.

But even that was not the worst of the horrors. Inside, they found chunks of flesh drying on hooks, they found jars containing human eyeballs preserved in alcohol, they found the remains of several corpses buried in a vegetable garden. They also learned that Yongming had been consuming the flesh of his victims and feeding some of it to his dogs.

Yet even as this macabre story was unraveling another equally disturbing one was revealed, one of police incompetence. With 20 people missing from a tiny hamlet within the space of two years, with citizens up in arms and local chatter rife about Yongming's activities, the police did nothing. The subsequent inquiry into the case would result in 12 local officials, including the police chief, losing their jobs.

Zhang Yongming went on trial in 2012 and was promptly found guilty and sentenced to death. Chinese justice is swift, and on

January 10, 2013, the state-run Xinhua News Agency reported that
Yongming had been "escorted to a place of execution and
executed."

96. Jack Unterweger

Country: Austria / USA / Czechoslovakia

Confirmed Victims: 11

Suspected Victims: 15

Born August 16, 1951, in Styria, Austria, Jack Unterweger was the illegitimate son of an American soldier and an Austrian prostitute. He grew up in the shadowy world of prostitution, drugs and violence. Little wonder then that he displayed early developmental problems, a volatile temper and a tendency to skip out on school whenever the mood took him.

Unterweger had his first major brush with authority when he was 16 years old. On that occasion, he was arrested for assaulting a prostitute, a precursor of what was to come. Over the next decade, he would be in and out of prison on a catalog of charges. Usually, they were for sexual assaults on women.

Given his history of violence, it was inevitable that Unterweger would eventually push things too far. In 1976 he was arrested for the murder of a prostitute. "She reminded me of my mother," was his only defense. He had bludgeoned the woman with an iron bar, then strangled her to death with her own brassiere.

Unterweger was sentenced to life imprisonment. Entering prison functionally illiterate, he applied himself to the task of learning to read and write. Then, amazingly, he launched a jailhouse career as a writer, with the publication of his autobiographical tale, "Purgatory." Poems, plays, and short stories followed and before long Unterweger was being hailed by Vienna's café society as an unheralded genius.

In time, a groundswell of support escalated into a clamor for his early release and with many prominent Austrians adding their voice to the cause, Unterweger was paroled on May 23, 1990. He had served just 14 years of his life sentence.

He claimed to be a changed man and Austrian society certainly seemed prepared to take him at his word. Unterweger became an overnight sensation, with TV appearances, newspaper interviews, and invitations to the most exclusive parties. He wore the best clothes, took to driving a Ford Mustang with a personalized license plate, and began dating a beautiful blonde model.

But the public persona that Unterweger projected was nothing more than a thin veneer. Even as he was being feted by the cream of Austrian society, he was stalking the streets of Vienna, raping and beating and strangling.

In October 1990, Brunhilde Masser, a prostitute from Graz, was reported missing. Two months later in early December another prostitute, Heidemarie Hammerer, disappeared. Her body turned up on New Year's Eve, discovered by hikers in a wood outside of town. She'd been severely beaten, before being strangled to death with her bra.

A few days after that gruesome discovery, came another. Brunhilde Masser's badly decomposed corpse was found in a quiet wood in Bregenz.

Despite the obvious similarities between the murders, the Austrian police were adamant that they were unrelated. That viewpoint would change on March 7, 1991, when yet another prostitute, Elfriede Schrempf, went missing from Graz.

Then, within the space of a month, four more prostitutes Silvia Zagler, Sabine Moitzi, Regina Prem and Karin Eroglu, all vanished, leaving the police in no doubt that they had a serial killer in their midst.

That killer was about to take his deadly show on the road.

In June 1991, an Austrian magazine hired Unterweger to write a piece on crime in Los Angeles. Gladly accepting the commission, Unterweger flew to L.A., where he arranged ride-alongs with the LAPD and began writing a series of articles focusing on prostitution in Hollywood.

But the police ride-alongs were not the full extent of Unterweger's research. On June 20, 1991, 35-year-old prostitute Shannon Exley was found strangled to death in Boyle Heights. Ten days later, Irene Rodriguez was found dead in the same neighborhood. And on July 10, another streetwalker, 26-year-old Peggy Booth, was found murdered in a canyon in Malibu. All three women had been brutally beaten before being strangled with their own brassieres; all three had been sexually violated with tree branches.

As the LAPD's investigation into the murders came up blank, the killer they sought was back in Austria. And he might never have come under suspicion had a vigilant Interpol officer not picked up similarities between the L.A. murders and the still unsolved Austrian series. Inevitably, suspicion began to fall on the man who had been in both locations at the time of the crimes, convicted murderer Jack Unterweger.

In February 1992, Austrian police were finally ready to bring Unterweger in for questioning. But by the time they raided his home, he had already fled, moving first to Switzerland, then France, then Canada, and finally back to the United States.

Throughout that flight, Unterweger was in touch with the Austrian media, alternately proclaiming his innocence and delivering "catch me if you can" taunts to the police.

Unterweger was eventually run to ground in Miami, Florida, a trail of credit card receipts leading to his capture. Then there was a fight over jurisdiction. Wanted for six murders in his native

Austria, three in the United States and two in Czechoslovakia, who would try him?

Eventually, a deal was struck whereby Unterweger would be returned to Austria but would be tried there for all 11 murders.

After several delays, the trial eventually got underway in Graz on April 20, 1994. Three months later, on June 28, Unterweger was convicted on nine counts and sentenced to life imprisonment.

He had no intention of serving that term. At 3:40 a.m. on his first night in prison, Unterweger was found hanging from a curtain rod in his cell. He had used the drawstring of his sweatpants to kill himself.

95. Henri Landru

Country: France

Confirmed Victims: 11

Suspected Victims: 25+

Henri Landru was a small, bow-legged man with a bald pate, bushy eyebrows, and a dense reddish-brown beard. Hardly the sort of man you'd expect would set a lady's heart aflutter. Yet over a criminal career spanning nearly three decades, this reprobate managed to seduce over 300 women, swindling many of them out of their life savings. These unfortunate ladies were left nursing broken hearts and facing uncertain financial futures. But they were the lucky ones. At least ten of the women seduced by Landru paid for his affections with their lives.

Landru was born into a working-class family in Paris on April 12, 1869. He attended a Catholic school and was a bright student, eventually gaining a place at the prestigious School of Mechanical Engineering. However, his studies were cut short when he was drafted into the army at age 18.

In 1891, while still serving in the military, Landru seduced his cousin, Mademoiselle Remy, who became pregnant and bore him a daughter. The couple was married in 1893, upon Landru's discharge from the armed forces. Soon after, he found employment as a clerk, but was left destitute after his employer absconded with money that Landru had given him to invest. Angered by this deception, Landru swore revenge.

The "revenge" that Landru exacted was directed at lonely, middle-aged women, who he'd seduce and then cheat out of their meager pensions. This scam worked well for a while, allowing Landru to set himself up in business as a second-hand furniture dealer. Inevitably, though, he fell foul of the law, earning a two-year prison term in 1900.

Over the next decade, Landru would be in and out of prison seven times and it was during one of these periods of incarceration that he struck on a new scam. He placed an ad in the matrimonial column of a newspaper, describing himself as a wealthy widower seeking companionship. A widow by the name of Madame Izore responded and was promptly relieved of 15,000 francs. She went to the police and Landru was in prison again.

He was released shortly before the opening salvos of World War I. Not yet ready to abandon his latest get-rich scheme, Landru decided to give it a fateful tweak. It was a move that would ultimately send ten women and a teenaged boy to early graves, and Landru to the guillotine.

In 1914, while still married (although estranged from his wife) Landru placed the following advertisement in a Parisian newspaper: "Widower with two children, aged 43, with comfortable income, serious and moving in good society, desires to meet widow with a view to matrimony."

The first woman to respond was Madame Cuchet, 39 years old, a lingerie shop employee with a 16-year-old son, Andre. Landru introduced himself as an engineer and said that his name was Monsieur Diard. Cuchet's family was suspicious of Landru and warned her about entering into a relationship with him. But the lovelorn woman ignored their counsel. In late 1914, she and Andre moved into "Diard's" villa near Chantilly. Neither was seen alive after January 1915. Soon after their disappearance, Landru gave his estranged wife Madame Cuchet's watch as a present.

The next victim was Argentine-born Madame Laborde-Line, the widow of a hotelier. She disappeared after moving in with Landru in July 1915. Shortly after, Landru cleared out her apartment, claiming all of her possessions for himself.

Fifty-one-year-old Madame Guillin was next, last seen alive in August 1915. Before the year was out, another of Landru's conquests, Madame Heon, visited him at his villa and was never seen again.

Landru, meanwhile, was running other scams, including a particularly callous one that deprived hundreds of disabled soldiers of their pensions. He was also carrying on an affair with a

19-year-old servant girl named Andree Babelay. She went missing in March 1917, never to be seen again.

Shortly after Babelay's disappearance, Landru was courting another wealthy widow, Madame Buisson. Like her predecessors, Buisson soon vanished without a trace. She was last seen alive in April 1917. In September of that year, Madame Louise Leopoldine Jaume was gone. The following year, two more women, Annette Pascal, and Marie Therese Marchadier, were missing.

At least ten women and one youth had now disappeared after meeting Landru. But he'd been so careful in covering his tracks – using numerous aliases, taking steps to separate the women from their families – that no one suspected him.

Yet it would be Landru's very efforts to cover his tracks that would lead to his eventual downfall.

Two years after Madame Buisson's death, her son passed away, leaving her family eager to contact her. They were unable to do so, but after one of Buisson's friends recalled receiving a postcard from Gambais, they contacted the mayor of that town. He replied that he had never heard of Madame Buisson, but put them in touch with the family of Madame Collomb. She had vanished under similar circumstances.

The combined efforts of the two families came to nothing. But Madame Buisson's sister (who had actually met Landru) was determined to find him and question him about her sister's whereabouts. She began staking out his old apartment in Paris and her determination eventually paid off when she spotted him on a street and followed him home. She then passed on his new address to the police and Landru was taken into custody.

Landru refused to discuss the missing women and, with no evidence against him, the authorities were forced to let him go. Over the next two years, the police dug up the gardens of his villa time and time again and came up empty; they tried to link him to the purchase of chemicals that might have been used to dissolve the bodies and found nothing.

The break in the case came after Landru's neighbors in Gambais recalled the noxious fumes that sometimes poured from the chimney of his villa. That led the police to search the large pot-bellied stove he'd had installed in his kitchen. There they found numerous small bones, undoubtedly human.

Landru's trial began in November 1921 and was a sensation throughout France.   Over the course of a month, the prosecution built up a damning case of multiple murder, while the accused maintained his stubborn silence, confident that he could not be found guilty, in the absence of a body.

He was, of course, wrong in that assumption.

In the end, it took the jury just two hours to convict him and sentence him to death. He was guillotined in February 1922, leaving in the custody of his attorneys a drawing, which many now believe constitutes a confession of sorts.

The sketch is of a pot-bellied stove. In the margin, Landru had written, "It is not the wall behind which a thing takes place, but indeed the stove in which a thing has been burned."

94. Leonard Lake & Charles Ng

Country: United States

Confirmed Victims: 12

Suspected Victims: 25+

On June 2, 1985, San Francisco police responded to a routine call about a shoplifting at a lumberyard. A sales clerk had seen an Oriental man smuggle a $75 vice out of the store and place it into the trunk of a Honda automobile. When another employee approached the man, he fled on foot.

The Honda was still parked outside when police arrived, a bearded man sitting at the wheel. Asked his name, the man produced a driver's license in the name of Robin Stapley, although it was plain to see that he bore no resemblance to the photograph on the I.D.

The officers then carried out a search of the vehicle. In the trunk, they found the stolen vice, as well as a .22 caliber pistol, equipped with a silencer. Calling in the Honda's license plate unearthed another inaccuracy. The plates belonged to a Buick, registered in the name of Lonnie Bond.

The bearded man was arrested and taken to South City police station, where he eventually admitted that his name was Leonard Lake and that his accomplice's name was Charles Ng.

"Who would have thought a lousy bench vice would bring me to this?" he said, and then brought his hand up to his mouth. Seconds later, his eyes rolled back and he began convulsing.

Lake was rushed to Kaiser Permante Hospital where it was determined that he'd swallowed two cyanide capsules. He'd eventually die four days later. In the meanwhile, detectives were puzzled. Why would a man kill himself over a stolen bench vice? They'd soon find out.

As the comatose Lake lay in hospital, the police began checking into his background. The license he was carrying in the name of Robin Stapley was real enough. Except that Stapley had been missing since April. The Honda, meanwhile, turned out to belong to Paul Cosner, a 39-year-old San Francisco car dealer who had disappeared in November 1984.

Armed with this information, detectives obtained a warrant to search Lake's residence in Wilseyville, California, consisting of a cabin and a concrete bunker with two secret compartments. Inside they found a large weapons cache, audio video equipment, torture devices and a collection of videotapes. They also found Leonard Lake's diary, outlining a plan by Lake and Ng to collect sex slaves.

"God meant women for cooking, cleaning house, and sex," Lake wrote. "When they are not in use, they should be locked up."

The officers looked next at Lake's video equipment, which serial numbers indicated was the property of Harvey Dubs, a San Francisco photographer. Dubs had gone missing in July 1984, along with his wife Deborah and infant son, Sean.

Which brought detectives to Lake's video collection. Slotting in a cassette, they watched in horror as the pictures flickered across the screen, pictures of young women being raped and tortured, at least one of them mutilated so savagely that it was unlikely she had survived the attack.

On another tape, Lake and Ng are seen sexually abusing Brenda O'Connor, Lake's neighbor who disappeared along with her husband, Lonnie Bond, their infant son, Lonnie Jr., and friend Robin Stapely, in May 1985. Brenda is seen tied to a chair, pleading for her life as her husband, son, friend Stapley, and others look on in horror. Lake is heard to say, "By cooperating with us, that means you will stay here as a prisoner, you will work for us, you will wash for us, you will fuck for us. Or you can say no, in which case we'll tie you to the bed, we'll rape you, and then we'll take you outside and shoot you. Your choice!"

In another segment, Ng is heard to tell the terrified woman, "You can cry and stuff like all the rest of them, but it won't do you no good. We're pretty cold-hearted."

Police estimated that 21 different women were shown on the tapes, being raped, sodomized and tortured. The cries of distressed children in the background were particularly hard to bear, even for hardened homicide detectives.

As the investigation progressed, attention turned to the grounds surrounding the bunker. On June 8, forensic teams working with search dogs unearthed four human skeletons. On June 13, a fifth victim was found, along with charred bone fragments and infant's teeth. A sixth victim was unearthed five days later, identified as Randy Jacobson, a 34-year-old drifter, last seen alive in October 1984. Two of Jacobson's neighbors, 26-year-old Cheryl Okoro and 38-year-old Maurice Wok, were also missing, and linked to Lake and Ng.

Three more skeletons were found on June 26, and police declared that Lake and Ng were connected to the disappearance of at least 25 persons. Among those; Mike Carroll, Ng's one-time cellmate; Donald Giuletti, a 36-year-old San Francisco disk jockey; Clifford Parenteau, age 24, who was last seen leaving a bar with Ng; and Jeffrey Gerald, an acquaintance of Ng's who disappeared after telling friends he was going to help Ng move some furniture.

On July 9, the remains of Robin Stapley and Lonnie Bond were found in a common grave and Charles Ng was formally charged with 12 counts of first-degree murder.

But where was the fugitive? Detectives tracked him to Chicago and from there to Canada. On July 6, 1985, he was caught shoplifting at a department store in Calgary. A scuffle ensued, during which a security guard was shot in the hand, an offense that would earn Ng four years in a Canadian prison.

With Ng in custody, US authorities began proceedings to extradite him back to California, a process that was eventually completed in 1991. Ng, though, had not wasted his prison time. He had spent it studying Californian law and now used that knowledge to exploit every legal loophole open to him.

The longest, most expensive criminal trial in California history finally concluded on May 3, 1999, with a guilty verdict and death penalty for Charles Ng.

Ng currently awaits execution at San Quentin.

93. Juana Barraza

Country: Mexico

Confirmed Victims: 11

Suspected Victims: 49

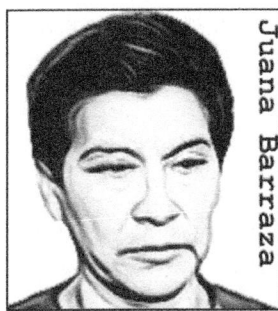

Between the years 2002 and 2006, 11 (and possibly as many as 49) elderly women were strangled to death in their Mexico City homes. The killer, dubbed by the press "La Mataviejitas" (The Old Lady Killer) struck at will, apparently talking his way into his victims' homes and then throttling them to death with a phone cable or item of clothing.

One after another, the strangled corpses turned up, throwing one of the world's most populous cities into a state of terror. Senior citizens were warned to be wary of strangers, not to let anyone they didn't know into their homes. Families and neighbors were told to look out for the elderly and to report strangers in their neighborhoods. When the first reports surfaced of a broad-shouldered woman seen in the location of the crime scenes, the police scoffed at the idea of a female serial killer. Bizarrely, they turned their attention to the city's transvestite population. It did nothing to stem the death toll.

Then, on January 25, 2006, a lodger at a boarding house in Venustiano Carranza was returning home when a strongly built woman exited the building and rushed past him. Inside, the man found his landlady, 82-year-old Ana Maria de los Reyes, lying on the floor, strangled to death. The man immediately called the police and they raced to the scene and made an arrest just a block away from the death house. The suspect was a 48-year-old mother of four, named Juana Barraza.

Juana Barraza was born on December 27, 1958, in a rural village just north of Mexico City. Her mother was poor and unwed, an alcoholic and, by all accounts, a callous and neglectful parent. Juana received no schooling and never learned to read or write. When she was 12 years old, her mother "sold" her to an unnamed man for a few beers. Not even a teenager yet, she was repeatedly raped by her new guardian, eventually becoming pregnant and giving birth to a son. She'd later have three more children by three different men.

Despite this insalubrious start to life, Juana was a devoted parent, who prided herself on being "both mother and father" to her children. Neighbors of the family described the kids as courteous and well behaved, and Juana as "quiet but pleasant." She supported her brood through a combination of domestic work and street vending, but she really harbored an ambition to become a professional wrestler.

Lucha libre, a form of masked wrestling, is massively popular in Mexico, and Barraza was passionate about the sport. Under the ring name "La Dama del Silencio" (The Silent Lady), she was a regular competitor in amateur bouts, staged at small town fiestas. In 2002, when the Mataviejitas murders began, she was still trying to make the breakthrough to the professional ranks and was living in a modest ground-floor apartment in the eastern suburbs of Mexico City with her three daughters. Her son had been killed in a mugging, years earlier.

Barraza's first victim was a 92-year-old woman named Maria de los Angeles Repper, found strangled to death in her home in early 2002. Why exactly Barraza started killing, and why she started at such a late age (48), is unknown. Robbery has been proffered as a motive, but the psychiatrists who examined Barraza believe it was secondary. The real motive, they say, was Barraza's accumulated anger at her mother for the abuse heaped on her as a child. As Barraza denies all but one of the murders, we will never know for sure.

We do however know something of Barraza's M.O. She appears to have used several ruses to gain her victims' trust, including helping them carry their shopping, and offering her services as a domestic worker. Her favorite ploy, though, was to approach elderly women claiming to be a social worker and offering to perform a free health examination in order to sign them up for government welfare programs. When she was arrested, she was found to be in possession of a social worker's identification card, social benefits forms, and a stethoscope. The stethoscope had been used to strangle a number of her victims.

Juana Barraza went on trial in Mexico City in March 2008, charged with 11 murders. She admitted to killing Ana Maria de los Reyes, claiming that the old lady had "angered her." However, despite fingerprint evidence linking her to the other crimes, she stubbornly maintained her innocence.

It did her no good. On March 31, she was found guilty on all counts and sentenced to 759 years in prison. Mexican law mandates that sentences must run concurrently and that no prisoner may be incarcerated for more than 60 years. Even so, it is highly likely that Juana Barraza will see out the rest of her life behind bars.

92. John Justin Bunting

Country: Australia

Confirmed Victims: 12

Suspected Victims: 12

John Bunting was born in Inala, Queensland, on September 4, 1966. As a child, he displayed at least one characteristic of the fledgling serial killer; he took pleasure in hurting animals. A favorite pastime of his was dropping insects and other small creatures into a vat of acid.

During his teenage years the undersized, near-sighted, and somewhat pudgy Bunting, became a neo-Nazi, buying completely into the warped ideology of that movement. As he reached adulthood, his hatred solidified into a loathing of gays, pedophiles, drug addicts and other "wasters" in society. By the time he moved to Salisbury North in 1991 and befriended future accomplice Robert Wagner, that loathing was primed to explode into a campaign of torture and murder.

Bunting's first known victim was Clinton Trezise, a 22-year-old who he suspected of being a pedophile. Luring Trezise to his home on the pretext of a social visit, he began accusing the man of molesting children. Trezise's protestations of innocence fell on deaf ears. Bunting bludgeoned him to death with a spade, then buried him in a shallow grave where his body would remain undiscovered until August 1994.

Three years passed before Bunting struck again. By now he'd indoctrinated the powerfully built Robert Wagner into his worldview and the duo targeted their deadly attention towards a mentally disabled man named Ray Davies.

Davies lived in a caravan on the property of Bunting's friend, Suzanne Allen. His "crime" was that Allen suspected him of making sexual advances towards her grandsons. Davies was murdered in December 1995, his body buried in the backyard of Bunting's home. After Davies's death, Bunting continued cashing Davies's welfare checks. He would continue to do so until his eventual arrest.

Not long after Davies's murder, Suzanne Allen herself disappeared. Her body would later be discovered in the same grave as Davies. Bunting claimed that she'd died of a heart attack, but he continued collecting her pension payments after her death.

There is nothing to suggest that the next victim, Michael Gardiner, was involved in abusing children. But he was openly gay and that was good enough for Bunting who freely professed his belief that all homosexuals were pedophiles.

Gardiner was killed in August 1997, his body stored in a barrel that would later be found in the vault of an abandoned bank in Snowtown. One of his feet had been severed in order to fit the body into its makeshift coffin.

The next to die was Barry Lane, a cross-dressing homosexual who had been Robert Wagner's lover and was the source of many of the names on Bunting's hit list. Despite their association, Bunting was openly critical of Lane, describing him as "dirty" and a "pedo." Lane's dismembered body would eventually be found in the Snowtown bank vault, alongside that of Michael Gardiner. All of the bones in his toes were crushed, suggesting that he'd been tortured prior to death.

Thomas Trevilyan, an accomplice in the Barry Lane killing, was the next victim. Trevilyan suffered from mental problems and following the Lane murder, Bunting had remarked to friends that he was afraid Trevilyan would give them away. Bunting and Wagner eliminated their risk in October 1997, driving Trevilyan into the Adelaide Hills and hanging him from a tree. When his body was found on November 5, 1997, it was assumed that he had committed suicide.

Bunting had by now married a woman named Elizabeth Harvey, whose son, James Vlassakis, looked up to him as a father figure. In 1988, a friend of Vlassakis, Gavin Porter, moved into Bunting's house as a guest. Porter was a heroin addict and Bunting took a dislike to him. The final straw came when Bunting found a used syringe that Porter had carelessly discarded on a couch. Not long after, Bunting and Wagner strangled Porter as he slept in his car in the driveway of Bunting's house. His body was stored in a barrel at the Snowtown vault.

Troy Youde, a half brother of James Vlassakis, was the next victim. Vlassakis had confided to Bunting that Youde had raped him when he was a child and Bunting, seething with rage, had decided to make him pay for it. In August 1998, Bunting, Wagner, and Vlassakis, dragged Youde from his bed and murdered him. Another accomplice, Mark Haydon, assisted in the removal of the body to Snowtown.

Haydon also helped with the disposal of the next victim. Frederick Brooks, 18, was Haydon's mentally disabled nephew. Bunting invited Brooks to his house on September 17, 1998. There, Bunting, Wagner, and Vlassakis brutally tortured the helpless teenager before killing him. Haydon continued collecting Brooks' disability payments after his death.

Bunting, Wagner, and Vlassakis murdered another mentally disabled man in November 1998. Gary O'Dwyer had been severely injured in a car accident and had no immediate family, making him an easy target for the vile trio. O'Dwyer was killed in his own home. His body, later discovered in the Snowtown vault, showed clear signs of torture.

For his next murder, Bunting turned closer to home. The victim was Elizabeth Haydon, wife of Mark. Elizabeth disappeared from her Adelaide home on November 20, 1998, and was reported missing by her brother. The police were immediately suspicious of Mark Haydon's failure to report his wife's disappearance. It would be this suspicion that would eventually provide the break in the case.

However, that break arrived too late to save Bunting's last victim. David Johnson, another half-brother of James Vlassakis, was lured to the Snowtown bank on May 9, 1999, on the pretense of viewing a computer for sale. Once there, he was overpowered and then tortured into providing his bank details and PIN number. Wagner and Vlassakis then drove to Port Wakefield and attempted to draw money from Johnson's bank account, leaving Johnson in the custody of Bunting. When they returned Johnson was dead.

Bunting and Wagner later dismembered Johnson's body and added a new perversion to their M.O. They fried and ate pieces of Johnson's flesh.

Fortunately, the net was closing on Bunting and his depraved apprentices. Police inquiries into Elizabeth Haydon's disappearance led eventually to the disused bank in Snowtown. On May 20, 1999, officers searched the premises and discovered eight bodies, concealed in drums in the vault. Bunting, Wagner, Vlassakis, and Haydon were arrested that same day.

In September 2003, John Bunting was found guilty on 11 counts of murder and sentenced to 11 consecutive life terms without the possibility of parole. His main accomplices, Wagner, and Vlassakis, were given seven and four life terms respectively. Mark Haydon pled guilty to the lesser charge of assisting in a murder and was convicted on two counts.

91. Linwood & James Briley

Country: United States

Confirmed Victims: 12

Suspected Victims: 12

Like many serial killers, Linwood and James (J.B.) Briley began their criminal careers early. Linwood was just 16 when he committed his first murder. On January 28, 1971, he spotted his 57-year-old neighbor, Orline Christian, hanging washing in her backyard. Fetching a .22 rifle, he drew a bead on the woman and fired, killing her instantly. When the police arrived to arrest him, he shrugged apathetically. "I heard she had heart problems," he said. "She would have died soon anyway."

On account of his youth, Linwood received only a one-year sentence for the murder. He was soon joined at the reform school by his brother, J.B., convicted for firing at a police officer. It was a warning of things to come. Yet few could have anticipated the extent of the carnage the siblings would unleash just years later.

The crime spree that would propel the Briley brothers to infamy began on March 12, 1979. At around 9 pm that evening, Linwood and J.B., along with their younger brother Anthony and a teenaged accomplice, Duncan Meekins, forced their way into the home of William and Virginia Bucher in Henrico County. They ordered the Buchers to lie on the floor and then tied them up and took them to separate rooms. They then ransacked the house before setting it alight and fleeing in William Bucher's car.

Fortunately, they had been sloppy in tying up their victims. As soon as they were gone, William Bucher wriggled free of his bonds, got a knife and cut his wife loose. They managed to get out of the house just as the blaze took hold. They were lucky. The next victims of the Brileys would not be.

On March 21, the gang broke into the house of Michael McDuffie, shooting him to death before ransacking his home. On April 9, they followed 76-year-old Mary Gowen back to her apartment, where they gang-raped the elderly woman, then robbed her and shot her to death. On July 4, J.B. spotted 17-year-old Christopher Philips hanging around Linwood's car. Suspecting that Philips might be trying to break into the vehicle, the gang surrounded him and dragged him into a nearby yard. There, J.B., Anthony, and Deekins pinned him to the ground while Linwood dropped a cinderblock on his head, crushing his skull.

On September 14, country-and-western musician John Gallaher was doing a gig with his band at the Log Cabin dance hall on Jefferson Davis Highway. Between sets, Gallaher stepped outside for a breath of air and had the misfortune of encountering the Brileys. Gallaher was overpowered and forced into the trunk of his Lincoln Continental. He was then driven to Mayo Island where he was pulled from the trunk and shot, his body dumped in the James River. The gang's take from the murder was $6 and a turquoise ring, which Linwood was still wearing when he was eventually arrested.

On September 30, the gang reverted to home invasions, following 62-year-old nurse, Mary Wilfong, back to her Richmond apartment. Mary's skull was crushed with a baseball bat and the gang then proceeded to loot her apartment of valuables.

Five days later, on October 5, they entered the 4th Avenue home of 79-year-old Blanche Page, bludgeoning her to death as she lay on her bed, the blows delivered with such force that blood splattered the ceiling. Her 59-year-old boarder, Charles Garner, was killed even more brutally. He was stabbed to death with an assortment of weapons, including five knives, a pair of scissors, and a carving fork. The body was found with these implements still embedded.

On October 19, the gang was out prowling when they spotted Harvey Wilkerson, a long-time friend of J.B. and Linwood. Wilkerson spotted them too. Sensing trouble, he went indoors and locked himself in, along with his pregnant wife, Judy Barton, and the couple's five-year-old son. Minutes later, Wilkerson heard a knock at the door and peered through the drapes. He saw the four men on his porch.

Wilkerson was put in an impossible position, allow the men in and they might hurt his family, refuse them entry and their response would be predictable, and violent. Given no choice, he opened the door.

The Brileys soon made their intentions clear. Both Wilkerson and Barton were bound and gagged. Judy was then manhandled into the kitchen where first Linwood and then Meekins raped her. She was then dragged back into the living room at which point Linwood left the house.

As the three remaining gang members covered their victims with sheets, J.B. instructed Meekins to kill Wilkerson, telling him, "You've got to get one." Meekins agreed to do it, placing a pillow over Wilkerson's head and firing, killing Wilkerson instantly. J.B. Briley then shot Judy Barton and her five-year-old son.

While this was going on, a police cruiser was patrolling the area and saw the Briley's car parked outside the Wilkerson residence. Later, the same officers saw the gang driving away from the scene. When the bodies were found three days later, the Brileys and Meekins were taken into custody.

Investigators quickly zeroed in on 16-year-old Duncan Meekins as the weak link in the gang. They offered him a deal if he testified against the Brileys and Meekins agreed, giving a full confession to their eight-month crime spree, linking the gang to crimes that investigators had no idea they'd committed.

As a result of his co-operation, Duncan Meekins escaped the death penalty and was sentenced to life plus 80 years. Anthony Briley, who had not participated directly in the killings, was given a single life sentence, with parole eligibility.

But the kingpins of the gang were Linwood and J.B. In their case prosecutors were determined to seek the death penalty. Linwood would eventually be sentenced to death for the murder of John Gallaher, while J.B. received two death sentences, one each for the murders of Judy Barton and her son, Harvey.

In May 1984, the Brileys masterminded an escape involving six death row inmates, making it as far as Philadelphia before they were apprehended 19 days later. There would be no further chance of reprieve. Linwood Briley went to the electric chair on October 12, 1984. J.B. followed him on April 18 of the following year, thus ending the murderous careers of two of the most vicious killers in Virginia's history.

90. Kenneth Bianchi & Angelo Buono

Country: United States

Confirmed Victims: 12

Suspected Victims: 12

Murders happen every day in a city the size of Los Angeles. And when the victims are prostitutes, they warrant hardly a mention. The lifestyle is dangerous, those who live it, well aware of the risks. And so the murders of three hookers, strangled and dumped on a hillside in October 1977, caused no more than a ripple.

But if the police and media were blasé about those crimes they'd soon have cause to pay attention. Close to Thanksgiving 1977, came a week of unprecedented carnage, with the bodies of five young women found in the vicinity of Glendale-Highland Park. These were not prostitutes, but ordinary girls, abducted from their middle-class neighborhoods, raped and tortured, then strangled and dumped in the hills.

The first of those discoveries came on November 20, the victim Kristina Weckler, a 20-year-old honors student at the Pasadena Art Center of Design. She'd been raped and sodomized and then strangled. The ligature marks on her wrists, ankles and neck, and the bruises on her breasts, bore witness to torture.

That same day, there was another gruesome find, two victims this time, their bodies in the early stages of decomposition, already infested with insects. The victims would later be identified as Dolores Cepeda, 12, and Sonja Johnson, 14. They'd last been seen talking to a man sitting in a large sedan. There was another man sitting in the passenger seat, confirming detectives' suspicions that they were looking for a pair of killers, working together.

On November 23, another young victim was found, this time near the Los Feliz off ramp on the Golden State Freeway. The level of decomposition suggested that she'd been there two weeks but made it impossible to determine whether she'd been raped. But she had been strangled, and her wrists and ankles bore the same ligature marks as the other victims. She was 28-year-old Jane King, a model and actress. She'd been an attractive and vibrant blonde before the strangler snuffed out her life

Less than a week later, on Tuesday, November 29, the naked body of a young woman was found lying partially in the street in Glendale's Mount Washington area. The ligature marks on her ankles, wrists, and neck, identified her as a Hillside Strangler victim. There was evidence of torture too, including burn marks on her palms.

The young victim was identified as Lauren Wagner, an 18-year-old student who lived with her parents in the San Fernando Valley. They had woken that morning to find Lauren's car parked across the street with the door open. Questioning the neighbors, Lauren's father had found that one of them, Beulah Stofer, had witnessed Lauren's abduction, even though she hadn't realized it at the time.

After the Wagner murder, the killers lay low for two weeks, emerging in mid-December to murder blonde call girl, Kimberly Diane Martin. On the night of her murder, her agency had sent Martin to Apartment 114 at 1950 Tamarind. She'd been found the next day, her body discarded on a steep hillside bordering Alvarado Street.

No significant progress was made in the case through December and January. Then, on Thursday, February 16, an attractive young woman by the name of Cindy Hudspeth was murdered. Like the other victims, she'd been raped and strangled. Her body was then crammed into the trunk of her car, which was pushed down a hillside on Angeles Crest. Ligature marks on the neck, wrists and ankles confirmed her as a Hillside Strangler victim.

Police continued working the case. But as the months passed with no new leads, nor any more killings by the Hillside Strangler, the trail began to go cold, the activities of the task force were scaled down, detectives began investigating fresher cases.

Almost a year later, police in Bellingham, Washington, arrested a security guard named Kenneth Bianchi on suspicion of murdering two Western Washington University students, Karen Mandic and Diane Wilder. Bellingham detectives were immediately struck by the way the two victims were bound. It reminded them of the Hillside Strangler case. They also noted that Bianchi had arrived in Bellingham shortly after the Hillside Strangler murders stopped. A call was therefore placed to Detective Frank Salerno at the L.A. County Sheriff's Office.

Salerno began looking into Bianchi's activities in L.A. and learned that he'd spent much of his time at an auto upholstery shop run by his cousin, Angelo Buono. Detectives called on Buono and within a few minutes were convinced that this crude, ugly man was the other Hillside Strangler.

However, despite the mounting evidence against them (including hair and fiber, plus jewelry from the victims found in Bianchi's possession) neither Bianchi nor Buono was talking. Bianchi, in fact, was working on an insanity defense, claiming multiple personality disorder. When that defense was proven to be a scam, Bianchi was convinced to confess and to testify against Buono in exchange for avoiding the death penalty.

Over the weeks that followed, Bianchi described to investigators how he and Buono had abducted, raped, tortured, and strangled their victims before dumping their bodies. They often posed as policemen to get victims to go with them, he said, then drove them back to Angelo Buono's auto upholstery shop. With neither remorse nor emotion, he described the brutal torture their victims had endured – sodomy, electric shocks, gassing, injection with acid-based cleaners, rape with various objects, including soda bottles. The descriptions sickened even hardened detectives. Bianchi seemed unmoved.

Based on his confession, Bianchi received two life sentences in the state of Washington. He was then transferred to California where he was sentenced to additional life terms.

Angelo Buono eventually went on trial in October 1983. Found guilty, he was sentenced to life and was sent to Folsom Prison, where he reportedly refused to leave his cell, so afraid was he of being attacked by other inmates. He died of a heart attack on September 21, 2002.

Kenneth Bianchi is currently serving his sentence at Washington's notoriously tough Walla Walla prison.

89. Enriqueta Marti

Country: Spain

Confirmed Victims: 12

Suspected Victims: 100+

From Spain comes the harrowing tale of Enriqueta Marti, a witchdoctor, serial killer, and procurer of children for pedophiles. Enriqueta was born in the small town of Sant Feliu de Llobregat in 1868. As a young girl, she moved to Barcelona, where she worked as a servant in the homes of the rich. However, the ambitious and beautiful Enriqueta quickly realized that she could make a lot more money selling her body than scrubbing floors. Before long she'd hung up her pinafore and found employment in one of the city's brothels.

Enriqueta was much in demand as a prostitute, but she was intelligent enough to know that her good looks were not going to last forever. Holding back a large percentage of her earnings, she eventually put together enough money to open her own brothel in 1909.

Hers, though, was not your typical bordello. Years of providing sexual favors to Barcelona's elite had taught her one thing – they were a depraved lot, prepared to pay a premium to have their perverted needs satisfied. With this in mind, she'd come up with an appalling plan, to kidnap children aged between five and fifteen and force them to work as prostitutes, catering to rich pedophiles.

This was easily achieved. Disguising herself as a beggar, she'd trawl the streets looking for child victims, luring them back to her apartment with promises of food or money. Her favorite targets were street children who she usually found waiting on the bread queues at convents, monasteries, and charity shelters.

But things did not start well for Enriqueta's new venture. She'd only been in business a few months when the police raided her Minerva Street apartment. A search of the premises turned up a ledger containing her client list, which included many of Barcelona's most esteemed citizens.

Enriqueta was arrested and thrown into jail. However, her powerful friends soon saw to it that she was released. The list of names also mysteriously disappeared.

Back on the streets, Enriqueta rented an apartment in El Raval, one of Barcelona's poorest neighborhoods. The location was perfect for her new business venture, one that involved the manufacture of elixirs and potions.

She began trawling again, sending some kids to the Minerva Street brothel, others to her squalid premises in El Raval. Here, they were slaughtered, their fat, blood, bones and hair used to make the ointments, facial creams, and tonics, which Enriqueta hocked to her wealthy clientele.

That Enriqueta's clients were aware of what her products contained, is not in doubt. Indeed, that was why they were prepared to pay a premium. It was believed at the time that the blood of children was an elixir for long life and that their fat was good for keeping the skin supple and wrinkle free. Another popular potion was a tonic containing powdered bone and bone marrow, believed to cure tuberculosis.

Enriqueta appears to have been living an extraordinary double life at this time. By day she donned her disguise as a beggar and wandered the streets. But when nightfall came, Enriqueta was transformed, emerging in the finest dresses and jewelry to rub shoulders with the rich and famous at the El Liceu Opera Palace and the Casino de la Arrabassada (and also to hock her wares to rich pedophiles and society donnas, of course).

Yet Enriqueta's enterprise was built on far from solid ground and already the sands were shifting. The disappearances of so many children could not go unnoticed forever. Rumors began circulating of witches kidnapping children for use in pagan ceremonies, of criminal gangs abducting kids and selling them into sexual slavery.

These rumors were, of course, not that far off the mark. But the authorities were reluctant to take action. In fact, the official word, issued by the mayor in late 1911, was that no children had been kidnapped. It seemed that Enriqueta's rich and powerful benefactors had come to her rescue again.

In the end, it was a nosy neighbor who brought about Marti's downfall. The woman was suspicious of the number of children entering Enriqueta's El Raval apartment never to re-emerge. She reported her suspicions to the police and they carried out a raid, rescuing two young girls. Unfortunately, they arrived too late to save a 5-year-old boy named Pepito. His tiny corpse was found already hacked up for processing into Enriqueta's macabre potions. It was not the last of the horrors the police uncovered.

Inside a closet, they discovered a bag of bloodied clothing and a gore-stained paring knife. In one of the rooms, they found at least thirty charred human bones, whose size suggested they were from children. But the worst was yet to come. Finding a locked door the officers forced it. Inside they found jars and bowls of various sizes, at least 50 in number. Contained within these receptacles were preserved human remains: lumps of fat, congealed blood, swatches of hair, tiny mummified hands and powdered bones. There were also jars of various potions, ointments, and salves ready for sale.

A search of Enriqueta's other apartments uncovered even more evidence. Behind concealed doors and false walls, the officers uncovered a number of corpses, the victims ranging in age from under a year to eight years. They also found preserved body parts from several children, as well as a collection of recipe books for preparing the various remedies.

Enriqueta Marti was arrested and sent to jail pending her trial. Meanwhile, the story broke in the newspapers, creating a sensation throughout Spain. A senior inspector was put in charge of the case and vowed to prosecute, not only Enriqueta, but her depraved clientele also.

That, of course, was never going to happen. Too many powerful people had too much to lose by allowing Enriqueta a public forum.

On the morning of May 12, 1913, Enriqueta Marti was attacked by fellow inmates and beaten to death. She was buried in an unmarked grave at Cementerio del Sudoeste, in Barcelona.

88. Charles Sobhraj

Country: Thailand / Nepal / India / Malaysia

Confirmed Victims: 12

Suspected Victims: 12+

Charles Sobhraj was born on April 6, 1944, in Saigon, Vietnam. His father was an Indian tailor, his mother a Vietnamese peasant. Shortly after his birth, his father abandoned the family. His mother later married a French soldier and moved to Marseilles, taking Charles with her.

Charles was unhappy in France, growing from a difficult child into a rebellious teenager who did poorly in school and often played truant. During his early teens, he became a prodigious shoplifter and petty thief. Inevitably, this led to more serious crimes and a burglary arrest saw him sentenced to three years at Poissy Prison.

Shortly after his release, Sobhraj met the woman who would become his wife. Chantal's parents were strongly opposed to the union but she went ahead with it anyway. Just months after the nuptials, Sobhraj fled Paris in the middle of the night with a pregnant Chantal in tow, and the gendarmes hot on their track.

They drove east, crossing Europe and the Middle East. Eventually, making it to Bombay, where Chantal gave birth to a baby girl.

Sobhraj soon set himself up in business, smuggling stolen luxury cars over the border from Pakistan and selling them at a handsome profit. Unfortunately, most of his ill-gotten gains went to feed his gambling addiction and by 1971 he was deep in debt to a number of Macau casino owners.

Given the opportunity to wipe out his gambling debts by carrying out a jewel heist, Sobhraj readily agreed. But the robbery went awry, Sobhraj was arrested and sent to the notorious Tihar prison. He escaped soon after and fled with his family to Kabul, Afghanistan.

Over the next few years, Sobhraj traveled around Europe and the Middle East, using various aliases and supporting himself through criminal schemes. Eventually, he abandoned his family in Kabul. Chantal returned to Paris, never to see Charles Sobhraj again.

Sobhraj showed up next in India, duping and robbing French and English-speaking tourists. While running these scams he met a French Canadian woman named Marie LeClerc, who would become his lover and criminal partner. The two moved to Bangkok, where they started assembling a criminal gang that included a French teenager named Dominique and two ex-policemen named Yannick and Jacques. The final member of the team was a sociopathic young Indian named Ajay Chowdhury, who became Sobhraj's right-hand man.

It is uncertain whether Sobhraj had murdered anyone up to this point, but that was soon to change.

His first victim was an American named Jennie Bollivar who fell in with the Sobhraj gang for a while before ending up dead in a tidal pool in the Gulf of Thailand. Then there was Vitali Hakim, who went on a trip with Sobhraj and Chowdhury and never returned. His badly burned body was found several days later, on the road to Pattaya. The police blamed Thai bandits.

In December 1975, Hakim's girlfriend, a French citizen named Charmayne Carrou, came looking for him. Within days, she was dead, the circumstances of her death almost identical to Jennie Bollivar. An autopsy would later reveal that she had been strangled.

Henk Bintanja and his fiancée, Cornelia Hemker, were Dutch students traveling around Southeast Asia when they met Charles Sobhraj in Hong Kong. He invited them to stay at his house in Bangkok, planning to rob them of their valuables.   Henk and Cornelia disappeared the day after Charmayne Carrou was found murdered. Their bodies were discovered days later, strangled and burned.

On December 18, Sobhraj and LeClerc entered Nepal where they befriended Canadian Laurent Carriere, 26, and Californian Connie

Bronzich, 29 years old. Just days later the bodies of Carriere and Bronzich were found in a field. They'd both been stabbed to death and then set alight.

A short while later, Sobhraj flew out of Nepal and re-entered Thailand on Carriere's passport.

Sobhraj was in for a surprise when he got home. Dominique, Yannick, and Jacques had fled the country. Before leaving, they'd clued the authorities in about Sobhraj's criminal activities.

With the Thai authorities after him, Sobhraj headed back to India, where he murdered Israeli scholar Avoni Jacob. He then returned to Bangkok, using Jacob's passport. Almost immediately, he was pulled in for questioning regarding the deaths of Jennie Bollivar and Charmayne Carrou.

The interrogation was half-hearted, but it spooked Sobhraj. As soon as he was released he headed for the airport and boarded a flight to Malaysia, taking LeClerc and Chowdhury with him. Shortly after their arrival, Chowdhury disappeared, never to be seen again. It appears that he'd outlived his usefulness to Sobhraj.

By now, the American, Canadian, French and Dutch embassies had begun asking questions about their murdered citizens. Fearful of being captured, Sobhraj returned to Bombay, where he felt he could disappear.

But Sobhraj wasn't exactly laying low. He quickly assembled a criminal team, including LeClerc, and new recruits, Barbara Sheryl Smith and Mary Ellen Eather. The first crime that they pulled off went horribly wrong. Sobhraj miscalculated the dosage required to knock out the mark, a Frenchman named Jean-Luc Solomon. The man died without regaining consciousness.

Unperturbed, Sobhraj tried drugging a tour group of 60 French students, but again miscalculated, causing the students to begin collapsing in their hotel lobby. Sobhraj and his gang were soon arrested.

Barbara and Mary Ellen quickly cracked under interrogation and told everything. In short order, Sobhraj was charged with murdering Jean-Luc Solomon and sent to Tihar. He'd eventually be sentenced to an extremely lenient 12 years in prison.

Not that Sobhraj was concerned. With the money he had, he could grease enough palms to live a life of luxury at Tihar. During his period of incarceration, it was said that he virtually ran the place.

On February 17, 1997, Sobhraj walked away from Tihar a free man. He returned to France where he became an instant celebrity. A movie company reportedly paid $15 million for the rights to a film about his life, while journalists queued to interview him at $5,000 a time.

But if anyone was due a healthy dose of bad karma, it was Charles Sobhraj, and so it proved.

In September 2003, for motives unknown, he traveled to Nepal, a country that still had two murder warrants out on him. Spotted on the streets of Kathmandu, he was quickly arrested, tried and sentenced to life imprisonment for the murders of Laurent Carriere and Connie Bronzich.

87. Maury Travis

Country: United States

Confirmed Victims: 12

Suspected Victims: 17

Although the police in St. Louis, Missouri, were reluctant to admit it, a serial killer was preying on the city's prostitute population. The first body – that of 34-year-old Alysa Greenwade – had turned up on April 1, 2001, in Washington Park. She'd been strangled and there were clear signs of sexual torture. Three days later, a woman was found in East St. Louis, severely beaten and close to death. She survived but was unable to identify her attacker. Then, on May 15, the body of Teresa Wilson, 36, was found in West Alton. From her injuries, it seemed that the same man might be responsible, but the police continued to play their cards close to their chest. The killer would slip up sooner or later. They didn't want to cause a panic.

Throughout the rest of the year, the bodies continued to show up with alarming regularity: Betty James, 46, found on May 23;

Verona Thompson, 36, found in West Alton on June 29; Yvonne Crues, 50, discovered on August 25; Brenda Beasley, 33, found in East St. Louis on October 8.

Neither did the new year bring any respite. On January 30, 2002, an unidentified female skeleton was found near Mascoutah. Two more sets of skeletal remains turned up in March, bringing the body count to ten. And yet the police had not a single clue they could tie to a suspect.

On May 21, an envelope arrived at the offices of the St. Louis Post-Dispatch. Inside were a typed letter and a map indicating the location of yet another body. The letter was passed on to police. Following the directions, they found another unidentified skeleton in West Alton, exactly where the map indicated it would be.

The dumpsite, like the others, carried very little in the way of physical evidence. The map, though, was an entirely different matter. Detectives soon found out that it had been downloaded from the Internet site, Expedia.com. Investigators contacted the company and learned that the information for the map site came from Microsoft. St. Louis PD then called in the assistance of the FBI, who issued Microsoft with a subpoena. What they wanted to know was whether anyone had requested a map of the West Alton area between May 18 and May 21, the dates either side of the postmark on the letter.

Four days later, they had an answer – of sorts. Microsoft was not able to provide a name, but they were able to provide a unique IP address. Next, the Feds contacted WorldCom Inc., the company that provides local telephone numbers to connect Internet services to their dial-up customers. WorldCom had an answer within a day. The temporary IP address had been provided on May 20 to user   MSN/maurytravis, who Microsoft later identified as Maury Troy Travis of Ferguson, Missouri.

Armed with this information, St. Louis PD immediately set up surveillance on Travis while they worked on obtaining a search warrant for his home. They learned that Travis was a 36-year-old waiter who had served time for robbery and for various drugs offenses.

Eventually, on June 7, they moved in to arrest Travis, simultaneously serving the search warrant. The search turned up a wealth of evidence including blood splatters found throughout the home, bloodstained belts and ligatures, and various torture paraphernalia. Most damning of all was a collection of videotapes found secreted inside a wall. The tapes showed Travis engaged in bondage and sadistic sex with several women, at least two of whom he appears to murder on film.

DNA evidence has subsequently linked Travis to ten murders. But of the victims whose bodies were found, only one, Betty James, is shown on the tapes. Which begs the question, just how many women did Maury Travis murder?

We shall never know. On June 17, Travis hanged himself in his cell. He had earlier told investigators that he would never go back to prison.

86. Fred and Rosemary West

Country: England

Confirmed Victims: 12

Suspected Victims: 20

Fred West was born in 1941, in Much Marcle, 120 miles west of London. He grew up to be a disruptive child who did poorly at school and was constantly in trouble. He also displayed a precocious interest in sex, reportedly molesting his younger sisters. At 17, West was involved in a motorcycle accident that left him with a metal plate in his skull. He'd later suffer a second serious head injury after a woman pushed him down a flight of stairs when he put his hand up her skirt.

1961 saw West arrested for statutory rape after he impregnated a 13-year-old neighbor. Given probation on that charge, be shortly thereafter started a relationship with a Scottish prostitute named Rena Costello, who was pregnant by an Asian bus driver at the time. In 1962, West married Costello and they moved to Scotland where she gave birth to a daughter, Charmaine. West explained the child's ethnicity by claiming that Rena's baby had been stillborn and that they'd adopted Charmaine as a replacement.

In Scotland, West found work driving an ice cream truck, a vocation that allowed him the opportunity to stalk young girls. In 1964, Rena gave birth to another daughter, Anne-Marie. Shortly after, West accidently struck and killed a young boy with his truck. Although cleared of wrongdoing, he moved his family back to Gloucester where he got a job at a slaughterhouse.

By 1965, Rena had had enough of Fred's constant sexual demands and fled back to Scotland, leaving the children behind. By the time she returned, in July 1966, Fred was living with another woman, Ann McFall.

Early in 1967, Ann announced that she was pregnant. Fred soon took care of the problem, murdering and dismembering Ann, then burying her remains in a field near Much Marcle, keeping her fingers and toes as a gruesome trophy.

In January 1968, 15-year-old Mary Bastholm disappeared from a Gloucester bus stop, with at least one witness claiming to have seen West lurking in the area. West was never charged with the crime. Later that same year, West met the woman who would become his wife and partner in crime.

Rosemary Letts was born on November 29, 1953, in Devon, England. Her father, Bill, was a violent schizophrenic, her mother a depressive who had endured electroshock therapy while pregnant with Rosemary. Known as Dozy Rosie, Letts was a slow-witted, obese child who suffered constant ridicule from her peers. There is evidence to suggest that she was involved in an incestuous relationship with her father as a teen. She certainly had involvements with other adult men.

One of those men was Fred West, and despite Bill Letts' protests, Rosemary refused to end the relationship. She was soon pregnant with Fred's child, conceiving a daughter, Heather, while Fred was imprisoned for theft in 1970. Rosemary was looking after Rena's daughters Charmaine and Anne-Marie during this time, but she resented the responsibility. In 1971, while Fred was still serving jail time, eight-year-old Charmaine disappeared. When Fred was released days later, he helped Rosemary bury the small corpse behind their house at 25 Midland Road.

In August 1971, Rena was back on the scene and asking questions about Charmaine. She disappeared soon after and would later turn up in a field near Much Marcle, her body dismembered and bearing Fred's signature mutilations, with toes and fingers missing.

In Rose, Fred had found his ideal partner, and the couple married in January 1972. Rosemary was every bit as depraved as he was. He enjoyed bringing men home and watching her having sex with them and Rose made no protest. In addition, they placed ads in swingers' magazines, advertising their kinky tastes. But even that wasn't enough. The depraved couple was soon taking long drives, looking for young girls who they could abduct and rape.

In June 1972, Rosemary gave birth to another daughter, Mae, and the family moved to a larger house at 25 Cromwell Street. There, Fred constructed a private torture chamber in the basement where he abused his own daughter and allowed her to be abused by other men he brought to the house. During this time Fred and Rose were arrested for abducting and sexually assaulting their babysitter, Caroline Raine, but they escaped with a fine after claiming that Raine had consented to "rough sex."

In 1973, 21-year-old Lynda Gough moved into the West household as a live-in nanny and promptly disappeared. In October of that year, the Wests kidnapped 15-year-old Carol Cooper, sexually abused and strangled her, then dismembered and buried her corpse in their cellar. 21-year-old Lucy Partington suffered a similar fate in December.

Swiss hitchhiker, Theresa Siegenthaler, 21, was murdered on April 16, 1974, 15-year-old Shirley Hubbard on November 14. In April 1975, 19-year-old Juanita Mott ended up buried in the West's basement graveyard.

In December 1977, Rosemary gave birth to another daughter, Tara. Shortly thereafter, 18-year-old prostitute, Shirley Robinson, moved into 25 Cromwell Street. Robinson was soon accommodating both Fred and Rosemary's sexual needs but when she started challenging Rose for Fred's affections she had to go. She was murdered in June 1978, her body buried in the garden. There was no room left in the cellar.

The next to die at Cromwell Street was 17-year-old Alison Chambers, tortured, murdered, dismembered, and confined to the garden bone yard in September 1979.

Between 1980 and 1983, Rosemary West birthed three more children. The first, Barry, was sired by Fred. The other two, Rosemary and Lucyanna, were of mixed race, their parentage unknown. Meanwhile, Anne-Marie had left home and Fred had turned his incestuous attentions towards Heather. When Heather began talking about the abuse outside the home, Fred decided to kill her. Heather died at her father's hands on June 19, 1987. Her dismembered remains were interred in the garden.

Fred and Rose told anyone who asked that their 16-year-old daughter had left home to work at a holiday camp. But they told a different story to their children, warning them to behave or they'd "end up under the patio like Heather." Eventually, those stories got out and the police arrived at Cromwell Street with a warrant to dig up the garden.

Fred West was taken into custody on February 24, 1994. He quickly confessed to killing Heather, then to the other murders as the police unearthed remains at his home. Later, he'd lead officers to the field in Much Marcle, where Rena West and Ann McFall lay buried.

West would eventually be charged with twelve murders. However, he would never be tried for any of them. He hanged himself in his cell on January 1, 1995, using strips torn from a bed sheet.

That left Rosemary to face the music alone and despite her protestations of innocence, she was charged with ten counts of murder. Found guilty of those crimes she was sentenced to life in prison, with the stipulation that she must never be released.

85. William Suff

Country: United States

Confirmed Victims: 12

Suspected Victims: 22

Shortly after dawn on October 30, 1986, a man was scavenging for scrap metal around the Rubidoux industrial area near Riverside, California, when he came upon the body of a young woman. She was lying on her back in a drainage ditch, her clothes ripped and covered in blood, her genital area severely mutilated. The man quickly ran for help.

The victim was 23-year-old Michelle Gutierrez, and an autopsy revealed that she had sustained multiple stab wounds to the face, chest, and buttocks, as well as severe trauma to the anal and vaginal areas. Death, though, was caused by strangulation.

Less than two weeks later, on December 11, investigators were called to the discovery of another corpse, that of 24-year-old

Charlotte Palmer. However, the body was so severely decomposed that it was impossible to determine how she'd died.

There was little doubt, though, about the next victim. 37-year-old Linda Ann Ortega was found in January 1987 along a stretch of dirt road in Lake Elsinore. Like the other victims, Ortega had a long rap sheet for prostitution and drug offenses. She had been strangled, and senior detectives were by now beginning to believe that there might be a serial killer on the loose in Riverside County.

Those suspicions were firmed up with the discovery of the next victim on May 2, 1987. Twenty-seven-year-old Martha Bess Young was found in a ravine close to the Ortega murder scene. She'd been strangled and then posed in a spread-eagled position, a deliberate taunt to investigators.

With the body count rising, local law enforcement agencies formed a task force to hunt the killer. But it appeared that the killer was aware of their activities. They'd barely begun working the case when he dropped out of sight. He'd remain dormant for nearly two years.

On January 27, 1989, twenty-one months since his last known murder, the killer was back. The body of 37-year-old Linda Mae Ruiz, a known prostitute, was discovered on a beach at Lake Elsinore. She'd been rendered unconscious with drugs before her head was buried under the sand, causing her to asphyxiate.

Six months later, on June 28, 1989, another prostitute was dead. 28-year-old Kimberly Lyttle was discovered in Cottonwood

Canyon, battered and strangled to death. But at least police had their first clues. Fibers and pubic hairs were discovered on the body, useless in finding the killer, but invaluable in proving his guilt, if and when he was captured.

And still, the killer wasn't done. On November 11, 1989, 36-year-old Judy Lynn Angel, died at his hands, so severely bludgeoned that her cranium was shattered.

On December 13, he killed 23-year-old Christina Leal at Quail Valley. Darla Jane Ferguson, a 24-year-old prostitute died on January 18, 1990. Three weeks later, on February 8, workers at an orchard in Highgrove discovered the nude body of 35-year-old Carol Lynn Miller.

Eight months passed. Then, on November 6, 1990, the body of 33-year-old prostitute Cheryl Coker was found at an industrial plant in northeast Riverside. She'd suffered severe mutilations, including the removal of her right breast, which was placed beside the body.

Victim number 12 soon followed. On December 21, a janitor at a factory complex discovered the nude body of Susan Sternfeld, a local prostitute. On January 19, 1991, a motorist spotted a body along a road northwest of Lake Elsinore. This latest victim was 42-year-old Kathleen Leslie Milne. She'd been bludgeoned into unconsciousness and then strangled to death.

By now, the case was national news and over 20 different law enforcement agencies were involved in the investigation. It did nothing to discourage the killer.

On April 27, 1991, he killed 24-year-old Cherie Michelle Payseur, a
hotel maid who sometimes supplemented her earnings by
prostitution. Just over a month later, picnickers near Railroad
Canyon Road found the remains of 37-year-old Sherry Ann
Latham. Like the other victims, Latham was a prostitute. She'd
been strangled to death.

The first break in the case came on August 15, 1991. On that day, a
man driving a gray van picked up a prostitute near the University
of California. He drove her to a quiet spot. Then, without warning,
he began assaulting her. Fortunately, the woman was able to get
out of the vehicle and run away. Looking back, she saw the man
drive off, then stop to pick up another girl, 23-year-old Kelly
Hammond. Later that evening, Hammond's strangled corpse was
found near the intersection of Sampson Avenue and Delilah Street.

The police now had a description of the killer and within hours
television stations were broadcasting a composite sketch. It did
nothing to stop the slaughter.

Catherine McDonald was killed on September 13, 1991, her right
breast removed and apparently carried from the scene. Six weeks
later, on October 30, Delilah Zamora Wallace turned up dead. On
December 23, it was Eleanore Ojeda Casares, her body left just half
a mile from Riverside Police headquarters. She'd been strangled
and her right breast was missing.

Then finally, on January 9, 1992, the police made an arrest after a
patrolman pulled up a gray Mitsubishi van for an illegal U-turn.

The driver identified himself as William Suff and was polite and cooperative. However, a computer check showed that his driver's license was suspended and that his vehicle registration had expired. He was therefore transported to the Riverside police station for questioning.

Back at the precinct, homicide detectives interrogated Suff for several hours and although he repeatedly denied any involvement in the prostitute killings, he was a good match for the description provided by the eyewitness. He was therefore charged with murder.

While blood and hair samples were obtained for comparison against evidence lifted from the victims, a warrant was obtained for Suff's home and vehicle. Meanwhile, detectives began looking into Suff's past and were astonished to find that he had served time for murder. In 1974, when Suff was 24-years-old, he and his former wife were convicted for beating their two-year-old daughter to death. Suff had received a 70-year sentence but had been paroled after serving just ten.

William Suff's trial began on March 25, 1995. He entered a plea of not guilty, his attorney describing the case against him as "largely circumstantial."

Unfortunately for Suff, it was forensic evidence that damned him. Hairs found at the murder scenes matched samples of Suff's hair; fibers from a blanket found inside Suff's van were similar to those discovered on the victims; fibers from the carpet in Suff's vehicle matched fibers found on the victims.

Suff was found guilty on 12 counts of first-degree murder on
August 17, 1995. He was sentenced to death and currently awaits
execution on death row at San Quentin.

84. Donald Gaskins

Country: United States

Confirmed Victims: 12

Suspected Victims: 80+

Donald "Pee Wee" Gaskins was born on March 13, 1933, in Florence County, South Carolina. He never knew his father, and was raised instead by a succession of his mother's brutal boyfriends.

In 1944, at the age of just 11, he quit school and started working at a local garage. He also began committing burglaries and during the course of one of those break-ins struck a young girl with an axe. Gaskins assumed that he'd killed the girl, but she survived to point the finger at him. He was shipped off to the South Carolina Industrial School for Boys.

On his first night at the reformatory, Gaskins was gang-raped by a group of 20 youths. Thereafter, he suffered habitual sexual and physical abuse before escaping in 1950, with less than a year of his sentence to run. He fled to Sumter, where he joined a traveling carnival, and married the first of his six wives, a 13-year-old member of the crew. She convinced him to return to the reformatory and he did, fulfilling the last three months of his sentence in solitary confinement.

Released on his 18th birthday, Gaskins got a job on a tobacco plantation, while also moonlighting as an arsonist for hire in a number of insurance scams. When his employer's teenage daughter teased him about his criminal activities, he picked up a hammer and cracked the girl's skull. That sent him back to prison for five years.

Gaskins entered the South Carolina state prison in the fall of 1952. Eager to make a name for himself, he attacked the most feared inmate in the penitentiary, cutting the man's throat. That murder added an additional nine years to Pee Wee's sentence. It was worth it. No one messed with him after that.

Paroled in August 1961, Gaskins landed a job as a driver for a traveling preacher named George Todd. A year later, he was arrested for statutory rape and sent back to prison for six years.

Pee Wee completed his latest period of incarceration in November 1968. Thereafter, he moved back to Sumter and got a job working construction. It was during this time that he first started taking long drives along the Carolina coast.

On one of these drives, in September 1969, he picked up a hitchhiker, a pretty blond girl, who he immediately started propositioning. The girl laughed him off. Pee wee, in a rage, knocked her unconscious, then drove her to an old logging road, where he raped and sodomized her. He then spent some time torturing the girl with a knife before dropping her weighted body into a swamp. She was still alive when she hit the water.

The murder thrilled Gaskins and made him eager for more. From then on, he trolled the coastal highways on weekends, looking for victims. By 1970, he was averaging one "Coastal Kill" (as he called them) every six weeks. His victims did not die easy. Gaskins would keep them alive for hours, sometimes for days, as he mutilated and tortured them. On one occasion, he emasculated two teenaged boys, then cooked and ate their severed genitals in front of them. Between September 1969 and December 1975, Gaskins estimated that he claimed between 80 and 90 victims.

Gaskins carried out the "Coastal Kills" purely for his own amusement. But from 1970, he also began committing what he called, "Serious Murders." That is, he began killing for profit or to hide evidence of other crimes.

His first two "serious" victims were his 15-year-old niece, Janice Kirby, and her 17-year-old friend, Patricia Alsobrook, picked up from a bar in November 1970, driven to an abandoned house, then raped and drowned in a water barrel.

A month later, Gaskins kidnapped, raped and murdered Peggy Cuttino, the 12-year-old daughter of South Carolina senator James Cuttino, Jr. Shortly after, he killed Martha Dicks, a 20-year-old African American woman who apparently became infatuated with him.

In late 1971, Gaskins murdered Eddie Brown and his wife Bertie. Brown was a gunrunner who Gaskins believed was trying to set him up. In July 1973, he moved to Prospect, South Carolina, where he committed three more murders, including that of a 14-year-old runaway, Jackie Freeman, who he claims to have cannibalized.

The following year, Gaskins committed his most heinous crime yet. He offered a ride to Doreen Dempsey and her two-year-old daughter Robin Michelle, then drove them to the woods, killed Doreen with a hammer, and raped the child before strangling her to death.

In 1974, Gaskins killed Johnny Sellars, a car thief who owed him money. He also killed Sellars' girlfriend, Jessie Ruth Judy, to prevent her from reporting Sellars missing. He followed that up by killing Horace Jones, after the man made a pass at Gaskins' wife.

The bloodshed continued in 1975, which Gaskins would later refer to as "my killingest year." He started it off by murdering a man and two women, "hippie types," as he described them. Then he carried out the contract killing of Silas Yates, a wealthy Florence County farmer. A woman named Diane Neely got to hear of the murder and tried to blackmail Gaskins. Bad mistake. Gaskins lured Neely and her lover, Avery Howard, to a wooded area where he shot them both.

Next, he killed Kim Ghelkins, a 13-year-old who angered him by rejecting his sexual advances. Not long after, he murdered 25-year-old Dennis Bellamy and 15-year-old Johnny Knight after he caught them trying to burgle his workshop.

In October 1975, Gaskins and his cohort Walter Neely were pulled in for questioning regarding the disappearance of Kim Ghelkins. Pee Wee steadfastly denied any knowledge of Ghelkins' whereabouts, but Neely quickly cracked under interrogation and told the whole sordid tale. In short order, he'd led investigators to the buried remains of Bellamy, Knight, Sellars, Judy, Howard, his sister Diane Neely, and Doreen Dempsey and her daughter Robin Michelle.

Gaskins went on trial in May 1976. Found guilty, he was sentenced to death, a sentence that was commuted just six months later, when the US Supreme Court vacated all death sentences

But Gaskins wasn't done yet. In 1982, he carried out the contract killing of a death row inmate named Rudolph Tyner. Tried and found guilty of that murder, Gaskins was again sentenced to death.

This time, there would be no reprieve. Pee Wee Gaskins died in South Carolina's electric chair on September 6, 1991.

83. Herb Mullin

Country: United States

Confirmed Victims: 13

Suspected Victims: 13

Herbert Mullin was born on April 18, 1947, one of two children. He was, by all accounts, a happy, well-adjusted boy who did well in school, had a steady girlfriend, and was voted by his classmates "most likely to succeed." He seemed destined for great things.

But then, something changed. After the death of a close friend in an automobile accident, Mullin's behavior became increasingly off kilter. He became obsessed with the idea of reincarnation and started spending all of his time in his room, studying Eastern religions, looking for answers. He changed his college major from Engineering to Philosophy and then dropped out of college altogether. He started smoking pot, then graduated to harder drugs. He began rambling on about an impending earthquake.

By 1969, Mullin's family were concerned enough about his behavior to have him admitted to Mendocino State Hospital. But whatever treatment he received had little effect. He continued ramblings about receiving messages from beyond, telling him to do things. He took to wearing a large black sombrero and speaking in a fake Mexican accent. Then he shaved his head and went on a crash diet to rapidly lose weight. Another time, he became aggressive when an Asian woman ignored his suggestion that they make a bi-racial baby together.

His behavior seemed to swing from one extreme to another, he declared himself a pacifist, then tried to join the U.S. Marines, he was an avid user of LSD and marijuana, yet said he hated hippies, he claimed to hate organized religion, yet attended Bible study groups.

In May 1971, when Herb Mullin was 24, he moved to San Francisco. There he lived in a squalid apartment building populated by drug addicts and alcoholics. Around this time, he decided to become a boxer, beating his opponent into a pulp in his first bout and having to be pulled away by his trainer. After losing his next fight, Mullin suddenly announced that he wanted to become a priest. He could often be heard late at night having screaming arguments with God, while he punched the floor until his knuckles bled. Eventually, he was evicted.

Mullin moved back in with his parents in September 1972, and declared that he was going to get his life together. But then some crackpot scientist made the news by predicting that a serious earthquake was about to devastate California. Herb Mullin had long predicted this himself. He took it as a sign.

On October 13, 1972, Mullin armed himself with a baseball bat and went for a drive. Along a quiet road, he spotted a homeless man, Lawrence White, walking alone. Pulling the car over, Mullin got out and beat the man to death, then dragged his body into the woods. He'd later claim that White had sent him a telepathic message asking Mullin to kill him so that others might be saved.

Days later, Mullin picked up a hitchhiker, Mary Guilfoyle. No sooner had Guilfoyle settled into the passenger seat than Mullin stabbed her in the chest with a hunting knife, killing her instantly. He then drove her into the woods, found a quiet spot and conducted a crude "autopsy," ripping the body apart and removing the organs.

The next murder occurred on November 2. Mullin had been drinking and decided to go to St. Mary's Catholic Church in Los Gatos. There, he attacked Father Henri Tomei, stabbing him through the heart. As the priest fell, a parishioner entered the church. She saw what was happening and ran away screaming. Mullin fled too, leaving fingerprints at the scene.

Needless to say, the murder of a priest, inside a church, sparked outrage in the community. But despite the fingerprints and the eyewitness account, no arrest followed.

In the meanwhile, Mullin's father had had enough of Herb's bizarre and unpredictable behavior. He told Herb to move out, which he did, moving into a   squalid apartment on January 19, 1973. By now the urge to kill was simmering again and he decided to murder a former high school buddy, Jim Gianera.

On January 25, 1973, Mullin drove to the home of Bob Francis, a drug dealer and known associate of Gianera. Obtaining Gianera's address from Kathy Francis, (Bob's wife), he drove to Gianera's apartment and shot both Jim and his wife, Joan, in the head. He then drove back to the Francis residence and murdered Kathy

Francis and her two sons, aged 9 and 11. Afterwards, he mutilated all three bodies with a knife.

Two weeks later, on February 10, Mullin was wandering in the woods in Henry Cowell State Park, when he came across an illegal campsite occupied by four teenaged boys - Brian Scott Card, David Oliker, Robert Spector, and Mark Dreibelbis. Mullin demanded that they leave. When the boys refused, he killed them, later claiming that they'd given their permission to be murdered. The bodies were found a week later by the brother of one of the victims.

And still, Mullin wasn't done. On February 13, he was bringing some firewood to his parent's home when he spotted Fred Perez at work in his driveway. Mullin was carrying a rifle in his car. He angled it out of a window and fired at Perez, hitting him in the heart and killing him instantly.

This time, though, there was a witness. A neighbor heard the shot and saw Mullin driving away from the scene. A lone officer later pulled Mullin over and arrested him. He offered no resistance.

Herb Mullin's trial began July 30, 1973. He proved himself a troublesome defendant, constantly interrupting proceedings with his outlandish outbursts.
He claimed that he had killed his victims in order to prevent a cataclysmic earthquake from destroying California, adding that his victims had given their permission for him to kill them.

When the matter went to the jury, on August 19, 1973, they deliberated for fourteen hours before finding Herbert Mullin guilty on two counts of first-degree murder and eight counts of second-degree murder. Mullin was sentenced to life in prison. He will be eligible for parole in 2025.

82. Lorenzo Gilyard

Country: United States

Confirmed Victims: 13

Suspected Victims: 13

It is a sad indictment of the times we live in, when a serial killer as prolific as Lorenzo Gilyard goes almost unnoticed. Over a 16-year period, from 1977 to 1993, Gilyard terrorized Kansas City, Missouri, strangling to death at least 13 women, all but one of them prostitutes.

The first victim was 17-year-old Stacie Swofford, killed in April 1977, her body dumped in a garbage-strewn lot. Three years later, Gwen Kizine, a 15-year-old just starting out in the dangerous world of prostitution, was found dead in an alleyway. Another teenaged prostitute, Margaret Miller, died at the hands of the same killer in May 1982.

Whether or not the police identified the three murders as a series, is unknown. Before any headway was made in the investigation, the killings suddenly stopped.

They resumed four years later, on March 14, 1986. The fourth victim, 34-year-old, Catherine Barry was not a prostitute, but she was homeless and living on the streets, easy prey for a serial killer.

In August 1986, another prostitute, 23-year-old Naomi Kelly showed up dead, her body discarded in a downtown park popular with drug addicts. Fourteen weeks later, the naked corpse of Debbie Blevins, 32, turned up outside a church in fashionable Westport.

The new year brought no respite from the killings. Five women – Ann Barnes, 36,
Kellie Ann Ford, 20, Angela Mayhew, 19, Sheila Ingold, 36, and Carmeline Hibbs, 30, were found murdered in 1987. All were prostitutes. All had been strangled.

By now, the police knew that they were dealing with a serial killer, but their response to the situation was tepid at best. Neither was the media particularly interested in the murder spree happening in their city. The Kansas City Strangler did attract some attention in the press but, as is often the case with prostitute victims, the coverage was muted. It was hardly the outcry you'd expect after ten brutal murders.

Over a year passed before the killer struck again. The victim was another prostitute, 26-year-old Austrian national, Helga Kruger. And four more years passed before the last victim, Connie Luther, was found dead in January 1993. Thereafter, the killings stopped entirely.

By 2003, the Kansas City Strangler investigation had long been consigned to a cold case file, with little prospect of a resolution.

DNA technology had, of course, advanced to the point where cold cases were being revisited and solved all over the country, but the Kansas City Police Department simply lacked the funds to reopen its hundreds of cold cases.

All of that changed in 2003, when the department was given $111,000 in federal funding, enabling it to run DNA tests on evidence from unsolved homicides. One of the cases chosen for evaluation was the 1986 murder of Naomi Kelly.

A match was soon obtained to a man named Lorenzo Gilyard, an ex-con who had served four years for felony assault. But then lab technicians got an unexpected bonus, linking Gilyard to twelve other murders, including all of the Kansas City Strangler killings.

Gilyard was well known to the Kansas City Police Department. He had, in fact, been a suspect at the height of the prostitute murders. Aside from that, he'd racked up a long list of rape arrests and yet had always managed to avoid serious jail time until his assault conviction in 1982. The four years he'd been away matched the break in the prostitute murders.

Gilyard was arrested in 2004. Aware that he'd likely face the death penalty if found guilty, his lawyers asked for a deal. Gilyard would waive his right to a jury trial, as well as his right of appeal, if the prosecutor did not seek the death penalty.

Jackson County Prosecutor Jim Kanatzar agreed, but it would be a full three years before the matter eventually came to trial in 2007. Charged with seven murders, Gilyard was found guilty of six. He was sentenced to life in prison without the possibility of parole.

81. The Boston Strangler

Country: United States

Confirmed Victims: 13

Suspected Victims: 13

Between June 1962 and January 1964, eleven Massachusetts women fell victim to a serial strangler. The killer entered his victims' homes without using force, apparently able to talk his way in. All of the women were then sexually assaulted before being strangled, usually with stockings or other items of clothing. The press dubbed this fiend, "The Boston Strangler."

The first Strangler victim was Anna Slesers, a 55-year-old divorcee who lived in the Back Bay area. On the evening of June 14, 1962, Slesers' son, Juris, arrived to take her to a church meeting. He found her lying on the bathroom floor, the cord from her robe drawn tightly around her neck.

A couple of weeks later, a retired 68-year-old physiotherapist named Nina Nichols was found sexually assaulted and strangled in her apartment. That same day, in the Boston suburb of Lynn, 65-year-old Helen Blake died in almost identical circumstances.

On August 21, 75-year-old Ida Irga was found dead in her apartment, strangled with a pillowcase, her nude body suggestively posed. Just 24 hours later, Jane Sullivan, a 67-year-old nurse, was found laid out in her bathtub. The condition of the corpse made it impossible to determine whether she'd been sexually assaulted or not.

As panic gripped the city of Boston, there was a three-month reprieve before the next murder. Sophie Clark was an attractive, 21-year-old African-American student. On December 5, 1962, Sophie's roommates discovered her nude body, legs apart, three nylon stockings knotted tightly around her neck.

As police began questioning Sophie Clark's neighbors, an interesting clue emerged, a young man had been knocking on doors in the building claiming to be a painter send by the building manager. According to the manager, he had not employed anyone to do painting work.

Three weeks after the murder of Sophie Clark, a 23-year-old secretary named Patricia Bissette was found raped and strangled to death in her apartment. On May 8, 1963, the body of 23-year-old graduate student Beverly Samans was discovered. She'd been stabbed, not strangled, but the way that the body was posed, provided a link to the other murders.

The summer of 1963 brought a break in the killings. Then on September 8, 1963, the strangler was back. 58-year-old divorcee, Evelyn Corbin, was found strangled in her home in Salem, Massachusetts, two nylon stockings knotted around her neck.

On November 25, while Bostonians grieved the death of assassinated President John F. Kennedy, another murder occurred. 23-year-old Joann Graff had been dead three days by the time her body was found. Two nylon stockings were tied in an elaborate bow around her neck. There were teeth marks on her breast and there was evidence that she'd been sexually assaulted.

As in the Clark case, a stranger was spotted in the building at around the time of the murder. Eyewitness descriptions were startlingly similar to the "painter" who had been seen near Sophie Clark's apartment.

Just over a month later, on January 4, 1964, two young women returned home to find their roommate, 19-year-old Mary Sullivan murdered. Mary was posed, sitting upright on a bed. Two stockings and a pink silk scarf were knotted around her neck, while a "Happy New Year" card resting against her feet. A thick liquid that looked like semen dripped from her mouth. A broomstick handle had been rammed into her vagina.

At this point in the story, it is necessary to take a detour to a bizarre series of sexual offenses that occurred in the Cambridge area a couple of years before the Boston Strangler appeared on the scene. Over a period of three months, a man took to knocking on doors, asking any woman who answered if she was interested in modeling work. If the woman said yes, he'd insist that he needed to measure her, to ascertain that she met the agency's requirements. That done, he'd thank the woman, and say he'd be in touch. Of course, he never called again. Eventually, some of the women complained to the police.

On March 17, 1961, Cambridge police apprehended a man trying to break into a house. Under questioning, the burglar confessed to being the "Measuring Man." He was Albert De Salvo, a 29-year-old Bostonian with numerous arrests for breaking and entering. De Salvo's was sentenced to 18 months and was released in April 1962, two months before the first Boston Strangler murder.

In November 1964, De Salvo was arrested on a more serious charge. A couple of weeks earlier, he'd entered a residence and placed a knife to a woman's throat. Then he'd stripped her naked and fondled her before fleeing the apartment. Before he left he apologized for what he'd done.

The woman's description of her attacker led investigators to De Salvo. He was brought in for questioning and quickly confessed to a spate of similar crimes committed by an offender known to police as "The Green Man."

De Salvo was sent to Bridgewater State Hospital where his cellmate was a man named George Nassar, accused of the execution-style killing of a gas station attendant.

Days later, Nasser called his attorney, F. Lee Bailey, and asked him to meet with De Salvo. Bailey walked away from that meeting with a taped confession to the Boston Strangler murders.

Bailey's next move was to sit down with Massachusetts Attorney General John Brooke to thrash out a deal. His offer was simple. De Salvo would plead guilty to the Green Man assaults and accept a life sentence, removing him from the streets. He would not face trial for the Boston Strangler murders.

The offer seemed less that favorable to the state of Massachusetts, but Brooke was acutely aware that there was no evidence against De Salvo other than his confession, which was inadmissible under attorney-client privilege rules. He knew also, the implications of losing such an important case during an election year. He therefore agreed to Bailey's terms.

Albert De Salvo duly went on trial for the Green Man charges on January 10, 1967, and received a life sentence. He'd serve less than six years before being stabbed to death by an unknown assailant.

But was De Salvo really the Boston Strangler? Most experts believe not. They find it incomprehensible that De Salvo could have been carrying out the Boston Strangler murders and the Green Man assaults at the same time. In the Strangler case, the victims were brutally slain, while the Green Man merely fondled his victims, always offering an apology before fleeing the scene.

So if not De Salvo, who then? It has not escaped notice that the two eyewitness descriptions of the Strangler bore a striking resemblance to George Nasser, De Salvo's cellmate and the man who convinced him to confess in the first place.

80. Duan Guocheng

Country: China

Confirmed Victims: 13

Suspected Victims: 13 +

At around midnight, on a sultry Thursday evening in 2001, 41-year-old Wang Guiyu was walking to her home in Wuhan, an industrial city in the east-central province of Hubei, China. Wang knew the neighborhood well, so she cut through a series of back roads and darkened alleys. Still, she trod carefully. These streets were far from safe at night. Just recently, there'd been rumors of a number of knife attacks on women. She was glad to eventually see the steel security gate of the middle-class apartment block where she lived.

Wang hurried across the street, then stopped to enter her access code. In the next moment, she heard faint footfalls and something heavy collided with the back of her head. Wang stumbled back, screaming, trying desperately to pull herself through the gate. She didn't make it. Gaining a handhold on her arm, her assailant spun her around and plunged a knife repeatedly into her chest, delivering seven brutal blows. Then, as lights began to come on in the apartment building, he fled, leaving the woman dead on the sidewalk.

Wang Guiyu was one of six women who fell to a vicious serial killer in the city of Wuhan during a frenzied three months in the summer of 2001. The night after her murder, the killer struck again, dragging down a 20-year-old migrant worker and hacking her to death.

And yet it might all so easily have been avoided. In fact, the police in Yueyang, just 80 miles away, knew exactly who was committing the murders and had passed this information on to their Wuhan colleagues. The Wuhan police had simply not paid attention.

Earlier that year, in February 2001, six police officers had arrived at a cramped, three-bedroom apartment in Yueyang. They were looking for Duan Guocheng, a 29-year-old security guard who lived there with his parents. Duan wasn't home, so they sat down to wait, ignoring Hu Yunxiang's pleas to tell them what her son had done wrong.

The officers waited all night, until Duan eventually appeared in the early morning hours. Spotting the policemen, he fled and although the officers gave chase he managed to evade them. The officers then returned to the apartment and revealed to Duan's parents why they were there. Their son was wanted on nine counts of murder.

The police were convinced that Duan had fled the city. Immediately, they transmitted bulletins to neighboring regions, providing details of their suspect, along with a photo and a list of aliases he might be using. They didn't hold out much hope though. Chinese police departments were notoriously insular. In all likelihood, their bulletin would be ignored.

The Yueyang police were right about Duan leaving the city. But he hadn't gone far, just 80 miles down the road to Wuhan, a city full to overflowing with migrant workers, the perfect hunting ground for a serial killer. He'd only been in the city a couple of months, when he picked up the threads of his murderous campaign.

Just after midnight on May 7, a young woman was stabbed to death while on her way home from work. The following day, another woman died and over the next month, six more were attacked, four of them succumbing to their injuries. One of those fatalities was Wang Guiyu.

With the body count climbing, the Wuhan police scrambled furiously to catch the killer. A task force of over one thousand officers was put together; detectives leaned hard on their contacts; undercover female cops walked the streets hoping to lure the killer into the open. None of it helped. The Red Dress Killer continued to claim victims at will. It was as though the police were hunting a phantom.

Part of the problem was the lack of public awareness of the crimes. An informed public would have been alert to the killer and might have passed on valuable information to the police. But newspapers in China generally report on crimes only after the perpetrator has been caught, so the dailies carried no stories about the murders, leaving the populace blissfully unaware of the savage creature in their midst.

On August 10, three months after the killings began, the Wuhan police finally decided to contact their colleagues in neighboring cities. From Yueyang they learned about Duan Guocheng, whose details had been sent to them back in February, before the murders had started. According to the original bulletin, Duan often used the alias Hu Cheng. Following that lead the police traced him in just three days.

He was staying at a guesthouse called the Aerospace Institute Inn, ironically just a few blocks from Wuhan's main police station. A unit was dispatched to the hotel and, after a brief struggle, took Duan into custody.

Duan Goucheng was charged with murder and went on trial in December 2001. In February 2002, he was found guilty and sentenced to death. Details of his execution are not recorded, but Chinese justice moves swiftly. He is likely to have been put to death soon after.

79. Francisco Antonio Laureana

Country: Argentina

Confirmed Victims: 13

Suspected Victims: 13+

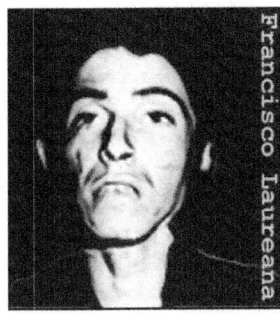

Argentina has produced very few serial killers and certainly none of the ferocity of other South American monsters like Garavito, Lopez, or Camargo. However, over a six-month period during late 1974 and early 1975, a particularly vicious predator was stalking the streets of Buenos Aires. His name was Francisco Antonio Laureana, and his reign of terror left at least 13 women brutally shot and strangled to death.

On the face of it, there was little reason to suspect that 35-year-old Francisco Laureana might be a serial killer. Raised in a religious family, Laureana had attended a seminarian college at Corrientes. He'd later moved to San Isidro, Buenos Aires, where he worked as a craftsman, making and selling earrings, bracelets, and necklaces. He married and fathered three children and was known to regularly warn them about going out on the streets because there were, "so many degenerates outside."

Yet, even while he was delivering these sermons, Laureana might have already been a murderer. While he was attending school in Corrientes, one of his fellow students had been raped, murdered and left hanging in a stairwell. The killer was never caught and no suspicion ever fell on Laureana. But given what we now know about the man, it isn't too much of a stretch to believe that he might have been responsible.

Exactly what it was that sparked Laureana's final killing spree is unknown. What is known is that between August 1974 and February 1975, 13 Buenos Aires women showed up dead, with little doubt that the same man was responsible. The killer always struck on a Wednesday or Thursday, always close to 6 p.m.

The victims fell generally into two categories. Some had been attacked while sunbathing on their own property, others were plucked from railway stations or bus stops. The outcome though was always the same, the woman ended up raped, then either strangled or shot to death with a .32 caliber pistol. Although the victims were not robbed, personal items were always taken. These would later be found in Laureana's home, hidden in a boot.

The Buenos Aires police, of course, had very little experience or expertise in dealing with a serial killer. Add to that the pointed denials from the Peron government that such a killer was loose on the streets and it is easy to see how Laureana was able to get away with his audacious crimes for so long.

Eventually, though, his luck ran out. An eyewitness spotted Laureana fleeing one of his crime scenes. Laureana fired at the man but missed and the man was later able to provide an accurate description. Within days, flyers were hanging from every lamppost in Buenos Aires, bearing the likeness of Francisco Laureana.

With so much heat on the street, you might have thought that Laureana would lay low. He didn't. On February 27, 1975, a woman spotted Laureana speaking to her daughter. Recognizing him from the wanted posters, she immediately called the police, who arrived to find the fugitive just a few blocks away.

But Laureana wasn't surrendering without a fight. A fierce gun battle ensued, during which Laureana was hit in the shoulder but managed to escape. Bleeding profusely, he hid in a henhouse but was tracked there by police. Still not prepared to surrender, he started shooting whereupon police officers returned fire and killed him.

Despite the sensational nature of the case, there was no coverage in the local media, the details having being suppressed by the Peron regime. It was only in later years that the story of Francisco Laureana, Argentina's most prolific serial killer, became public knowledge.

78. Peter Sutcliffe

Country: England

Confirmed Victims: 13

Suspected Victims: 15

Peter William Sutcliffe was born in Bingley, Yorkshire, on June 2, 1946, the first son of John and Kathleen Sutcliffe. He was a frail baby, who grew to be a shy, introverted boy with little interest in sports and games. At school, he was often a target for bullies and he dropped out at 15, working for a while in a mill, then finding work as a gravedigger at Bingley Cemetery.

In 1966, Sutcliffe started dating Czech immigrant, Sonia Szurma, the couple eventually marrying in August 1974. By then, Sutcliffe had moved on from his grave-digging job and was working as a truck driver.

But all was not well in the Sutcliffe's marriage. The couple was desperate to have children but after a series of miscarriages, Sonia was told that she'd never be able to conceive. Meanwhile, Peter enjoyed bragging to his drinking buddies about his exploits with prostitutes.

Sutcliffe's first recorded attack on a woman occurred on July 4, 1975, when he bludgeoned Anna Patricia Rogulskyj with a hammer and then inflicted deep slashes across her body with a knife. She survived, but the next victim, Wilma McCann, was not so lucky. She was bludgeoned and stabbed to death in Leeds on August 29.

On January 20, 1976, the Ripper was back in Leeds where he bludgeoned to death, Emily Jackson, a middle-aged housewife moonlighting as a prostitute to make ends meet. Thereafter, he took a 13-month hiatus, returning in February 1977 to murder prostitute Irene Richardson, again in Leeds.

In April he showed up in Bradford, killing prostitute Tina Atkinson in her own apartment, severely mutilating her body after death.

Despite the brutality of the murders, they had thus far caused no great outrage in the media. But that was to change on June 16, when the Ripper cut down Jayne MacDonald, a 16-year-old schoolgirl killed while walking to a relative's house. Jayne's killing caused panic throughout the northeast since it was now evident that all women, not just prostitutes, were at risk.

In July, Sutcliffe attacked Maureen Long, a Bradford prostitute, fracturing her skull with a flurry of blows but failing to kill her. In October, he crossed the Pennines to slaughter Manchester prostitute, Jean Jordan. Jordan lay undiscovered for over a week, during which time Sutcliffe returned to the scene to inflict more damage on the corpse.

In January 1978, Sutcliffe appeared for the first time in the Yorkshire town of Huddersfield, where he murdered prostitute Helen Rytka. He followed that up with the slaughter of three "non-prostitute victims," Josephine Whittaker, Marguerite Walls, and Barbara Leach.

The police, of course, had not been sitting idle while the Ripper rampaged across northeast England. But their manhunt, the biggest ever launched in England, was hampered by the sheer weight of evidence and insufficient resources to manage the thousands of tips that were coming in daily. In addition, they were being taunted by a hoaxer claiming to be the Ripper. Countless hours were wasted as the police chased down false clues delivered in a series of letters and tape recordings.

The real Ripper meanwhile, carried out two non-fatal attacks in October and November, before dropping out of sight. He returned to his favorite hunting ground of Leeds in November 1980, to snuff out the life of student Jacqueline Hill.

The case eventually broke on January 2, 1981, when police in Sheffield arrested a man while he sat in a car with a known prostitute. The man identified himself as Peter Sutcliffe and asked the officers if he could go to some nearby bushes to relieve himself before they took him in. The officers allowed him to do so.

Sutcliffe was taken to the police station where he was interrogated. As he had been found parked with a prostitute in an isolated spot, Sutcliffe was questioned about the Yorkshire Ripper murders but denied any involvement. Detectives had meanwhile returned to search the area where Sutcliffe had been picked up. In the bushes close to where he had stood to urinate, they found a ball-peen hammer and a knife, his instruments of murder. Confronted with this new evidence Sutcliffe eventually cracked and admitted to the Yorkshire Ripper murders.

Peter Sutcliffe went on trial on May 5, 1981. He entered not guilty pleas to the 13 counts of murder, claiming diminished responsibility. According to Sutcliffe, he'd been instructed to kill prostitutes by a voice he'd heard coming from a gravestone in the cemetery where he'd worked. He believed it to be the voice of God.

The prosecution appeared willing to accept the plea after four different psychiatrists diagnosed Sutcliffe with paranoid schizophrenia. However, the trial judge, Justice Boreham, rejected the diminished responsibility plea. It would be up to the jury to decide on Sutcliffe's sanity and hence his responsibility for the crimes.

The verdict came on Friday, May 22, after a trial lasting 14 days. Sutcliffe was found guilty on all counts and sentenced to life imprisonment with the stipulation that he must serve at least 30 years. This was later extended to a whole life term, meaning that Sutcliffe will never be free.

Five years of terror were at an end, but for the surviving victims, as well as the parents, relatives, friends and children of the deceased, a lifetime of pain and suffering still lay ahead.

Peter Sutcliffe began his sentence at Parkhurst Prison but was later transferred to Broadmoor Hospital, under section 47 of the Mental Health Act of 1983. He has been attacked three times while incarcerated, suffering serious knife wounds and the loss of an eye.

Sonia Sutcliffe obtained a separation from Sutcliffe in 1982 and a divorce in April 1994.

The author of the Yorkshire Ripper letters, which had so hindered the police in their search for the killer, was finally arrested in October 2005. He was John Humble, an unemployed alcoholic who lived in Sunderland. In March 2006, he received an eight-year prison sentence for perverting the course of justice.

77. Richard Ramirez

Country: United States

Confirmed Victims: 13

Suspected Victims: 20+

For a thirteen-month period, from June 1985 to August 1986, the residents of Los Angeles County lived in terror of a vicious murderer known as the Night Stalker. The phantom came after dark, sneaking into his victims' bedrooms as they slept, dispatching the male occupant with a gunshot to the head, then raping and brutalizing the unfortunate woman. He would eventually be identified as Richard Ramirez, a high school dropout from El Paso, Texas.

Ramirez had arrived in Los Angeles in 1978. With neither friends nor prospects in his new hometown, he'd taken to supporting himself by burglary and petty theft. He'd been arrested twice, in 1981 and again in 1984. On each occasion, he walked on the charges. Yet nowhere was there any inkling of the reign of terror he was about to unleash.

Ramirez committed his first murder on June 28, 1984. In the early hours of that day, he broke into the Glassel Park home of 79-year old, Jennie Vincow, raping the elderly woman before stabbing and slashing her to death, the cuts so deep that the victim was almost decapitated.

After the Vincow murder, Ramirez lay dormant for eight months. On March 17, 1985, he re-emerged to murder 20-year-old Dayle Okazaki in her Rosemead, California apartment. Okazaki's roommate, Angela Barrios, narrowly escaped when she arrived home during the murder. Ramirez fired at her but missed. He then fled the scene, arriving soon after in nearby Monterey Park, where he shot 30-year-old Tsia-Lian Yu to death, as she walked along a sidewalk.

Ramirez waited just three days before he struck again, raping and murdering an 8-year-old girl in Eagle Rock, California. Then, on March 27, he committed a double homicide, shooting Vincent Zazzara, stabbing and mutilating his wife Maxine.

Six weeks after the Zazzara murders, Ramirez returned to Monterey Park, where he broke into the home of Harold and Jean Wu. 66-year-old Mr. Wu was shot. Mrs. Wu, 63, was savagely beaten, then raped, before Ramirez fled.

Two weeks passed before Ramirez broke into the home that Ruth Wilson shared with her 12-year-old son. Using threats of violence against the boy, he raped and sodomized Mrs. Wilson, before fleeing. She was later able to provide police with a description -

her attacker had been tall, with long dark hair, and of Hispanic origin.

By this time, the media was awash with stories of a serial killer running loose in the city, sparking widespread panic. There was a run on new locks and security systems. Police were on high alert. None of this seems to have bothered Ramirez. Instead of slowing down, his reign of terror was escalating.

On May 29, he attacked Malvia Keller, 83, and her sister Blanche Wolfe, 80, beating the two old women to death with a hammer. A month later, on June 27, he raped a 6-year-old girl in Arcadia. A day after that, he murdered 32-year-old Patty Elaine Higgins in her Arcadia home. Five days later, he committed another murder in Arcadia, slitting the throat of 75-year old Mary Louise Cannon. And he surfaced again in Arcadia on July 5, savagely bludgeoning 16-year-old Deidre Palmer with a tire iron. She survived her injuries.

Two days later he was back in Monterey Park, where he battered 61-year-old Joyce Nelson to death. Later that same night, he entered the home of 63-year-old Linda Fortuna. He tried to rape Mrs. Fortuna but couldn't get an erection. When she started screaming, he fled, leaving her unharmed.

On July 20, the Night Stalker switched his attention to Glendale, killing and mutilating Maxson Kneiling and his wife, Lela, both 66. Later that night, he shot 32-year-old Chitat Assawahem as he slept, then raped his 29-year-old wife Sakima. Before he fled, he sodomized the couple's 8-year-old son.

By now, Ramirez had a well-established M.O. and he used it again on August 6, breaking into the home of Christopher and Virginia Petersen. But this time, the killer had taken on more than he could handle. Despite a bullet that lodged in his brain, Christopher Petersen, a powerfully built man, chased the intruder from his home. Miraculously, Petersen survived the bullet wound.

Ramirez had more success two nights later, in Diamond Bar, California. Ahmed Zia, 35, was shot in the head while he slept. His wife, Suu Kyi Zia, was subjected to a prolonged attack during which she was raped, sodomized, and forced to perform oral sex.

Then, with police attention in Los Angeles County intensifying, the Night Stalker shifted his focus north.

Peter and Barbara Pan were attacked on August 18, in Lake Merced, a San Francisco suburb. Mr. Pan was pronounced dead at the scene. His wife survived, but would be an invalid for the rest of her life. A man matching the Stalker's description later sold a pair of Mr. Pan's cufflinks to a pawnbroker.

While San Francisco police were following this lead, Ramirez headed back south. On August 24, he attacked a young couple in Mission Viejo, shooting the man in the head, raping and sodomizing the woman.

But Ramirez had made his first mistake. Earlier that evening a teenager had noticed an orange Toyota cruising the neighborhood. The behavior of the driver struck the boy as suspicious, so he jotted down the license plate number. Next morning, when news of the attack came out, he passed the license number on to police.

The vehicle turned out to have been stolen from L.A.'s Chinatown district and police were able to lift a print from it, a print that belonged to Richard Ramirez. His name and photograph were immediately released to the media.

But could they stop the Night Stalker before he killed again?

With his face receiving blanket coverage on TV and in the newspapers you might have thought Ramirez would have lain low for a while. He didn't. A week after the Mission Viejo attack, Ramirez tried to steal a car in East L.A. Unfortunately for him, the owner was under the car at the time, working on the transmission. He gave chase, and along with several of his neighbors, managed to apprehend Ramirez, beating him severely and holding him until the police arrived.

Ramirez was charged with fourteen murders and thirty-one other felonies.

On September 20, 1989, after almost two months of deliberation, the jury pronounced a guilty verdict. Two weeks later, they voted for the death penalty. It was a sentence that would never be carried out.

Richard Ramirez died of complications arising from B-cell lymphoma on June 7, 2013. He had been on death row at San Quentin for 23 years.

76. Kaspars Petrovs

Country: Latvia

Confirmed Victims: 13

Suspected Victims: 38

The tiny Eastern European nation of Latvia has produced few serial murderers during its long history. However, between the years 2000 and 2003, a particularly vicious killer was stalking the capital city of Rigo, claiming one elderly victim after the other, 38 of them strangled to death in their apartments within the space of three short years. And yet the police seemed incapable of catching the monster until he got careless and left a fingerprint behind. That turned up a match to a man who had a single conviction on file, for a theft in 1998. His name was Kaspars Petrovs.

Kaspars Petrovs was born in Rigo in 1978. He was the son of a prominent surgeon and his family was well off, if not exactly wealthy. He certainly lacked for nothing growing up. However, Kaspars was a problem child, always in trouble for some or other ill-advised prank or caper. He would later say that he got into trouble because he was looking for attention. Finding none, he sought solace in books. Like most serial killers, he also spent much of his time in a fantasy world of his own creation.

His family might have hoped that Kaspars would follow in his father's footsteps. However, although undoubtedly bright, the boy lacked application, eventually dropping out of school and drifting from one menial job to another. By the time he committed his first murder, he had been homeless for three years.

Petrovs developed a simple but effective M.O. He targeted elderly women because they were easy to overpower. He sought out smartly dressed victims because he believed they probably had money. He'd follow them from the post office or from local markets. Often he'd approach them and strike up a conversation, then offer to carry their shopping bags home. Once there he'd attack them, strangle them and then rob the place of money, jewelry, even food. He'd then tuck the victim up in bed, as though she were asleep.

Another ruse was to knock on doors and pretend to be an employee of the gas company wanting to read the meter. Petrovs had worked out that older, single women tended to occupy the small apartments located on the middle floors of apartment buildings. On occasion, he'd use this knowledge to murder two victims in quick succession. He described one such attack as follows;

"I came into the stairway and walked up to the third floor, where I knocked on the middle door. An old woman opened it. I presented myself as a gas company official and went into the kitchen. I washed my hands, took the towel and went into the other room, where the woman was, and strangled the woman with the towel. Then I put her on the sofa, checked the closet and found the money, approximately 60 lats.

"I looked at the woman and saw the blood running from her nose. I went back to the kitchen, took the other two towels and cleaned the blood. I put those towels in the bag, closed the room and threw away the bag with the towels and a key.

"Afterwards, I felt terrible and started to vomit, but then I went to the next stairway and knocked again on the middle door."

This door was opened by another elderly woman. But after Petrovs grabbed her by the throat, she started screaming, causing him to flee. She was one of only eight victims who survived his deadly attentions. Thirty-eight other women would not be so lucky.

Petrovs was arrested on February 3, 2003, and charged initially with five murders. By November, the indictment had swelled to 38 murders, although the prosecutor had to be satisfied with trying him on 13 counts, where forensic evidence linked him inextricably to the crime scene.

Brought before the courts in April 2005, Kaspars claimed that he had not wanted to kill his victims, merely to render them unconscious so he could rob them. The judge, however, was not prepared to consider a plea of manslaughter. He sentenced

Kaspars to life in prison on May 12, 2005. The possibility of parole was not ruled out, although it is unlikely that Petrovs will ever be released.

75. Belle Gunness

Country: United States

Confirmed Victims: 13

Suspected Victims: 40+

Belle Gunness was born Brynhild Poulsdatter Storseth on November 11, 1859, in Trondheim, Norway, the eighth child of stonemason Paul Pedersen Storseth and his wife Berit. As a young woman, she immigrated to the United States where she settled in Chicago and married a man named Mads Sorenson.

The couple was keen to start a family, but as their union was not blessed with children, they adopted four orphans – Caroline, Axel, Myrtle, and Jennie. Of those, Caroline and Axel died in infancy, allegedly of acute colitis. Both were insured and the insurance company paid out on each occasion.

On July 30, 1900, Mads Sorensen developed similar symptoms to those shown by the children – nausea, fever, diarrhea, lower abdominal pain, and cramping. He died soon after, his death attributed to heart failure. A day later, his grieving widow collected a payout of $8,500 from the insurance company. She used her windfall to buy a farm on the outskirts of La Porte, Indiana.

Not long after she arrived in La Porte, Belle had a new husband, a tall, handsome, Norwegian named Peter Gunness. Just one week after the couple married on April 1, 1902, Peter's infant daughter died while alone in the house with Belle. Eight months later, in December 1902, Peter himself met with a tragic accident. According to Belle, an iron, sausage-grinding machine fell from a high shelf, striking him on the head. He died that same night.

The death of her second husband netted Belle $4,000. But not everyone was convinced that his death had been an accident. In fact, the district coroner convened a coroner's jury to look into the matter. The verdict came down in Belle's favor.

Over the next few years, the Gunness farm prospered, even though Belle seemed to have rotten luck with help, as her farmhands always seemed to abscond in the middle of the night. Then, in late 1906, Belle's adopted daughter, Jennie Olsen, disappeared. Belle said she'd gone away to attend a Lutheran College in Los Angeles and no one thought to question her explanation.

In the spring of 1907, Belle hired a dim-witted handyman named Ray Lamphere to help her around the farm. The two were soon lovers, but that didn't stop Belle placing ads in the matrimonial columns of various daily newspapers. A typical ad read as follows;

Comely widow who owns a large farm in one of the finest districts in La Porte County, Indiana, desires to make the acquaintance of a gentleman equally well provided, with view of joining fortunes. No replies by letter considered unless sender is willing to follow answer with personal visit. Triflers need not apply.

Several well-heeled, middle-aged men responded to Belle's ads, among them John Moe, of Elbow Lake, Minnesota. Moe arrived carrying more than $1,000 in cash to illustrate his credentials. He disappeared from the Gunness farm within a week. Other suitors also disappeared, including Ole B. Budsberg of Iola, Wisconsin, and Andrew Helgelien, a bachelor farmer from Aberdeen, South Dakota.

But by now, Belle's little matrimonial murder scam was running into problems. First, there was Ray Lamphere, jealous of the many men arriving to court Belle. After one flare up too many, she fired him in February 1908.

The other problem was more difficult to overcome. Asle Helgelien was querying his brother's whereabouts and insisting on traveling to La Porte to conduct a search.

With the odds stacking up against her, Gunness started making plans to flee, drawing up a will in favor of her children and cleaning out her bank accounts.

In the early hours of April 28, 1908, Joe Maxson, Belle's new farmhand, woke to find the Gunness house on fire. Maxson tried to get to his employer and her children but was driven back by the flames. He escaped the blaze by jumping from a second-floor window.

By morning, the farmhouse was a gutted ruin, with four bodies found inside, Belle's three children and the headless corpse of a woman. Suspicion immediately fell on Ray Lamphere, who had been heard around town uttering threats against Belle. He was taken into custody and charged with murder and arson.

But who were the victims? The identity of the three children wasn't in doubt, but there was much debate about the headless woman. At 5-foot-3 and 150 pounds, it was too small to be Belle Gunness, surely.

The argument was eventually settled by Belle's dentist, Dr. Ira Norton, who identified a piece of bridgework and stated categorically that it belonging to Belle. As a result, Coroner Charles Mack officially concluded that the body was Belle Gunness.

Meanwhile, Joe Maxson had come forward and told of a number of depressions in the earth behind the hog shed, which Gunness had ordered him to fill in. It sounded suspicious, so the sheriff put together a work detail and got them digging.

On May 3, 1908, the diggers unearthed the body of Jennie Olson, then the bodies of two unidentified children and then that of Andrew Helgelien. As the gruesome work continued, one body after another was disinterred, including those of Ole B. Budsberg and John Moe, former suitors of Belle Gunness.

But Belle wasn't around to take the rap, and Ray Lamphere was. In May 1908, he went on trial and was found not guilty of murder, but guilty of arson. He received a 20-year prison term but served only one before dying of tuberculosis on December 30, 1909.

Shortly after Lamphere's death, the Rev. E. A. Schell came forward with a confession that Lamphere had made to him. In it, Lamphere gave a detailed description of the crimes committed by Belle Gunness.

Lamphere said that Gunness had killed at least 42 men, amassing a fortune of $250,000 in the process ($6 million in today's money). Her method was simple. She'd drug her victim, then wait for him to pass out before caving in his head with a meat cleaver, later burying the body behind the hog shed.

The mystery of the headless corpse was also cleared up by Lamphere. It was not Belle, he insisted, but a woman she'd lured from Chicago with the promise of work as a housekeeper.

Lamphere's version of events is borne out by much of the evidence found at the Gunness farm. And if Belle Gunness really did fake her own death she managed to remain at large for the rest of her life. She was a true female Bluebeard, a heartless killer who got away with murder.

74. Jake Bird

Country: United States

Confirmed Victims: 14

Suspected Victims: 44

Jake Bird had a stock answer for anyone who asked where he was from. "Somewhere out in Louisiana where they got ain't no post office," he'd say. Wherever that town was, Jake remained there until he was 19 years old. Then he hit the road and would remain a transient for the rest of his life.

Work was plentiful in those days for anyone with the strength and stamina to wield a pick, a sledgehammer or a shovel. Jake found employment as a manual laborer on road crews and on the railroads. It was tough, backbreaking work, but it built up his strength and allowed him to travel the country in search of recreation.

And recreation to Jake Bird meant rape and murder. By the time of his capture in 1947, he'd racked up 44 victims, one for each year of his life.

The double homicide that would eventually end Jake Bird's murderous career, occurred on October 30, 1947. On that day, Bird was scouting a neighborhood in Tacoma, Washington, when he spotted 52-year-old Bertha Kludt and decided to attack her.

Finding an ax in the woodshed, Bird stripped off his clothes and entered the home where he raped Mrs. Kludt before hacking her and her 17-year-old daughter, Beverley, to death.

Unfortunately for Bird, the victims' dying screams were heard by a neighbor, who called the police. Officers Andrew P. Sabutis and Evan "Skip" Davies were dispatched to the scene and immediately encountered a barefoot man running from the house. The two patrolmen gave chase, eventually trapping Bird in an alley. Seeing that he was cornered, Bird pull a knife and attacked the officers, cutting Davies' hand and stabbing Sabutis in the shoulder. Sabutis, though, was a former prizefighter, and a left-hook to the jaw soon put Bird's lights out. The officers then returned to the house where they found the two women, brutally slain.

Bird's trial was set for Monday, November 24, 1947. As was customary in those days, he was charged with only one murder, that of Bertha Kludt. The logic was that, should he somehow be found not guilty, he could then be tried for the other murder.

Of course, there was never any prospect that Bird, a black man who'd murdered two white women, would be found not guilty. After a trial lasting just one-and-a-half days, he was convicted and sentenced to hang.

Unlike the modern era, where condemned prisoners can sit for years or even decades on death row, justice moved swiftly in those days. It was rare for an execution to be delayed by more than a couple of months. But Bird and his lawyer played the system well. Through a series of stays and reprieves, they managed to delay the inevitable for nearly two years.

Many of those stays were achieved by offering to clear up unsolved homicides. During that time, Bird confessed to 44 murders and was visited by law enforcement officers from all over the country. At least 11 murders were definitely attributed to him, occurring in locations as far flung as Evanston, Illinois; Louisville, Kentucky; Omaha, Nebraska; Kansas City, Kansas; Sioux Falls, South Dakota; Cleveland, Ohio; Orlando, Florida; and Portage, Wisconsin.

In addition, police in Houston suspected Bird in the murder of a Mrs. Richardson, and Chicago authorities believed him responsible for a weighted body retrieved from Lake Michigan, near Kenosha. Los Angeles detectives wanted to question Bird about the murder of a black youth and a Jewish grocer, while in New York City, he was linked to the robbery and murder of a delicatessen owner.

Bird's favored targets though, were women, specifically white women. A psychiatrist who examined him in prison said that Bird derived sexual satisfaction from the sight of women cowering from him in terror.

Time eventually ran out for Jake Bird in July 1949. On Thursday, July 14, he ate his final meal and spoke with his attorney for two hours. Later that night, he was moved to a holding cell, where he shaved and dressed in a new suit.

Just after midnight, he was marched ten feet from the death cell to the gallows. Prison chaplain, Reverend Arvid Ohrnell, started to read a note from Bird, saying he bore no malice toward anyone and sought forgiveness. Before he had finished, the trapdoor was sprung, and Jake Bird plunged to his death.

73. Arthur Shawcross

Country: United States

Confirmed Victims: 14

Suspected Victims: 14+

On March 24, 1988, police in Rochester, New York, pulled a body from the waters of Salmon Creek, a tributary of the Genesee River. She was Dorothy Blackburn, a 27-year-old prostitute who had gone missing on March 18. She had suffered a severe beating prior to her death, with vaginal trauma and bite marks. She'd also been strangled.

Prostitution is a high-risk occupation and prostitute murders a fact of life for most city police departments. Rochester PD did what they could, but the meager leads they had led nowhere. A year passed without any progress. Then other prostitutes started showing up dead.

On September 9, 1989, a man out searching for empty bottles, stumbled on a set of skeletal remains, later identified from dental records as Anna Steffen. On October 21, hikers walking a trail along the Genesee River Gorge came across a decomposing, headless corpse. Six days later, a boy retrieving a soccer ball from a site close to the Gorge, saw a foot sticking out from beneath a pile of debris. Police arrived to find the maggot-infested corpse of Patty Ives, a once-attractive streetwalker.

The discovery of three dead prostitutes in such quick succession suggested to that a serial killer might be at work. And as the police had no viable leads to follow, they decided to focus their attention on Lyell Avenue, the preferred prostitute pick-up spot in Rochester. Officers began working the area, questioning hookers about any suspicious punters. Meanwhile, detectives cruised the streets in unmarked cars, hoping to catch a break.

It didn't come. What's more, prostitutes were still going missing.

Maria Welch disappeared in November. Her body had not yet been discovered, when another dead hooker, Frances Brown, turned up in the Genesee River. She'd been beaten to death.

Not long after, a man reported his 26-year-old girlfriend, June Stott, missing. He said she'd been gone eighteen days. He hadn't reported it earlier because she often disappeared for long periods.

On November 15, Kimberly Logan, a black prostitute, well known in the Lyell Avenue area, was found dead beneath a pile of leaves the backyard of a residence. She'd been viciously beaten and kicked and leaves had been stuffed down her throat. Her file was added to the growing list of prostitute murders in the Rochester area.

Eight days later, a man out walking his dog discovered a corpse concealed under a strip of carpet. The corpse had been somewhat preserved by the cold weather and the medical examiner determined that she'd originally been laid out on her back but had later been flipped onto her stomach. This suggested that the killer had revisited the murder site and the sickening reason was soon revealed. The corpse had been anally penetrated after death. Not only that, but she'd been gutted, cut from her breasts to her vagina. The victim was soon identified as the missing June Stott.

The weeks before New Year brought three more missing prostitutes, Darlene Trippi, June Cicero, and Felicia Stephens. In an effort to find their bodies, the police sent a helicopter into the Gorge, to search for likely dumpsites. They found nothing until January 3, 1990, when a team working along Highway 31 spotted a body lying on the icy surface of Salmon Creek, near a bridge.

As they flew in closer, they noticed a man standing on the bridge, looking towards where the body lay. The man was tall and heavy-set and he appeared to be relieving himself. Then he got into his car – a Chevy Celebrity – and drove off. The helicopter unit alerted their colleagues on the ground and they set off in pursuit, eventually pulling the Chevy over at a municipal parking lot in Spencerport.

The driver identified himself as Arthur John Shawcross. When asked for his driver's license, he confessed that he didn't have one. He also admitted that he was an ex-con, having served time for manslaughter.

The officers then asked Shawcross to accompany them to State Police Barracks for further questioning, which he agreed to willingly, even signing forms giving them permission to search his house and car.

Shawcross remained under interrogation for five hours. At first, he was coy, but as investigators pressed him on his manslaughter conviction he opened up, describing in sickening detail how he'd killed a ten-year-old boy and an eight-year-old girl, sodomizing the child before he strangled her. He'd served just 14 years for the crimes on a plea agreement that had reduced the charges to manslaughter.

Asked again about his presence at Salmon Creek, he insisted that it was purely coincidental. He knew nothing about murdered prostitutes. Officers were sure that he was lying, but with no evidence, they were forced to let him go.

The task force now moved into overdrive, checking the details of Shawcross's previous convictions. One detail jumped out at them. Leaves had been forced down the female victim's throat. They'd seen the same thing in some of the Genesee River victims.

Shawcross was brought in for a second round of questioning. Except, this time, detectives drove him out to the various crime scenes. Still, Shawcross maintained his composure, giving nothing away. However, as the day wore on he began to become agitated and asked to terminate the interview, saying he didn't want to leave his girlfriend, Clara Neal, alone any longer. One of the detectives immediately seized on the opportunity.

"Is Clara involved?" the officer asked.

"No," Shawcross said, hanging his head, "Clara's not involved."

In the next minute the floodgates opened up and Shawcross began recounting his sordid tale of murder and mutilation. In true serial killer fashion, he offered a justification for each killing – some of them had ridiculed him, others had tried to steal from him, some had threatened to tell Clara that he was seeing prostitutes, one had bitten his penis, another talked too much.

Arthur Shawcross went on trial in November 1990 and was found guilty on ten counts of first-degree murder and sentenced to 25 years on each charge, for a total of 250 years. He would serve only eighteen.

On the afternoon of November 10, 2008, Shawcross complained of pains in his leg. He was taken to Albany Medical Center, where he suffered a fatal heart attack at 9:50 p.m.

72. Joachim Kroll

Country: Germany

Confirmed Victims: 14

Suspected Victims: 14+

Joachim Kroll was born in Hindenburg, Upper Silesia (now Zabrze, Poland) on April 17, 1933. His father was a coalminer and Joachim was the youngest of eight children. A weakling as a boy, he had a chronic bed-wetting problem that persisted into his teens. He was also considered mentally challenged, getting no further than Grade 3 in school and recording an IQ of 78.

During the war, Kroll's father was drafted into the German army. He'd later be captured by the Russians and would never return to his family. The rest of the Kroll clan escaped the newly communist east in 1947 and settled in North Rhine-Westphalia.

In 1955, Kroll's mother died, leaving him devastated. Not long after, he claimed his first known victim, a 19-year-old girl named

Inngard Strehl, who was raped, strangled and left in a barn near the village of Walstedde, in February 1955.

Kroll's next victim was 12-year-old Erika Schuletter, raped and strangled at Kirchhellen in 1956. Three years later, he stabbed Klara Jesmer to death in the woods near Rbeinhausen, on June 17, 1959.

Joachim Kroll was not an intelligent man. But he possessed a criminal cunning and a strong sense of self-preservation. So far, he'd been careful to spread out his murders, both in terms of time and location. With his next murder, though, he'd add a perversion that would alert the police to the presence of a serial killer. On July 26, 1959, he raped and murdered 16-year-old Manuela Knodt in a park near Bredeney, south of Essen. When Manuela's body was discovered, it was clear that several chunks of flesh had been sliced from her thighs and buttocks.

The same mutilations were found on the next victim, 13-year-old Petra Giese, whose body was discovered at Walsum on April 23, 1962. This time, though, the killer had gone even further, slicing off both buttocks, along with the child's left forearm and right hand. Less than two months later, also in Walsum, 13-year-old Monica Tafel vanished on her way to school. She was found in a rye field, the now familiar cuts made to her buttocks and thighs.

With the police alerted to the presence of a cannibal killer, Kroll varied his M.O. with the next murder. Twelve-year-old Barbara Bruder was killed at Burscheid in July 1962, although this time the body was left intact.

Three years passed during which the police discovered no new cannibal killings, but also made no progress in the case. Then, in August 1965, the Ruhr Hunter was back.

Spying young lovers Hermann Schmitz and Marion Veen making out in a car in Duisburg–Grossenbaum, Kroll crept up and punctured a tire. He then hid in the bushes until Schmitz tried to pull off. When the young man stopped the vehicle and got out to see what the problem was, Kroll charged him and stabbed him to death. Marion Veen, however, escaped by driving off on the flat tire, leaving Kroll frustrated at missing his prime target.

A year later, on September 13, 1966, Kroll raped and murdered Ursula Roling in Foersterbusch Park near Marl. Three months on, he struck again, raping five-year-old Ilona Harke before drowning her in a ditch near Wuppertal. When Ilona's body was found, there were steaks cut from her buttocks and shoulders.

Kroll's murderous career was almost ended in 1967, soon after he moved to Grafenhausen. Luring a 10-year-old girl to a field with the promise of showing her some rabbits, he instead produced a pack of pornographic pictures. The girl ran off and told her parents who alerted the authorities. By the time they arrived to arrest him, Kroll had fled.

Perhaps frightened by that close call, Kroll lay low for the next two years. When he resumed his murderous career on July 12, 1969, he targeted a victim outside of his usual profile. Maria Hettgen, 61, was strangled to death in her home in Hueckeswagen. Kroll then raped her corpse.

In May 1970, Kroll claimed yet another child victim, raping and strangling 13-year-old Jutta Ranh in Breitscheid. Thereafter followed his longest "cooling" period yet. It was six years before he waylaid 10-year-old Karin Toepfer on her way to school in Dinslaken Voerde, raping the little girl and then strangling her.

In May 1976, Kroll moved to a new apartment in the Duisburg suburb of Laar. Shortly after his arrival, on July 3, 1976, a four-year-old named Marion Ketter went missing from a local playground. The police were called and began knocking on doors, asking if anyone had seen Marion. They got a very curious response from one man. The man said that the toilets in their apartment building had been backed up and he'd asked his upstairs neighbor, Joachim Kroll, if he knew what might be causing the blockage. "Guts," had been Kroll's nonchalant reply. The officers decided to pay Kroll a visit. They were unprepared for what they found.

Bubbling away on a stove was a stew of carrots and potatoes that also contained a child's hand. Plastic bags of human flesh were stored in the freezer, while Marion's tiny corpse lay on the kitchen floor with her hand hacked off and chunks of flesh carved from her buttocks. When a plumber later arrived to clear the blocked drains, a child's lungs and viscera were flushed from the drainage.

Kroll was unrepentant about his crimes. He said that he enjoyed rape and murder and had only taken to cannibalism to save money on his grocery bills. He did, however, admit that he had come to enjoy the taste of human flesh. As to the number of victims, he said that he remembered 14, but that there might be more.

At his trial in April 1982, Kroll seemed genuinely unable to grasp the gravity of his situation. He believed that at its conclusion the authorities would give him an operation to clear his homicidal urges and then set him free. Instead, he was found guilty on eight counts of murder and sentenced to life in prison.

Joachim Kroll died of a heart attack at Rheinbach Prison, near Bonn, on July 1, 1991.

71. Marcelo Costa de Andrade

Country: Brazil

Confirmed Victims: 14

Suspected Victims: 21+

Marcelo Andrade was born on January 2, 1967, the son of poor migrants from northeast Brazil. He grew up in Rocinha, a sprawling Rio de Janeiro ghetto, where over 150,000 people live in abject poverty, many in tin shacks and lean-tos without running water.

Andrade's childhood followed the path of many fledgling serial killers. He was physically abused by both his parents and grandfather and sexually abused by an older boy at age ten. By 14, he'd racked up his first arrest, for prostitution; by the time he was 16, he was a hardened veteran of Rio's homosexual flesh trade. At 17, he tried to rape his 10-year-old brother.

But then Andrade's life seemed to change for the better. He became involved in a stable relationship with an older man, an affair that lasted six years. He was devastated when the man left him.

Now 23, Andrade moved to the Itaborai slum, to live with his mother. There, he began attending the controversial, "Universal Church of the Kingdom of God." The teachings, which focused on the eradication of demons, must have struck a chord with Andrade, because he attended four times a week, each service lasting five hours. It was during this time that he began killing.

According to Andrade, his killing spree was sparked by an encounter with a young transvestite. After having sex with the boy, Andrade became obsessed and tried to find him again. Unable to do so, he turned his attention to other children and began forcing himself on them.

Andrade developed a simple but efficient M.O. Once he found a child he liked, he'd approach him with an offer of money for some minor chore, usually for lighting candles at a church. He'd then lure the boy to an isolated spot and rape him. It wasn't long before he turned to murder, strangling a boy named Anderson with his own shirt, then hiding the body and returning to the scene several times over the weeks that followed. The act of murder, he later admitted, thrilled him.

Over the next nine months, Andrade claimed 13 more victims. As someone who had grown up in the slums, he knew the byways and alleyways well and knew also how to approach the streetwise and naturally suspicious kids. Those who fell for his smooth talk ended up raped and strangled. Andrade practiced necrophilia on several of the bodies, decapitated one of the boys, crushed the head of another. On other occasions, he drank the blood of his victims (so that he could, "become as beautiful as them," he later explained).

In December 1991, Andrade persuaded Altair de Abreu, 10, and his brother Ivan, 6, to help him light candles at a local cathedral. As they were crossing a vacant lot on the way to the church, Andrade turned on the younger boy and began strangling him. Paralyzed with fear, Altair did not run away but stood watching as Andrade murdered and then raped his brother.

"When he was finished with Ivan," Altair later told police, "he turned to me, hugged me, and said he loved me."

Andrade then asked Altair to come and live with him. Scared of what might happen if he refused, Altair agreed. He spent the night sleeping with Andrade in some bushes behind a gas station. The next morning, Andrade took him to Copacabana, where the terrified boy managed to give him the slip.

Altair hitchhiked home, but afraid of the consequences, he withheld from his parents what had happened to his brother, saying only that he'd lost Ivan. It was several days before Altair finally broke down and told his sister what had happened.

Andrade meanwhile, was calmly maintaining his daily routine, his only deviation a trip to revisit Ivan's tiny corpse. There he tucked the little boy's hands inside his shorts, "so that the rats couldn't gnaw his fingers." When the police came for him, he told the arresting officers, "I thought you would come yesterday."

Andrade would eventually confess to 14 murders, claiming he'd killed the boys because they were guaranteed a place in heaven if they died before they were 13 years old. Declared insane he was confined to the Heitor Carrilho psychiatric hospital in Rio. It is unlikely that he will ever be released.

70. Coral Eugene Watts

Country: United States

Confirmed Victims: 14

Suspected Victims: 80+

Carl Eugene Watts was born on November 7, 1953, in Killeen, Texas. His parents, Richard and Dorothy Mae had been childhood sweethearts, but their marriage was an unhappy one that eventually ended in divorce in 1955, after which Dorothy Mae moved with her children to Inkster, Michigan. During this time, the family traveled regularly to Coalwood, West Virginia, to visit relatives, and Carl loved the southern town so much that he later changed his name to Coral - a southern pronunciation of his name.

In 1962, Coral's mother re-married, a situation that greatly distressed the boy. He hated having a competitor for his mother's affections. Around this time another life-changing event occurred. Coral developed meningitis, and although he eventually recovered, he seemed to have undergone a personality change.

The first indicator was the deterioration of his academic performance. Then there were the dreams, violent dramas in which he tussled with the evil spirits of women and killed them. More worrying was his assessment of these nightmares. They didn't frighten him, he said. In fact, he enjoyed them.

In 1968, those fantasies manifested in reality, when 15-year-old Coral knocked at the door of 26-year-old Joan Gave. When Mrs. Gave answered, he forced her back into her apartment, pushed her to the floor and started beating her. When he was done, he continued his newspaper delivery route as if nothing had happened.

Gave immediately called the police, and they were waiting for Coral when he returned home. Brought before a judge, he was ordered to undergo psychiatric treatment at the Lafayette Clinic in Detroit. Here, psychiatrists diagnosed him with strong homicidal tendencies and flagged him as a danger to others. Nonetheless, he was released just a few months later, on his 16th birthday.

Coral returned to school, where with extensive tutoring by his mother, he eventually graduated at age 19. Despite his low grade point average, he won a football scholarship to Lane College in Jackson, Tennessee. But he remained at the school only a few months before returning home. He just couldn't bear to be away from his mother.

Watts found work as an apprentice mechanic in Detroit, remaining at that trade for a year before enrolling at Western Michigan University in Kalamazoo. Soon after, there was a rash of attacks in the area around the campus.

On October 25, 1974, Lenore Knizacky, 23, answered her door to a young black man who forced her inside and then began strangling her. She managed to fight him off. Gloria Steele was not so lucky. The 19-year-old was stabbed to death in her apartment on October 30, suffering 33 stab wounds during a frenzied attack.

On November 12, another student was attacked and managed to escape, writing down the license plate number of her assailant's vehicle as he fled. The car belonged to Coral Watts.

Watts readily admitted to two counts of battery but insisted that he hadn't killed Gloria Steele. He was placed under psychiatric evaluation for six months and diagnosed with antisocial personality disorder. When his case eventually came to trial he was sentenced to a year in prison on the battery charges. The police lacked sufficient evidence to charge him with murdering Gloria Steele.

Watts was released in 1976 and returned to live with his mother. Shortly after, he began seeing a woman named Delores, fathering a child by her before the couple split. In 1979, he married a woman named Valeria, but she walked out on him after just six months, citing his bizarre behavior.

Valeria would later describe how Watts would always leave the house for several hours after they had sex. He never explained where he went, but it is likely that he was out stalking victims. Several women were attacked and murdered during this period, including Detroit News reporter Jeanne Clyne, high school student Shirley Small and Glenda Richmond, a 26-year-old restaurant manager. Then there was the frenzied attack on University of Michigan student Rebecca Huff, 20, who suffered at least 50 knife wounds.

In the wake of the Huff murder, Watts was identified as a suspect and brought him for questioning. Shaken up by the police attention, he quit town, moving to Columbus, Texas, where he found work at an oil company. Columbus is just 70 miles from Houston. Soon Watts took to cruising that city, looking for new victims.

Watts managed to fly under the radar until May 1982, when he was apprehended after attacking two young women in their Houston apartment. One of those women, Melinda Aguilar, escaped by jumping from a second-floor window. Watts was trying to drown the other, Lori Lister, in the bathtub when the police arrived.

Under interrogation, Watts refused to talk. Then Assistant District Attorney Ira Jones made him an incredible offer, immunity on all murder charges, in exchange for a confession to any murders committed in Harris County. Watts was no fool. He grasped the deal with both hands.

On August 9, 1982, Watts confessed to 13 murders, including the drowning of University of Texas student Linda Tilley in her apartment complex swimming pool in September 1981, and the fatal stabbing of 25-year-old Elizabeth Montgomery, one week later.

That same day Watts also killed Susan Wolf, 21, stabbing her to death as she returned from the grocery store. In January 1982, he strangled 27-year-old Phyllis Tamm, while she was out jogging. Two days later, he murdered 25-year-old architecture student Margaret Fossi. Her body was found in the trunk of her car at Rice University.

During that month, he attacked three more Houston women, slashing one across the throat, stabbing one with a knife and another with an ice pick. Miraculously, all three survived.

His next victims were not as lucky. Between February and May 1982, Watts killed Elena Semander, 20; Emily LaQua, 14; Anna Ledet, 34; Yolanda Gracia, 21; Carrie Jefferson, 32; Suzanne Searles, 25, and Michele Maday, 20.

Watts admitted to at least 80 more murders in Michigan and Canada but refused to give details, because his immunity deal applied only to murders committed in Texas.

Eventually brought to trial for the attack on Lori Lister and Melinda Aguilar, Watts pled guilty to one count of burglary with intent to kill, the plea bargain he'd agreed. He was sentenced to 60 years in prison, parting with these chilling words, "You know, if they ever let me out, I'll kill again."

Fortunately, Watts would never get the chance to make good on that promise. He died in prison on September 21, 2007, of prostate cancer. He was 53 years old.

69. Elifasi Msomi

Country: South Africa

Confirmed Victims: 15

Suspected Victims: 15+

Post-apartheid South Africa has produced a veritable plague of highly prolific, extremely brutal, black serial killers. Moses Sithole, the so-called ABC killer is perhaps the most infamous, luring at least 38 young women to their deaths with promises of employment. But there are others. Cedric Maake, the Wemmer Pan serial killer, clubbed 27 victims to death with a hammer between 1996 and 1997; Christopher Zikode, a necrophile, strangled upwards of 18 women in and around the tiny Kwazulu-Natal town of Donnybrook; Sipho Twala turned the Sugarcane fields around Phoenix into his personal killing ground, claiming 18 lives.

Before any of these monsters emerged, there was Elifasi Msomi, a vicious axe murderer, who blamed his killing spree on a Tokoloshe, an evil gnome of African folklore.

Elifasi Msomi was a burly young Zulu man, a novice Sangoma (witchdoctor) who was not doing very well at his trade. Desperate for help, he turned to a more experienced Sangoma for advice. The elder witchdoctor, according to Elifasi's later testimony, introduced him to a Tokoloshe, who appeared in the form of the man's son. "You will go with this son of mine," the elder told him, "and get me the blood of 15 people. First I want the blood of a girl."

Over the next 18 months, Msomi wandered the hills and valleys of Umkomaas and Umzimkulu in Kwazulu-Natal, seeking out suitable victims. The Tokoloshe was always by his side, advising him who was to die. When he eventually found a girl that the Tokoloshe approved of, he hacked her to death, then gathered her blood in a bottle in order to fulfill his promise to the older witchdoctor. The Tokoloshe then asked for a child, so Msomi obliged him, hacking to death five young victims in the months that followed.

His method was to use his status as a Sangoma in order to lure his victims to remote areas, where he'd attack them with a hatchet, a knife or a knopkierie (a club of seasoned ironwood). After each murder, he'd faithfully collect blood in a bottle as he'd been instructed to do.

Unsurprisingly, the murders caused alarm among the local populace, but the South African police were not overly concerned by black-on-black violence and while an investigation was launched, it was hardly given much priority.

Msomi was, in fact, in police custody at the height of his murder spree, after being arrested on an unrelated theft charge. However, he soon escaped and resumed killing. He'd later insist that the Tokoloshe had aided his getaway by making him invisible.

Serial killers seldom stop killing of their own volition, but that is exactly what happened with Elifasi Msomi. Having collected the blood of his fifteenth young victim, he said that the Tokoloshe thanked him for his service, then bathed with him in the river before they parted company.

Msomi returned to his village, presumably to resume his career as a witchdoctor. However, his girlfriend spotted the bottles of blood he'd collected and promptly reported him to the police. When items in his possession proved to be from the murder victims, he was arrested.

Once in custody, Msomi admitted freely to the murders and even led police to the remains of those he'd killed. But it was not he who was responsible, he said. He had been acting under the influence of the Tokoloshe and had been powerless to refuse.

Msomi carried that story with him into his murder trial and, bizarre though it seems, it might well have saved him from the gallows. However, he could not explain why he'd raped some of his victims and robbed others. It appeared that Elifasi was just a common, garden-variety psychopath after all. He was accordingly found guilty of murder and sentenced to hang, his execution scheduled for February 10, 1956.

The case had one final twist to offer. Local Zulu chieftains, while pleased with the court's decision, insisted on attending the execution. They wanted to be sure that the Tokoloshe did not intervene to save Msomi from the gallows. Fifteen chiefs were accordingly flown to Pretoria to watch Msomi hang, thereafter declaring themselves satisfied that the danger had passed.

68. Dennis Nilsen

Country: England

Confirmed Victims: 15

Suspected Victims: 16

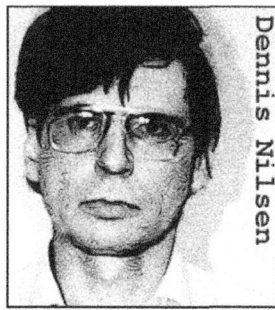

Dennis Andrew Nilsen was born in Fraserburgh, Aberdeenshire, on November 23, 1945. His father was a Norwegian soldier, Olav Magnus Nilsen, who deserted the family when the boy was 6-years-old. Despite this, Dennis had a fairly ordinary childhood, even though he was somewhat of a loner. At 15, he left school and joined the army, serving with the catering corps. It was during his military service, while posted in Germany, that Nilsen had his first homosexual encounter.

In 1972, having served eleven years and three months, Nilsen quit the military. Thereafter, he joined the Metropolitan Police but resigned after just one year. He later became a counselor at a job center.

By 1974, Nilsen was a regular at the gay bars in the north London suburb where he lived. He was also involved in a relationship, with a man named David Gallichan. When that relationship ended two years later, he became a heavy drinker, cruising the bars for casual sex partners who he'd bring to his home at 195 Melrose Avenue.

Nilsen committed his first murder in December 1978, picking up a 14-year-old named Stephen Dean Holmes, bringing him home, and strangling him with a necktie after they had sex. According to Nilsen's later confession, he killed Holmes because he didn't want him to leave.

Later that day, Nilsen bought an electric carving knife, intending to dismember the body. But he found the corpse "too beautiful" and couldn't do it. Instead, he dressed it in new underwear, then crept into bed beside it. Later he got up, made dinner and watched television. Finally, he pried some floorboards loose and hid the body in the floor space. The corpse would remain there for seven months before Nilsen eventually burned it in a fire in his garden. During the first weeks it was there, he'd regularly take it out from under the floorboards to wash and dress it. Sometimes he even climbed into the tub with it.

In October 1979, nearly a year after the first murder, Nilsen brought home a young student from Hong Kong named Andrew Ho. He tried to strangle the man, but Ho escaped and reported the incident to the police. They took no action.

Nilsen committed his second murder on December 3, 1979. The victim was Kenneth Ockendon, a Canadian tourist who Nilsen met at a pub. They drank together for several hours, ending up back at Nilsen's flat, where Ockendon was strangled with a cord from some headphones. Nilsen then washed the body and spent the night with the corpse in his bed, fondling and caressing it.

Over the days that followed, Nilsen regularly washed the corpse, dressed it, and placed it in a chair beside him as he watched television. He also slept with it at night, pushing its legs together so that he could have sex between the thighs. Finally, the corpse was placed beneath the floorboards, although Nilsen retrieved it several times, to sit with him as he watched television and to share his bed.

Five months later, on May 13, 1980, Nilsen murdered 16-year-old Martyn Duffey. In the months that followed, he claimed seven more victims, including 27-year-old male prostitute Billy Sutherland, a skinhead, and an Irish laborer. Nilsen claims that he barely remembers these victims.

Nilsen now had half–a-dozen corpses hidden in various spaces in the small apartment. After a neighbor complained about the smell, he realized that he was going to have to get rid of them. Stripping to his underwear, he dissected them on the kitchen floor, calling on his butchering skills from his army days. He boiled the flesh from the heads using a pot that he'd bought for that purpose. Then he packed the body parts into plastic bags and stored them back under the floorboards. Some of the organs he threw over a fence to be consumed by rats and foxes. The rest he destroyed in three large bonfires in the back garden.

But Nilsen was soon going to be deprived of the use of his garden. After an argument with his landlord, he was asked to move out of 195 Melrose Avenue.

His new residence was a small attic apartment, one of six units at 23 Cranley Gardens. Here there were no floorboards to be lifted for the convenient storage of corpses, there was no garden to build bonfires in. It should have dissuaded Nilsen from home-based murder. But it didn't.

Just six months after moving to Cranley Gardens, Nilsen picked up a petty criminal named John Howlett at a pub, brought him home and strangled him. He then hid the corpse in a closet, while he tried to figure out how to get rid of it. Eventually, he decided to cut the body into small pieces and flush it down the toilet. He also boiled some of the flesh in his kitchen, along with the head, hands, and feet. The bones were separated and put into the trash, with some of the larger ones tossed over the back fence into a waste area. Other bones were sprinkled with salt and stored in a tea chest.

Two more victims, Archibald Graham Allan and Steven Sinclair, met a similarly horrendous fate at Cranley Gardens. It was the disposal of Sinclair's remains that would eventually bring about Nilsen's undoing.

During the first week of February 1983, Cranley Gardens residents began complaining to their landlord that the toilets were not flushing properly. A plumber was called to investigate but said that there appeared to be a blockage in the drains that required a specialist. Two days later, Michael Cattran, a technician from a drain cleaning company, arrived to take a look at the problem. Shortly after, he called his supervisor and reported what looked like chunks of flesh on the sewer floor.

The supervisor told Cattran to close the drain and said he'd make an inspection himself the following day. When they arrived, Cattran commented that the drain cover had been moved. It was soon clear why. It appeared someone had climbed into the drain during the night and cleaned out the suspicious chunks of flesh.

But whoever had done it had been less than thorough. One piece remained, along with several small bones. The supervisor called the police.

Detective Chief Inspector Peter Jay was assigned to the case and soon learned that one of the tenants, Dennis Nilsen, had been seen tampering with the drain cover during the night. The detective went immediately to Nilsen's apartment and informed him of the discovery of human flesh in the drains. He then demanded that Nilsen show him where the rest of the body was.

Nilsen paused only a moment before replying. "In two plastic bags in the wardrobe," he said. "I'll show you."

Later, with Nilsen under arrest and on his way to the police station, he was asked whether there was one body or two. "Fifteen or sixteen," was his reply, "since 1978."

Denis Nilsen went on trial at the Old Bailey on October 24, 1983. Found guilty of six murders, he was sentenced to life in prison, with the stipulation that he should never be released. He is currently incarcerated at Full Sutton maximum-security prison in Yorkshire.

67. Angel Resendiz

Country: United States

Confirmed Victims: 15

Suspected Victims: 18+

Angel Resendiz was born in Izucar de Matomoros in the Mexican state of Puebla, on August 1, 1960. As a child, he spent much of his time on the streets, begging, scavenging and stealing. By his teens, this latter endeavor had lured him into making regular crossings into Texas, where the pickings were much richer.

Resendiz first came to the attention of the U.S. authorities in August 1976, when, at age 16, he was caught trying to cross illegally into Brownsville, Texas. Over the years that followed INS agents picked him up in Stirling Heights, Michigan, and in McAllen, Texas. Each time he was deported. Each time he barely paused for breath before crossing the border again.

In September 1979, Resendiz was arrested in Miami, Florida. The charge was auto theft and assault and it earned him a 20-year sentence. He served six before being paroled and deported.

But if the US authorities thought they'd seen the last of Angel Resendiz they were sorely mistaken. Over the next decade, he reappeared regularly on US soil, acquiring a lengthy arrest record in the process. He was charged variously with, falsely claiming citizenship, carrying a concealed weapon, Social Security fraud, and burglary. After each of these infractions, he was put on a bus and returned back to Mexico. But international borders meant little to Angel Resendiz. Often he'd be back in the United States within the day.

Yet the string of deportations was having an effect on Resendiz. He became more and more resentful, angry at what be perceived as unfair treatment. Eventually, that simmering anger exploded into violence.

According to Resendiz's later confession, he committed his first US murder in 1986, when he killed a woman who he met in a homeless shelter. The woman disrespected him, he said, so he shot her four times with a .38 caliber pistol and left her body at an abandoned farmhouse. When the woman's boyfriend started asking questions about her whereabouts, he killed him too, dumping his body in a creek near San Antonio.

Resendiz next killed a 33-year-old man named Michael White, battering him to death with a brick in July 1991, after White made homosexual advances towards him.

Six years later, in 1997, Resendiz bludgeoned Jesse Howell, 19, to death with an air hose coupling, then raped and strangled his 16-year-old girlfriend, Wendy Von Huben. The bodies were buried in a shallow grave in Sumter County, Florida. That same year, an unidentified transient was beaten to death with a piece of wood in a rail yard in Colton, California. Police consider Resendiz the prime suspect in that case.

The first murder of the spree that would elevate Resindez to the FBI's Most Wanted List occurred on August 29, 1997, in Lexington, Kentucky. Christopher Maier, a 21-year-old University of Kentucky student was walking along the railroad tracks near the college with his girlfriend, Holly Dunn, when Resendiz attacked them. Maier was bludgeoned to death with a rock, Dunn beaten, raped and left for dead. Miraculously, she survived.

Thirteen months later, on October 4, 1998, 87-year-old Leafie Mason was bludgeoned to death with a tire iron inside her home, just 50 yards from the railroad tracks in Hughes Spring, Texas.

On December 17, 1998, Resendiz broke into the home of Dr. Claudia Benton, 39, in Houston, Texas. When Dr. Benton returned home, he raped her before stabbing and beating her to death. Resendiz fled the scene in the victim's Jeep Cherokee, which was later found in San Antonio, Texas. Fingerprints lifted from the steering column were matched to Resendiz, and a warrant was issued for his arrest.

Despite the warrant, Resendiz struck again on May 2, 1999, in Weimar, Texas. Reverend Norman "Skip" Sirnic, 46, and his wife Karen, 47, were bludgeoned to death with a sledgehammer in the parsonage of the United Church of Christ. The couple's red Mazda was found in San Antonio three weeks later, again with forensic evidence linking the murders to the Railroad Killer.

A month later, on June 2, a Border Patrol apprehended Resendiz near El Paso as he was trying to cross. While he was in custody, the INS ran a computer check that somehow missed the warrant for the Benton murder. Resendiz was driven back to Mexico and released. He immediately returned to Texas. Within 48 hours, he committed two more murders.

On June 4, Resendiz battered 26-year-old Noemi Dominguez to death in her Houston apartment. That same day, the brutal killer bludgeoned 73-year-old Josephine Konvicka. As with the other victims, Konvicka's home was located close to the railway lines.

By now, the elusive Railroad Killer had struck terror into the hearts of communities along the tracks from Texas all the way to Illinois. In small towns where doors had traditionally stood unlocked at night, deadbolts were fixed. Meanwhile, law enforcement agencies stepped up railyard security and began hauling in vagrants for questioning. Freight trains were stopped and searched. It did nothing to stop the killer.

On June 15, 1999, Resendiz broke into a mobile home in Gorham, Illinois where he shot 80-year-old George Morber Sr. in the head with a shotgun, before clubbing Morber's daughter, Carolyn Frederick, to death.

Later that month, the FBI placed the Railroad Killer on its Ten Most Wanted list and offered a $50,000 reward for information leading to his capture. In the meantime, arrest warrants were issued in Jackson County, Illinois, Louisville, Kentucky, and Fayette County, Texas, as DNA evidence linked Resendiz to the murders committed there.

Two hundred agents were now hunting Resendiz, and over 1,000 tips came in from members of the public, but still he evaded them. In fact, Resendiz had already fled back to Mexico and was laying low.

In July 1999, the Harris County D.A. offered Resendiz a deal guaranteeing his personal safety in prison, as well as regular visitations from friends and family. He also promised that Resendiz would undergo a psychiatric evaluation, something the killer was apparently keen on. That offer was forwarded to Resendiz via relatives and on July 12, he handed himself over to US authorities in El Paso.

Angel Resendiz went on trial on May 8, 1999. On May 17, after 10 hours of deliberation, the jury returned a guilty verdict for first-degree murder. Despite his lawyer's contention that he had been guaranteed immunity from execution, the Railroad Killer was sentenced to death.

He was executed by lethal injection in Huntsville, Texas, on June 27, 2006.

66. Robert Hansen

Country: United States

Confirmed Victims: 15

Suspected Victims: 21

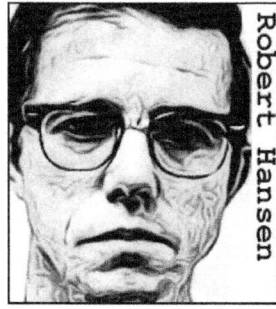

On September 12, 1982, off-duty Anchorage police officers, John Daily and Audi Holloway were hunting in the Knik River Valley, when they discovered the half-buried corpse of a woman. The officers immediately jogged back to camp and called in the find, summoning forensic teams to the scene.

The victim was later identified as Sherry Morrow, a 24-year-old topless dancer who worked at the Wild Cherry Bar in downtown Anchorage. She had last been seen on November 17, 1981, when friends said she'd gone to meet a man who had offered her $300 to pose for some pictures. Morrow had died from three gunshot wounds, delivered by a .223 caliber rifle.

It looked like an execution-style shooting and investigators were afraid that it might not be an isolated incident. A number of strippers and prostitutes had gone missing from Anchorage over the previous year. In addition, two bodies had been found, one of an unnamed victim who investigators nicknamed "Eklutna Annie," the other of a topless dancer named Joanne Messina. Unfortunately, both corpses were badly decomposed and no trace evidence had been recovered.

Months passed, with the investigation into Sherry Morrow's murder going nowhere. Then, on June 13, 1983, there was a break in the case.

A trucker was driving into town when a young woman ran into the road, trying frantically to flag him down. The trucker brought his rig to a stop and the woman scrambled aboard and told him to drive. She looked terrified and he noticed a pair of cuffs dangling from her wrist. She said a man was after her and asked him to drive her to the Big Timber Motel. After dropping her off, the trucker reported the incident and a police cruiser was dispatched. The officers found the woman standing outside the motel, the handcuffs still attached to her wrist. She told them a peculiar story.

She said that she'd been approached by a man who had offered her $200 for oral sex. She'd gotten into his car and they'd driven to an isolated spot. But halfway through the act, he'd produced a gun, and then handcuffed her. He'd driven her to a house in Muldoon where he'd raped and tortured her, biting her nipples and forcing the handle of a hammer into her vagina. When he was done he told her that he was taking her to his cabin in the mountains and said that if she co-operated she would not be hurt. He drove her to an airfield where he forced her into a small plane. The woman realized that if she went with him, she'd be killed, so she waited until he was getting into the plane himself, then pushed open the door and ran. The man chased her for a distance but stopped when he saw the truck approaching.

Investigators thought the story extraordinary, but they drove the young prostitute to Merrill Field airport anyway, and asked her to identify the plane. It belonged to a local businessman named Robert C. Hansen.

After dropping the woman off at the hospital, officers stopped at Hansen's house. He reacted angrily to the girl's accusations, insisting that she was probably trying to set him up for blackmail. He also offered an alibi, which checked out. Officers left without charging him.

Three months after the police questioned Hansen, another body turned up along the Knik River. The partially decomposed remains were identified as Paula Golding, a 17-year-old prostitute and topless dancer. She'd been missing for five months. An autopsy revealed that she'd been killed by a .223 caliber bullet.

The Alaska State Police were by now certain that they had a serial killer in their jurisdiction and, despite his denials, they still considered Robert Hansen their main suspect. The problem was that Hansen had an airtight alibi for the night of the attempted abduction. In an effort to break that alibi, they brought in the two men who had claimed to be with Hansen on the night in question.

Threatened with charges if they were found to be lying, the men quickly cracked and admitted that they hadn't been with Hansen.

They also added another useful tidbit of information. Hansen, they said, had pulled off a series of insurance scams. Property that he claimed had been stolen was, in fact, hidden in his basement. It was enough for investigators to obtain a search warrant.

On October 27, 1983, police hauled Robert Hansen in for questioning, while simultaneously serving search warrants on his house and plane. The search of the house produced plenty of weapons but none that would match the .223 that had killed Sherry Morrow and Paula Golding.

Then, when they'd all but given up, the searchers discovered a secret compartment hidden in the rafters of the attic. Inside, they found an aviation map with specific locations marked off; pieces of jewelry; newspaper clippings about the case; and several ID cards, some of which belonged to the dead women. They also found a .233 caliber rifle, potentially the murder weapon.

On November 3, 1983, an Anchorage grand jury returned indictments on all of the charges. Then, after ballistics confirmed Hansen's .233 as the murder weapon, his attorney called the D.A. and asked for a deal. Hansen would give a full confession in exchange for serving his time in a Federal prison rather than a maximum security one.

When Robert Hansen eventually got to telling his story, it revealed one of the most unique M.O.'s in the annals of serial murder. He said that he'd lured his victims by soliciting them for sex or asking them to pose for photographs. Once inside his car, he'd produce a gun, threaten the woman and then cuff her. He'd then drive her to his plane and fly her out to his remote cabin. There he would rape and torture the woman. Afterwards, he would strip her naked, blindfold her, then set her free in the woods and tell her to run. After a brief wait, he'd follow, sometimes armed with a high-powered rifle, other times with just a hunting knife.

Hansen would later lead police to 15 burial sites. On February 18, 1984, he entered guilty pleas to the first-degree murders of Paula Golding, Joanna Messina, Sherry Morrow, and "Eklutna Annie." One week later, he was sentenced to 461 years plus life, without the possibility of parole. He was remanded to Lewisburg Federal Penitentiary in Pennsylvania.

65. Lainz Angels of Death

Country: Austria

Confirmed Victims: 15

Suspected Victims: 200+

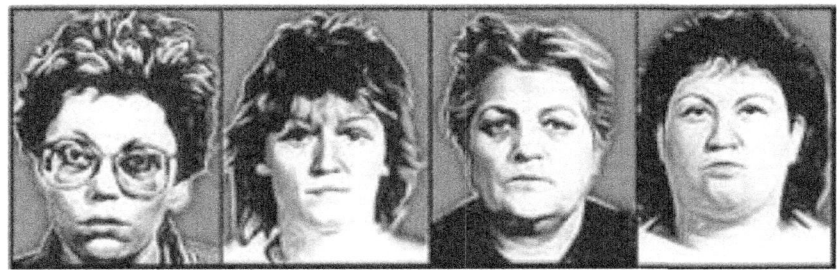

The Lainz General Hospital is one of the largest medical facilities in Vienna, Austria, a sprawling complex with a staff of some 2,000 medics and support personnel. Within Lainz General, Pavilion 5 is reserved for elderly patients, many of them in the latter stages of terminal illness. Unsurprisingly, the ward has a high mortality rate.

But between the years 1983 and 1989, not all of the deaths in Pavilion 5 were from natural causes. A killer was at work among the elderly patients, claiming at least 42 lives, and possibly as many as 300.

It all began in the spring of '83, when a 77-year-old female patient approached a nurses' aide named Waltraud Wagner with an unusual request. She wanted Wagner to overdose her with an injection of morphine, thereby ending her suffering. At first, Wagner was reluctant, but eventually, she agreed to carry out the mercy killing. She duly delivered the lethal shot and, to her surprise realized that the act of murder, of playing God, thrilled her. She could hardly wait for an opportunity to "terminate" another patient.

Nobody knows how many patients Wagner killed on her own, before she decided to enlist others into her death scheme. What we do know is that over time, she recruited three accomplices, all of them nursing aides working the night shift in Pavilion 5.

Maria Gruber, 19, Irene Leidolf, 21, and Stephanija Mayer, a 43-year-old immigrant from Yugoslavia, all agreed to join in the deadly game. And their targets were no longer the terminally ill. Any patient who annoyed them was at risk. These annoyances didn't have to be serious. Anyone who snored too much, who wet the bed, who refused to take medication, who buzzed the nurses' station too often or at inconvenient times, might be targeted.

Once a patient was marked for death, Wagner would announce to her followers, "This one gets a ticket to God." The victim would then receive a visit from the deadly foursome during the night.

At first, they dispatched their victims with lethal injections of morphine or insulin. When those methods failed to deliver the requisite thrill, Wagner devised another, which she called the 'water cure.' The patients' nose would be pinched, her head forced back and the tongue depressed. Water would then be poured down her throat, slowly drowning her, a particularly slow and painful death. As it is common for elderly patients to die with fluid in their lungs, these deaths did not arouse suspicion.

Yet, initially, the killers restrained their murderous instincts. It was only after Mayer joined the group in 1987 that the murders accelerated. However, Wagner remained the prime mover and de facto leader. She decided who would die, when and how.

By 1988, the rate of killings had accelerated to such an extent that Pavilion 5 had acquired the nickname, "Pavilion of Death," and there were rumors of a killer working the ward. Yet nothing could be proven. It would take an act of recklessness to finally uncover the heinous scheme.

The "Death Angels" were in the habit of adjourning to a local tavern for a few drinks after their shift, when the topic of conversation often turned to the murders they'd committed. In February 1989, they were giggling together as they discussed the murder of an elderly patient named Julia Drapal. Mrs. Drapal had been given the water cure for refusing medication and insulting Waltraud Wagner. The foursome appeared particularly amused by the expression on the old woman's face just before she died.

Unfortunately for the "Angels," a doctor was seated at the next table and overheard snatches of their conversation. He took the information to the police and a six-week undercover investigation was launched, leading to the arrest of all four suspects on April 7.

Once in custody, the four women had no problem admitting to their crimes. Wagner, in particular, seemed the relish her role, claiming 39 murders on her own and ten more with various accomplices. "I killed those who got on my nerves," she proclaimed proudly. "Dispatched them directly to a free bed with the good Lord."

The other "Angels" meanwhile, were determined to shift most of the blame to Wagner, accusing her of more than 100 killings over the previous two years. Once Wagner heard that her cohorts had turned against her, she changed her story. She now claimed that she'd killed only 10 patients and that all of those had been mercy killings.

The Lainz Death Angels went on trial in March 1991, charged with the most brutal murder spree in Austria's history. The prosecution sought to prove 42 counts of murder, but in the end had to be satisfied with 15 convictions against Wagner and five against Leidolf. Both were sentenced to life in prison.

Stephanija Mayer and Maria Gruber were convicted on various charges of manslaughter and attempted murder. They each drew terms of 15 years in prison.

Mayer and Gruber were released in 2003, Wagner and Leidolf in 2008, amidst widespread public outrage.

64. Jose Antonio Rodriguez Vega

Country: Spain

Confirmed Victims: 16

Suspected Victims: 16

Jose Antonio Rodriguez Vega is Spain's most prolific serial killer, a classic psychopath who targeted vulnerable old women, raping them and then strangling them to death.

Vega was born in Santander, a coastal city in northern Spain, on December 3, 1957. Like many serial killers, he grew up in a highly dysfunctional household with a dominant mother who terrorized her family and even beat up her terminally ill husband.

Perhaps because of his mother's dominance Vega grew up with a deep-seated hatred toward women, although in typical psychopathic fashion he managed to hide it behind his good looks, his easy charm, and his engaging smile.

He married in 1977, but all the while he was concealing from his wife his criminal career as a prolific rapist. That is, until October 17, 1978, when the police eventually caught up with him. He was convicted and sentenced to 27 years in prison. With time off for good behavior, he served just 8.

Vega emerged from prison in 1986, to find that his wife had left him. This "betrayal" served only to fuel his hatred and he soon found a target for his anger in a mentally disabled woman who he wooed and married and then proceeded to abuse both physically and emotionally. To his neighbors, he projected the image of a hard-working and long-suffering husband, who endured his wife's disability with patience and good humor.

Nothing could have been further from the truth. Even as Vega was playing the cheerful and good-natured neighbor he was stalking the elderly women of Santander. Soon he'd unleash himself upon them with a fury not seen before or since in that city, indeed in the whole of Spain.

Jose Antonio Rodriguez Vega was an obsessively neat man and he carried that fastidious nature into the horrendous crimes he committed. A highly organized killer, he'd identify a victim and then begin stalking her, learning every aspect of her routine. When the time was right, he'd introduce himself to the victim, gaining her trust with his impeccable manners. Eventually, he'd gain entrance to her home, usually on the pretext of doing some handyman work.

Everything we know about this type of killer tells us that this period of stalking and isolating the victim is as much of a thrill as the kill itself. However, once Vega had the victim alone inside her house, he'd normally be overcome by excitement and would attack immediately. His usual method was to fall upon the unfortunate woman and choke her into submission. He'd then remove her underwear and fondle her before raping her or violating her with objects like bottles or broom handles. Sometimes the rapes occurred post mortem.

Once he was done with the victim, he'd tuck her up in bed with such care that many of his murders went unnoticed at first, with death ascribed to natural causes.

The first murder that was recognized as such, related to the death of 82-year-old Margarita Gonzalez, killed in her home on August 6, 1987. The crime might have gone unnoticed had Vega's attack not caused the woman to swallow her false teeth. A few weeks later, on September 30, 1987, Vega entered the home of Carmen Gonzalez Fernandez, 80 years old, raping and strangling her. The following month he killed Natividad Robledo Espinosa, 66, this time beating the victim to death.

With the police now on high alert, Vega lay low for a while, emerging again on January 21, 1988, to murder Carmen Martinez Gonzalez. Then, on April 18, he raped and suffocated Julia Paz Fernandez, aged 66.

A month later, on May 19, police followed up an anonymous tip and arrested Vega near his apartment on Cobo de la Torre. Under questioning, he almost immediately implicated himself in the murders and the police soon had all of the corroborating evidence they needed.

At Vega's apartment, they found a macabre shrine constructed of trophies he'd collected from each of his victims. Not only did this link him to the murders of which he was already suspected, but once pictures of the shrine were shown on television, shocked members of the public came forward to identify items that had belonged to their recently deceased relatives. The deaths had previously been ascribed to natural causes.

Jose Antonio Rodriguez Vega went on trial under heavy police guard in November 1991, in Santander. Despite the overwhelming evidence against him including his prior confession, he now claimed complete innocence for all of the murders, his attorney suggesting that the victims had died of natural causes.

It was a strategy that was doomed to failure. Vega was found guilty and sentenced to 440 years in prison. Impressive though that sentence sounds, it effectively meant that Vega would be a free man in 2008, when he'd be 51 years old and still potentially a danger to society.

He didn't make it that far. On October 25, 2002, the Old Lady Killer was walking in the exercise yard at the Topas jail in western Salamanca, when he was attacked by two inmates and stabbed to death. He was 44 at the time. Few, if any, missed his passing.

63. Saeed Hanaei

Country: Iran

Confirmed Victims: 16

Suspected Victims: 16

To most westerners, Iran is a closed shop, a country run according to the strict tenets of Islam, where crime and immorality are unheard of. It might surprise you to learn, therefore, that Iran has a serious problem with drugs and prostitution, the former in the shape of opium pouring over the border from neighboring Afghanistan, the latter in desperate, drug addicted women, prepared to do anything to pay for their next fix.

In 2000, one man decided to do something about the problem.

Saeed Hanaei was a 39-year-old construction worker, living in a working-class neighborhood in Masad, one of Iran's holiest cities. By all accounts, he was an unremarkable man, married with three children. He had served in the 1980-1988 Iran-Iraq War.

Then in 2000, an incident occurred that transformed Hanaei from a loving father and husband to a brutal killer. While walking home from the market, his wife was mistaken for a prostitute and propositioned by a taxi driver. When Hanaei heard about the incident he flew into a rage and swore vengeance.

At first, he began harassing the men who cruised for streetwalkers in his neighborhood. But that only got him beaten up, so he turned his attention to the women themselves. Now, though, his revenge went way beyond harassment.

Over the next year, 19 women were found dead on the streets of Masad. Each was a known prostitute. Most were drug users. Each had been strangled with her own headscarf and wrapped in her chador, the flowing black garment that covers a woman from head to toe.

As the body count mounted word began to spread about the so-called, "Spider Killer," sparking furious debate across the country. In more conservative circles, the murderer was hailed as a folk hero, someone who had taken it upon himself to clean the streets of immoral women.

Iranians of a more progressive bent, though, voiced fears that an extremist religious group might be behind the slayings and accused the police of laxity in pursuing the killer.

Whether that was true or not, the mounting death toll could not be ignored and the police were forced into action. They began by removing over 500 prostitutes from the streets as a 'safety measure.' Then they launched a major operation to catch the killer. Saeed Hanaei was arrested after an intended victim escaped and reported him to the police.

In custody, Hanaei had no problem in admitting to the murders. In fact, he appeared proud of what he'd done and seemed to relish the adoration directed at him from various extremist groups.

"They were as worthless as cockroaches to me," he said. "Toward the end, I could not sleep at night if I had not killed one of them that day. It was as though I had become addicted to killing them."

According to Hanaei, he'd go cruising for prostitutes whenever his wife and three children were away. He'd bring them back to his home, where he would strangle them and then dump their bodies on the streets or in open sewers. With some of his later victims, he'd even waited around for the body to be discovered, then helped the police load it into the ambulance.

Despite a significant public outpouring of support for Hanaei, he was found guilty of murder and sentenced to die, his pseudo-religious motivation for the crimes not helped by his admission that he'd had sex with the women before killing them.

He was hanged at Masad Prison on April 16, 2002. Reportedly, he went to the gallows kicking and screaming. He had believed right until the end that his powerful supporters would get his conviction overturned.

62. Charles Ray Hatcher

Country: United States

Confirmed Victims: 16

Suspected Victims: 16+

Charles Ray Hatcher was born on July 16, 1929, in Mound City, Missouri, the youngest of four children. His father was an ex-con and an abusive alcoholic who doled out regular beatings to his kids. Hatcher endured a difficult childhood. When he was just 6 years old, his brother was accidentally electrocuted right before his eyes. His parents divorced soon after and his mother remarried several times, landing the boy with a succession of abusive stepfathers.

Hatcher's first brush with the law came in 1947, when he was convicted of stealing a truck from his employer and received a two-year suspended sentence. Undeterred by this setback, he fell into a life of petty crime and served time variously for auto theft, forgery, and burglary. By 1959, the 30-year-old Hatcher had already served six prison terms. Soon, though, he'd graduate from petty crimes against property to violent offenses against people.

On June 26, 1959, Hatcher was arrested after attempting to abduct a 16-year-old boy at knifepoint. Sent down for five years, Hatcher was returned to the Missouri State Penitentiary, where he boasted that he was the state's most notorious criminal since Jesse James.

On July 2, 1961, inmate Jerry Tharrington was found raped and stabbed to death in the prison kitchen. Hatcher was suspected of the murder but there wasn't enough evidence to convict him. Instead, he spent time in solitary confinement before being returned to the general prison population. He remained there until August 24, 1963.

After his release, Hatcher drifted for a while, eventually ending up in California. On August 27, 1969, he abducted twelve-year-old William Freeman in Antioch, California, took him to a creek, then sexually molested and strangled him. Two days later, he abducted six-year-old Gilbert Martinez in San Francisco. Hatcher was arrested in the act of beating and sexually assaulting the boy.

Facing another extended prison term for the crime, Hatcher claimed insanity, alleging that he heard voices. There followed an extended round of psychiatric evaluations, some doctors declaring him unfit to stand trial, others convinced that he was exaggerating his symptoms.

Eventually, on May 24, 1971, Hatcher was sent to trial and pleaded not guilty by reason of insanity. A new round of evaluations followed, during which time Hatcher escaped from the hospital and went on the run. Captured a week later, he was declared unfit to stand trial and sent to the prison hospital at Vacaville.

It was only in August 1972, that Hatcher finally faced the music for the abduction and attempted rape of Gilbert Martinez. In December 1972, he was found guilty and sent to the California State Hospital as a mentally disordered sexual offender.

In June 1976, the California Parole Board declared that Hatcher's condition had improved dramatically and in May 1977 he was released to a halfway house.

On May 26, 1978, four-year-old Eric Christgen disappeared in downtown Saint Joseph, Missouri. His body was later found along the Missouri River. He had been sexually abused and then strangled.

The police focused their investigation on Melvin Reynolds, a mentally retarded 25-year-old and despite a lack of evidence, they eventually coaxed a confession out of him. Reynolds was tried and sentenced to life in prison, while the real killer, Charles Hatcher, was free to kill again.

On July 29, 1983, hikers found the nude, battered body of 11-year-old Michelle Steele on the banks of the Missouri River near St. Joseph. She had been raped, strangled and beaten to death. Arrested for the murder the following day, Hatcher broke down and started confessing. He claimed to have killed 15 other children between 1969 and 1983, the murders traversing California, Iowa, Missouri, and Illinois.

Among his victims, he named James Churchill of Davenport Iowa and drew investigators a map, which allowed them to recover the boy's body. He also confessed to killing Eric Christgen, a crime for which Melvin Reynolds had already served four years.

Hatcher was convicted of the Christgen murder in October 1983, and sentenced to life imprisonment with no parole for at least 50 years. A year later, he went on trial for killing Michelle Steele. Hatcher asked for the death penalty but the jury opted for life imprisonment. It was a term Charles Hatcher would never serve. On December 3, 1984, he hanged himself in his cell at the state prison in Jefferson City.

61. Vladimir Mirgorod

Country: Russia

Confirmed Victims: 16

Suspected Victims: 16+

Serial killers are generally classified into two broad categories, organized and disorganized. The organized killer is usually socially adept, relying on persuasion to gain control over his victim. The disorganized killer relies on surprise and force, springing on an unsuspecting victim without warning. Vladimir Mirgorod is unusual in that he started out as an organized killer and then later devolved towards disorganized behavior.

In the summer of 2003, a series of gruesome murders played out in Moscow's northern and northeasterly suburbs. At least ten women were found, tied up, strangled and raped. Several more women were sexually assaulted but managed to escape. They described their assailant as a dark-haired young man with mad, glassy eyes.

The early victims had all been found indoors and had apparently invited the killer into their homes. Then, for some inexplicable reason, he changed his M.O. and began attacking women in parks and on the streets. This caused some confusion, and the Moscow police, always quick to deny rumors of serial murder, confidently stated that the murders were unrelated. Privately, though, they must have been aware that they were hunting a serial killer.

The murder that first alerted the police to that possibility was the third in the series, the strangulation of a 25-year-old woman, recently arrived in Moscow from Minsk. She was found indoors, a slipknot pulled tightly around her neck. She'd been raped and several valuables were noted as missing from her apartment. That was in January 2003.

In March of that year, a 20-year-old Moscow University student was raped and then strangled with her own scarf. A few days later, another 20-year-old girl was killed in similar fashion. A month later, a 34-year-old woman from Novosibirsk was found dead in her rented apartment on Matros Zheleznyak Street. June 2003, brought a double homicide, a 43-year-old woman strangled and raped, her 16-year-old son hung with a leather belt. It appeared that the boy had walked in on his mother's murder.

With the onset of warm weather in July, the killer took his murderous activities outdoors. First, a 28-year-old woman was found gagged and strangled at the city's Botanical gardens. Then another 28-year-old, Irina Gero, was found strangled to death with a leather belt on Yablochkova Street. Both of the women had been raped.

Then, as suddenly as they'd started, the killings stopped. The police, who despite several eyewitness reports had made very little progress in catching the killer, breathed a collective sign of relief and got on to other, more solvable cases.

In 2010, the Moscow police department was in the process of digitalizing its archives when detectives made a chance discovery. They matched fingerprints from the unsolved serial killer case to a man who had recently completed a 5-year term for robbery. The man's name was Vladimir Mirgorod and his term of incarceration coincided neatly with the cessation of the Moscow murders.

Mirgorod was quickly tracked down and re-arrested. Charged initially with seven murders, the docket later expanded to incorporate 16 cases. Found guilty on those charges, and on numerous related rapes and assaults, he was sentenced to life in prison.

60. Vladimir Kondratenko & Vladislav Volkovich

Country: Ukraine

Confirmed Victims: 16

Suspected Victims: 16+

On June 18, 1996, police in Kiev, Ukraine, were called to the site of a murder. The victim was a 44-year-old factory worker named Evgeniy Osechkin, found dead near Karavaevy Dachi train station. He'd been killed by a .22 bullet to the head. He'd also been stabbed several times in the chest.

The murder had police stumped. Osechkin, as far as they could determine, had no enemies. And robbery was quickly ruled out as a motive when it was discovered that he was still carrying his weekly wages in his pocket. Why then, had he been killed?

An interesting clue soon emerged. Some months before the Osechkin murder, a homeless man had been shot and killed just 100 yards from the same train station. The bullet, in that case, had also been a .22.

Believing that they might have a serial shooter on their hands, the police placed the station under surveillance. They had made no further progress in the case when the next murder occurred.

On July 2, a local doctor named Aleksandr Egorov was gunned down in broad daylight, as he sat in his car. The police had barely begun questioning witnesses to that crime when word came of another murder, the male victim shot and stabbed to death just blocks from the Egorov crime scene. In each case, the perpetrator was described as a man of about 30. Fingerprints were discovered at both scenes but no match was found on record. Ballistics, however, confirmed that the same weapon had been used in all four shootings.

Two weeks later, a man named Aleksandr Shpack was at a party with his girlfriend when he got into an argument with two men who had gatecrashed the event. The men soon departed. Later, Shpack left the party somewhat the worse for wear. He was found the next morning, shot and stabbed to death. His girlfriend was able to describe the two men, adding that one of them had been named Vladimir. The clue looked promising but ultimately led nowhere.

Another man fell victim to the elusive killers on September 4. Then, at around 10:30 p.m. on September 28, 36-year-old Petr Gromov was found shot to death, his body discarded in a gutter. The police found his vehicle about a block away. It appeared that the killer (or killers) had tried to drive off in the car, then abandoned that idea and fled on foot. Ballistics linked this latest murder to the series.

By now, the police were convinced that they were hunting a serial killer team. Armed with a description of the suspects, they began canvassing residents in the general area of the shootings. They soon hit paydirt when a woman said that she recognized one of the men. His name was Vladimir, and he lived in an apartment nearby. The police quickly converged on the building where a search located an unlocked door. Inside, a man named Aleksandr Bykov sat slumped in a chair, a bullet wound to his head.

The bullet that had killed Bykov was soon matched to the weapon used in the other murders. Also in the apartment, the police found a photograph of a young man who looked a lot like their main suspect. Desperate for a break in the case, they placed the apartment under surveillance.

Three days later, the suspect showed up. Unfortunately, the surveillance team jumped the gun, spooking him. Several officers gave chase but lost him in a local marketplace.

With the suspect now alerted, the police were afraid that he might flee the area. They therefore stepped up their efforts to identify him and found a clue in the most unlikely of places. A young man had accompanied Aleksandr Bykov's wife to the morgue to formally identify his body. He'd even been overheard promising the woman that he'd do whatever it took to find Aleksandr's killer. He had provided his details to the duty officer. His name was Vladimir Dmitrievich Kondratenko.

Now the other pieces fell quickly into place. An I.D. soon followed on Kondratenko's partner in crime, a man named Vladislav Volkovich. An arrest warrant was issued but unfortunately arrived too late to save the murderous pair's final victim, an unidentified woman who they struck and killed (albeit accidentally) while fleeing a crime scene in a stolen vehicle.

Soon after, Volkovich and Kondratenko were taken into custody. They quickly confessed to the crimes they'd committed, 20 murders as well as numerous robberies, carjackings, and burglaries.

The killers offered a highly unusual motive for their crime spree. They said that they had been looking for a way to make money and had hit on the idea of becoming contract killers. However, they were not sure if they'd actually be able to kill anyone, so they'd decided to go on a few practice runs. At first, they'd targeted homeless men. But they'd discovered that they actually enjoyed the act of murder and had added to their M.O.

A favorite tactic was for one of the men to stand hitchhiking. Once someone gave him a ride he'd ask the driver to make a small detour, so that he could pick up a box from a friend. The second of the men would be standing at the side of the road. The minute the driver pulled to a stop he'd open fire, while the man inside the car would simultaneously begin stabbing the driver.

The case came to trial in May 1997, the two men charged with 16 murders. Kondratenko, however, opted out of the punishment waiting for him. Two days into the court proceedings, he overdosed on prescription medication and died in police custody. His death was ruled a suicide.

Left to face the music alone, Vladislav Volkovich attempted to shift most of the blame to his deceased partner. It didn't work. He was found guilty and sentenced to life in prison.

59. The Death Angels

Country: United States

Confirmed Victims: 16

Suspected Victims: 16+

The city of San Francisco was under siege. Over a period of just two months, from October to December 1973, eleven people had been shot to death on the street, one more killed in a horrendous machete attack. In addition, a number of people had been seriously wounded, among them future San Francisco mayor, Art Agnos. And yet the police had nothing, other than that the attackers were black, the victims white, the killings apparently without motive.

The murder spree had begun on October 19, 1973, when Richard Hague, 30, and his 28-year-old wife, Quita, were dragged from the street into a white van. Mrs. Quita was sexually molested by the abductors before being hacked to death with a machete. Her husband was severely injured by the same weapon but survived.

Ten days later, on October 29, a man stepped into the path of Frances Rose's car as she approached the entrance gate of the University of California. The man first demanded a ride, then produced a pistol and shot Rose several times.

On November 25, Jordanian shopkeeper Saleem Erekat, was tied up and executed in the restroom of his grocery store. On December 11, Paul Dancik, a 26-year-old artist, was shot three times in the chest as he stood making a call at a pay phone. Two days later, Art Agnos was shot twice in the back and seriously injured as he stood on a sidewalk in Potrero Hill. That same evening Marietta DiGirolamo, 31, was shot and killed on Divisadero Street.

On December 20, a 20-year-old college student was shot three times but survived. 81-year-old janitor, Ilario Bertuccio, shot that same evening, was not so lucky. He died at the scene having been hit four times in the chest and shoulder.

Two days passed. Then on December 22, two more victims were dead. Neal Moynihan, 19, was walking near Civic Center when a man stepped in front of him and shot him in the chest, face, and neck. Just six minutes later, the same killer   executed 50-year-old Mildred Hosler as she stood at a bus stop.

With the city reeling under this spate of attacks, the killers lay low for a week before re-emerging on December 28 to carry out their most deadly spree yet. Five people were shot that night, only one of them surviving. Roxanne McMillian, 23, would spend the rest of her life confined to a wheelchair.

Needless to say, the attacks caused widespread panic in San Francisco, with the streets of this vibrant city all but deserted after dark. The police, meanwhile, had put extra patrol units on the streets and formed a task force to catch the killers.

Thus far, they had very little to go on. They knew that the offenders were black, that they used a .32 caliber pistol and that they typically walked up to the victim, fired off a burst and then fled on foot. Most baffling of all was the motive. There seemed neither rhyme nor reason for the crimes.

The task force (designated Zebra, after the radio frequency it used) had barely begun its investigation when the killers dropped out of sight. They would remain concealed for three months.

On April 1, 1974, Thomas Rainwater, 19, and Linda Story, 21, were walking to a Salvation Army meeting when a man overtook them and then turned and started firing. Rainwater was killed instantly. Story survived but was seriously injured. Shell casings from a .32 caliber handgun suggested that the serial shooters were back.

On Easter Sunday, a merchant seaman named Ward Anderson, and a 15-year-old student named Terry White, were shot as they stood at a bus stop on Fillmore Streets. Both survived and described their attacker as a black man

Three days later, on the evening of April 16, 23-year-old Nick Shields was shot and killed as he was loading a rug into the back of his station wagon. An eyewitness reported seeing a black man fleeing the scene.

In the wake of this latest murder spree, the SFPD began to take drastic measures, including stopping and questioning any African American man who resembled the suspect. Over 500 individuals were interrogated on the first weekend that the program was in effect, but the move soon drew outrage from the NAACP and the

ACLU. Within days an interdict had been issued outlawing the operation.

The other measure applied to the case was much more productive. The offer of a $30,000 reward encouraged a man named Anthony Harris to contact the police. Harris said that he knew who had carried out the attacks and that he had been present during several of them, although he hadn't been an active participant. He also told police about a murder that they hadn't connected to the series.

A homeless man had been kidnapped from Ghirardelli Square and taken to the premises of a company called Black Self-Help Moving and Storage. There he was gagged and bound and then hacked to death with machetes. His body was later dumped in the bay. The police had pulled a John Doe from the water on December 24, bearing exactly the injuries that Harris described, so they knew he was telling the truth.

With the offer of immunity and a new identity for himself and his girlfriend, Harris eventually gave up the names and addresses of the suspects.

On May 1, SFPD officers carried out a number of pre-dawn raids and arrested the seven men named by Harris. Three of the men subsequently had to be released due to lack of evidence, leaving Larry Green, J.C.X. Simon, Manuel Moore, and Jessie Lee Cooks to face the music. Cooks admitted to his involvement in the shootings, while the other three defendants went to trial, their defense funded by Black Muslim leader John Muhammad's Nation of Islam.

That trial began on March 3, 1975, with the prosecution presenting a mountain of evidence against the "Death Angels," including ballistics and the testimony of 108 witnesses. Most convincing of all was the testimony of Anthony Harris and the detailed confession given by Jessie Lee Cooks.

Found guilty of murder and conspiracy to commit murder, Green, Simon, Moore, and Cooks were sentenced to life imprisonment.

58. Il Mostro

Country: Italy

Confirmed Victims: 16

Suspected Victims: 16+

On the evening of August 21, 1968, Barbara Locci and her lover, Antonio Lo Bianco, were shot to death as they sat in a car parked on a rural lane near Florence, Italy. The murder appeared to be an open and shut case. Locci's husband was soon arrested tried and found guilty of the murders. He'd spend six years in prison before the killer struck again, proving his innocence.

The second pair of victims were young lovers Pasquale Gentilcore and Stefania Pettini, slain on September 14, 1974, with the same .22 caliber weapon used in the Locci / Lo Bianco murders. This time, though, the killer added a new perversion, sexually mutilating the female victim.

Another long break followed before the killer emerged on June 6, 1981, to murder 30-year-old Giovanni Foggi and 21-year-old Carmela Di Nuccio. Again, the killer directed most of his rage at the female victim, inflicting over 300 stab wounds on her body.

Up until now, there had been long breaks between murders, but this time, the killer waited just three months before he struck again, killing 26-year-old Stefano Baldi and 24-year-old Susanna Campi. As he'd done in 1974, the killer again mutilated the female victim, hacking Susanna Campi's vagina from her body and removing it from the scene.

Over the next four years, Il Mostro (as the press was now dubbing him) reappeared with deadly regularity to commit his trademark double homicides. On June 19, 1982, Paolo Mainardi, 22, and Antonella Migliorini, 22, were shot with a .22 pistol matching the previous crimes. Migliorini was mutilated after death. Fifteen months later, Il Mostro varied his pattern, shooting to death two male tourists from Germany, Horst Meyer and Uwe Rusch Sens. On June 29, 1984, he killed Claudio Stefanacci and Pia Rontini, removing Rontini's genitals and left breast. On September 8, 1985, he murdered French tourists, Jean-Michel Kraveichvili and Nadine Mauriot, hacking Mauriot's breast from her body. A day later, part of Mauriot's genitalia was mailed to the police.

But despite eight double homicides committed out in the open, the police had very little to go on. The crimes were all linked by ballistics but the killer had been careful not to leave evidence at the scenes and was believed to wear surgical gloves. That and the possible use of a scalpel to inflict the horrendous wounds on the victims, suggested a medical connection. An exploration of that theory provided no answers.

The police, quite frankly, were stumped and despite carrying out more than 100,000 interviews and retaining six different suspects in the case, they were nowhere near to catching the killer until January 17, 1993, when they arrested 71-year-old Pietro Pacciani.

On the surface, Pacciani made a good suspect. He'd been convicted of murder before, after shooting a salesman who he accused of having an affair with his girlfriend. He'd also done time in prison for assaulting his wife and for molesting his two young daughters. Yet the evidence against Pacciani was scant and although he would be convicted of the Il Mostro killings, the verdict would later be overturned by an appellate court.

In December 1996, ten months after that reversal, the Italian Supreme court reversed the appeal court's decision and ordered a new trial for Pacciani, along with three accomplices, 70-year-old Mario Vanni, 77-year-old Giovanni Faggi, and 54-year-old Giancarlo Lotti. Prosecutors now had a new theory. They believed that the murders had been carried out by a criminal gang, with Pacciani as their leader.

Pacciani would never attend that trial. He died at his home on February 22, 1998. Meanwhile, his three confederates had all had their day in court, with mixed results. Giovanni Faggi was acquitted on all counts; Giancarlo Lotti was convicted of involvement in eight murders; Mario Vanni was convicted of involvement in five. The remaining cases are officially unsolved, and many would argue that the real "Monster of Florence" is still out there.

57. Carroll Cole

Country: United States

Confirmed Victims: 16

Suspected Victims: 16+

Carroll Edward Cole was born in Sioux City, Iowa, on May 9, 1938, the second son of LaVerne and Vesta Cole. In 1939, the family moved to Richmond, California, where LaVerne Cole worked in the shipyards.

During WWII, LaVerne Cole was drafted into the army and it was then that young Carroll's life began to go awry. His mother began engaging in casual sexual relationships and beating Carroll to ensure that he kept his silence. This continued until his father returned from the war.

Carroll had problems at school too, constantly teased and bullied for having a "girl's name." His main tormentor was a boy named Duane, but in 1946, Carroll got his revenge. One afternoon in 1946, a group of boys went swimming at Richmond's yacht harbor, Cole and Duane among them.

While no one was watching, Cole pulled Duane under the water, holding him there until he stopped struggling. The death was ruled accidental. Carroll Cole was eight years old and had just gotten away with his first murder.

By the time Cole reached high school he was already a heavy drinker and a habitual burglar. He dropped out in 1957 and joined the Navy. That lasted just 18 months before he was dishonorably discharged after a burglary conviction.

On June 1, 1960, Cole launched a hammer attack on a couple parked in a lover's lane, earning 30 days on the county work farm. In January 1961, he flagged down a police car and told the stunned patrolmen about his urge to rape and strangle women. He was sent to Napa State Hospital for 90 days of observation.

After his release, Cole moved to Dallas, Texas, where he hooked up with an alcoholic stripper named Billie Whitworth. The couple married in November 1963, but it was a bad match from the start, characterized by drunkenness and domestic violence. Eventually, Carroll burned down the hotel they were staying in, after accusing Billie of sleeping with other men. That earned him a two-year prison term.

Cole served nine months, then drifted to Oklahoma City, then to Lake Ozark, Missouri, where he was arrested in May 1967 for breaking into the bedroom of an 11-year-old girl and trying to strangle her. Sent to prison for five years, he was released on parole in 1970.

Cole continued to drift, first back to San Diego, then to Reno, Nevada. On September 19, 1970, he handed himself over to Reno police and confessed his urge to murder women. He was sent to a state hospital in Sparks, Nevada, then discharged and put on a bus back to California.

By now, Carroll Cole had given up asking for help. On May 7, 1971, he picked up Essie Buck in a San Diego tavern and strangled her in his car. Two weeks later, he strangled a woman named Wilma and buried her in the foothills outside San Ysidro. A third victim was consigned to a similar fate a week later.

In March 1972, Cole picked up two Hispanic women in a bar in San Ysidro, later convincing them to join him on a drive into the desert. There he bludgeoned one of the women to death with a hammer and strangled the other.

In July 1973, Cole married again. His new bride was a barmaid named Diana Pashal and the union was every bit as tempestuous as his first. Police were regularly called to their home to break up drunken brawls.

In August 1974, the couple moved from San Diego to Las Vegas, where Cole got a job transporting coins from the slot machines at McCarran Airport to the downtown casinos. One day he simply fled with the day's receipts, leaving Diana behind.

On August 9, 1975, he showed up in Casper, Wyoming, where he murdered a woman named Myrlene Hamer. After that, he returned to San Diego and convinced Diana to take him back. He was soon in trouble again. Arrested for trying to cash a stolen government check, he got a one-year sentence.

In April 1977, Cole skipped out on his parole and headed back to Las Vegas, where he strangled a prostitute named Kathlyn Blum on May 14. He headed next for Oklahoma City, where he committed his most horrendous murder yet.

On November 23, Cole picked up a woman in a topless bar, taking her back to his place for sex. The following morning, he woke to find the woman's mutilated corpse in the bathtub. Both of her feet and her right arm had been severed and were later found in the refrigerator. A chunk of flesh from the woman's buttocks lay in a skillet on the stove, another piece, half-eaten, was on a plate on the kitchen table. Using kitchen knives and a hacksaw, Cole finished dismembering the corpse, then placed the pieces in plastic garbage bags and dropped them at the city dump. He later claimed that he'd blacked out, and had no recollection of the murder.

From Oklahoma, Cole moved on to Denver City, Texas, then back to San Diego, and another reunion with Diana.

On August 27, 1979, he strangled Bonnie Sue O'Neil, leaving her body behind the appliance store where he worked. The body was found the next day. The police didn't even bother questioning the employees of the store.

Things with Diana, meanwhile, had assumed their customary cycle of binges and fights. On September 17, 1979, Cole strangled Diana, wrapped her body in a blanket, and pushed it into a closet. When the corpse was eventually found, cause of death was recorded as "alcohol poisoning."

Cole, meanwhile, was back in Vegas. On November 3, he picked up Marie Cushman, took her to the Casbah Hotel and strangled her. Her body was found the next day, by which time Cole was headed for Texas. He'd murder three more women there before his eventual arrest on December 1, 1980.

Cole went on trial on April 6, 1981, the jury taking just 25 minutes to convict and sentence him to three life terms. On March 30, 1984, he was extradited to Nevada to stand trial for the murders of Marie Cushman and Kathlyn Blum. This time, the sentence was death.

Over the next 11 months, Carroll Cole stubbornly refused all attempts to lodge appeals on his behalf. He kept his date with the executioner on December 6, 1985, and became the first man executed by lethal injection in Nevada.

56. Michel Fourniret

Country: France / Belgium

Confirmed Victims: 16

Suspected Victims: 19+

On June 26, 2003, Belgian police arrived at a stone farmhouse near the village of Sart-Custinne in the Ardennes. They carried with them a warrant for the arrest of 65-year-old French national, Michel Fourniret. Earlier in the day, Fourniret, along with his 59-year-old wife, Monique Olivier, had tried to abduct a 13-year-old girl in the nearby town of Ciney. The girl had managed to escape and had reported the crime, providing the police with Fourniret's license plate number. It had brought the police directly to his door. Little did they know that they'd just captured the sadistic killer of at least ten women and young girls.

Michel Fourniret was born in Sedan, France, on April 4, 1942. Not much is known about his childhood or upbringing, but in later life, he qualified as a draftsman, and developed a keen interest in DIY, classical music, and chess. He also acquired a taste for pedophilia and an obsession with abducting and raping young virgins.

Fourniret was 24 years old when he racked up his first conviction, for kidnapping and sexually assaulting a 10-year-old girl in his hometown of Sedan. Two more rape convictions followed before he was arrested in 1984 for a series of sex attacks on young girls in and around Paris. That sent him back to prison, although the sentence was ludicrously lenient, just seven years for the repeat sex offender.

Fourniret's period of incarceration would prove eventful, with two particular events that shaped the course of his life. Firstly, he was placed in a cell with Jean-Pierre Hellegouache, leader of France's notorious 'Wig Gang' of bank robbers. Hellegouache confided in Fourniret that the gang had buried their loot in a cemetery. After Fourniret's release, Hellegouache sent his girlfriend to ask for Fouriniet's help in recovering the money. Fourniret agreed, but once the whereabouts of the loot was revealed, he murdered the woman and kept the money for himself.

The other event to occur while Fourniret was locked up, was even more significant. Advertising for a pen pal, he attracted the attention of Monique Olivier. Twice divorced and with two estranged children, Olivier was desperate for attention and soon infatuated by Fourniret and his ideas of abducting and raping virgins. When Fourniret was released on October 26, 1987, Olivier was there to collect him.

The couple set up home in the northern Burgundy village of St Cyr-les-Colons. Just six weeks later, on Friday, December 11, 1987, 17-year-old Isabelle Laville was walking home from school in the Auxerre suburb of St Georges-sur-Baulche, when Monique Olivier pulled up alongside her, driving a Peugeot panel van. She asked Laville for directions, then convinced the girl to get into the vehicle and show her the way.

A couple of miles down the road Fourniret waited, standing in the emergency lane with a fuel can, playing the part of a stranded motorist. Olivier obligingly stopped to pick him up.

Fourniret got into the back seat and Olivier had hardly pulled away when he looped a rope around Isabelle Laville's neck. He then forced her to swallow sleeping tablets. By the time they arrived at Fourniret's home in St Cyr-les-Colons, Laville was unconscious. Fourniret carried the girl inside where he instructed his wife to examine her, to ensure that she was still a virgin. Satisfied that she was, he tried to rape her. However, despite Olivier's efforts to stimulate him orally, he was unable to sustain an erection. He then strangled Laville. Her body was later dumped in an abandoned well.

In 1988, the Fournirets moved from St Cyr-les-Colons to the Ardennes town of Floing. Olivier was by now heavily pregnant, but that didn't stop her joining her husband on his "virgin hunts."

Using her condition as a ruse, Olivier approached 20-year-old student, Fabienne Leroy, and told her she urgently needed to get to a doctor. Leroy was convinced to get into the car, where

Fourniret sat behind the wheel. He drove to a field where he forced Leroy from the vehicle at gunpoint. There, Olivier subjected the girl to a crude examination, before Fourniret raped and then shot her. Leroy's body was found in the field the next day. Soon the area around Floing would be plagued by a number of similar murders.

In March 1989, Jeanne-Marie Desramault, 22, disappeared. In December that same year, 12-year-old Elisabeth Brichet, went missing. There were other murders too, bearing Fourniret's unique signature, most notably that of British student, Joanna Parrish. Fourniret denies involvement in this and other murders.

In the spring of 1990, Fourniret and Olivier moved from their bungalow to the nearby Château de Sautou, bought in 1989 with the money stolen from Jean-Pierre Hellegouache.

In November 1990, 13-year-old Natacha Danais was snatched from a street in Loire-Atlantique. Her body was found on a beach in western France three days later. She had been raped and stabbed to death.

Two more victims followed. Celine Saison, 18, was murdered in May 2000, 13-year-old, Mananya Thumpong, a year later. Both bodies were discovered in the Belgian Ardennes.

Now, two years later, Michel Fourniret was in custody, but confident that he'd receive no more than a slap on the wrist for the attempted abduction. He could not have anticipated that his loyal wife, Monique, would betray him.

At around that time, the Marc Dutroux child murder case was big news in Belgium and around the world. Monique had been following the story and was dismayed when the court handed down a 30-year sentence to Dutroux's wife for complicity in the crimes. Fearful that she'd get the same treatment, she called for a meeting with investigators. She then told the stunned detectives that her husband had murdered "at least six" women.

Confronted with his wife's accusations, Fourniret readily confessed to the earlier murders, believing that he couldn't be tried for them due to France's statute of limitations, which decrees that a person cannot be charged for a murder if the investigation has been formally closed for more than 10 years.

What Fourniret wasn't aware of, was that the statute does not apply to serial murder. Once investigators informed him that he could, and would, be tried for the crimes, he cracked and admitted to seven murders. He would eventually lead the police to the burial sites of his victims.

Michel Fourniret went on trial in the French town of Charleville-Mezieres in May 2008. Convicted on seven counts of murder he was sentenced to life in prison. Despite insisting that she'd been under Fourniret's psychological control, Monique Olivier got the same sentence.

55. Robert Lee Yates Jr.

Country: United States

Confirmed Victims: 16

Suspected Victims: 20+

Someone was slaughtering the prostitutes of Spokane, Washington, a mysterious shooter brandishing a small caliber firearm. Between February 1990 and August 1997, the killer had appeared intermittently, claiming one or two victims before dropping out of sight. And the police still had no clues when, on Tuesday, August 26, 1997, the body of 16-year-old Jennifer Joseph was discovered just off Forker Road.

Like the nine victims that had preceded her, Jennifer was a prostitute. But in this case, there was a lead. She had been seen getting into a white Corvette with a Caucasian male, approximately 30 to 40 years old.

About a month later, on September 24, an officer pulled over a similar vehicle in the vicinity of Sprague and Ralph, a popular pick-up spot for hookers. The driver identified himself as Robert L. Yates Jr. He was ticketed for a minor traffic infraction and allowed to proceed. Unfortunately, the patrolman mistakenly wrote up Yates vehicle as a Camaro, rather than a Corvette.

Meanwhile, the killer was accelerating. On November 5, 1997, a decomposing corpse was discovered in a shallow grave on Hangman Valley Road. A month later, another body was found, in Tacoma, Washington. Like the other victims, she'd been shot with a small caliber weapon. She also had a plastic grocery bag pulled over her head, a signature of the killer.

Less than a fortnight later, another corpse turned up. She was 36-year-old Shawn Johnson, a Spokane prostitute. She'd been shot, her head shrouded in a plastic bag.

Friday, December 26, 1997, brought a double discovery, Laurel Wason and Shawn McClenahan. Both were prostitutes, both had been shot and both had their heads covered with plastic bags.

The next victim was found on Sunday, February 28, 1998. Sunny Oster was a 41-year-old prostitute and drug user. Found in a ditch beside Graham Road she'd died of gunshot wounds. Three plastic bags were drawn over her head.

And the killer wasn't done yet. Over the next three months, three more slain prostitutes were discovered, bringing the official body count to 17. And yet, police were no closer to identifying a suspect.

On Tuesday, November 10, 1998, Robert Yates appeared on police radars again, when he was stopped by a patrolman after picking up a known prostitute, Jennifer Robinson. Yates claimed he'd been sent by Robinson's father to pick her up and Jennifer backed up his story. The officer allowed them to drive on. Shortly thereafter, the killer again dropped out of sight.

On August 1, 1999, he was back. A prostitute named Christine Smith reported that she had been picked up by a man driving a black van. She described him as white, approximately 50-years-old, about 5'10", 175 pounds, with a medium build, sandy blond hair, and a pockmarked face.

They drove to a parking lot behind a clinic on East Fifth Street. En route the man revealed some facts about himself. He said he was a helicopter pilot with the National Guard and that he was married with five kids. After they parked they got into the back where Christine started to perform oral sex on the man. A moment later, she felt a blow to her head, delivered with such force that it almost knocked her unconscious. She staggered backwards and somehow managed to get out of the vehicle. She ran to the nearby St. Luke's Rehabilitation Center. From there a security guard drove her to Sacred Heart Hospital, where she received stitches to close the wound in her head. According to doctors, it was caused by a bullet graze.

Smith was unable to identify her attacker, but her description stayed with one of the detectives who revisited the lengthy suspect list and turned up Robert Lee Yates, only on the list because of his two traffic stops. The detective also noted that Yates was a helicopter pilot who served with the Washington National Guard.

On Tuesday, September 14, 1999, Yates was asked to meet with members of the task force at the Public Safety Building. He complied with the request and answered questions in a calm and courteous manner. However, when asked to provide a blood sample for DNA comparison, he refused, leaving detectives frustrated.

Yates' wife, Linda, was more forthcoming. She told investigators about his late night sorties, and about how he'd once come home with the back of his van covered in blood. He said that he'd hit a dog and had had to transport the animal to a vet, but thereafter he'd spent a great deal of time scrubbing the van and had destroyed the bloodstained cushions.

Other evidence also began stacking up against Yates. Investigators learned that he'd lied about his reasons for picking up Jennifer Robinson and that he'd neglected to tell them about the black van he owned. They also learned that he'd had the carpets in his Corvette changed twice in two years.

Yates had since sold the Corvette but detectives traced the new owner and obtained a sample of the carpet fibers. They turned out to match fibers found on one of the victims, Jennifer Joseph. Even more tellingly, flakes of dry blood were found in the vehicle, and matched by DNA typing to Joseph.

Yates was arrested on April 18, 2000. After his arrest, a search warrant was executed enabling the police to obtain a sample of his blood. Subsequent tests matched the DNA profiles of sperm taken from eight of the victims.

On Monday, October 16, 2000, Yates' attorneys approached prosecutors and offered a deal. In exchange for receiving life in prison, Yates would plead guilty to 13 counts of first-degree murder. They agreed.

Robert Lee Yates Jr. was sentenced to 408 years in prison.

54. Herb Baumeister

Country: United States

Confirmed Victims: 16

Suspected Victims: 25+

In June 1994, 28-year-old Alan Broussard disappeared shortly after leaving a gay bar in downtown Indianapolis. His parents reported him missing but, dismayed by the tepid response they received from the police, they turned to a private investigator named Virgil Vandagriff, a former Marion County sheriff.

Vandagriff's inquiries turned up an alarming number of gay men missing from local taverns, and he quickly became convinced that a serial killer was at work in the area. When he took his suspicions to Indianapolis PD, they were less than enthused by the idea. Not even the disappearance of 34-year-old Roger Goodlet a month later could shake them from the belief that the men had simply left town.

Unperturbed by their rebuttal, Vandagriff continued working the case, canvassing gay bars across the city, speaking to owners and patrons, putting up missing person posters. That line of inquiry eventually provided him with a lead in August 1994, when a man named Tony Harris contacted him. Harris had an interesting story to tell.

He said that he'd met a tall, dark-haired man named Brian Smart at a bar called the 501 Club. They'd had a few drinks together and had then gone back to Smart's home, a Tudor mansion to the north of the city, in what Harris described as, "rich people territory." There, Smart had suggested that they engage in autoerotic asphyxiation, something he insisted would increase the intensity of their orgasms. Harris had allowed Smart to choke him but had quickly become convinced that Smart was trying to kill him. He'd feigned unconsciousness whereupon Smart had released his grip.

Smart had seemed dazed afterwards and had shortly thereafter passed out. When he came to, Harris convinced him to drive him back to the city, which Smart did reluctantly. They made arrangements to meet at the 501 Club the following Wednesday but Smart didn't show.

The lead sounded promising, and Vandagriff decided to have another crack at getting Indianapolis PD involved. This time, he went directly to Detective Mary Wilson, who was working the missing persons cases on several of the disappeared gay men.

Wilson admitted that the story was worth looking into. However, her inquiries could find no record of a Brian Smart. Vandagriff had no better luck circulating Smart's description among the city's gay bars. Neither was Tony Harris able to find his way back to the house where he'd been taken. The lead quickly petered out. It would remain dormant for almost a year.

Then, on August 29, 1995, Vandagriff got a call from an obviously excited Tony Harris. He'd bumped into "Brian Smart" again, this time at a bar called the Varsity Lounge. Harris had followed him out and written down his license plate number. Indianapolis PD ran the plate. It turned up a match to Herbert R. Baumeister, of Westfield, Indiana.

Looking into Baumeister's background, Vandagriff and Wilson were at first certain they had the wrong man. Baumeister was a successful local businessman, married with two children. He was also from a prominent family, his father Herbert Sr., a leading anesthesiologist.

But as they began to scratch below the surface, a different picture began to emerge. Both Baumeister's marriage and his businesses were in trouble. The thrift shops he managed were on the verge of bankruptcy and he and his wife were separated, pending a divorce.

Detective Wilson decided it was worth questioning Baumeister. She approached him at his place of business and told him that she was investigating the disappearance of several young men in Indianapolis, that he was a suspect, and that she wanted permission to search his home. Baumeister flatly refused and told her to speak to his lawyer in future. Wilson then approached Julie Baumeister and got a similar refusal.

Six months went by, during which time Wilson tried without success to obtain a search warrant on the Baumeister property. Then, on June 23, 1996, Julie Baumeister finally gave permission for a search.

While Herb was visiting his mother at Lake Wawasee, Mary Wilson drove to the Baumeister home with a forensic search team. They'd barely begun their search of the grounds when they came across a charred piece of bone, about a foot in length. Then as the searchers eyes focused in, they realized that the pebbles and pieces of rock they were standing on, were not pebbles at all, but literally hundreds of bone fragments.

By the following day the search team had swelled to 60, and their activities had turned up an incredible 5,500 bone fragments. Then neighbors showed up to lead investigators to yet another boneyard, which they'd discovered on their property.

The corpses here were more intact, some with ribcages showing, others with handcuffs still fixed to their wrist bones. But only four of the victims would ever be identified; Roger Goodlet, 34; Steven Hale, 26; Richard Hamilton, 20; and Manuel Resendez, 31.

Meanwhile, a search had been launched for Herb Baumeister. On June 29, he phoned his brother, Brad, from Michigan, asking him to wire some cash. Brad sent the money, but after he learned of the discoveries at Herb's home, he called the police.

The following day, Baumeister entered Canada. He arrived in Sarnia on June 30, staying a few days before heading east to Grand Bend, Ontario. There, on the evening of July 3, Herb Baumeister put a .357 Magnum revolver to his forehead and ended his life.

53. Randy Kraft

Country: United States

Confirmed Victims: 16

Suspected Victims: 67

Randy Kraft was born on March 19, 1945, in Long Beach, California. In 1948, his family moved to Midway City, in Orange County. There, Randy grew up to be a conservative young man with a right-wing worldview. After graduating, however, he underwent a radical change, growing his hair and taking a job as a bartender in a gay bar. He also began consuming copious amounts of Valium. Kraft acquired his first arrest in 1966, for propositioning an undercover police officer.

In 1968, Randy Kraft underwent another change. After gaining a bachelor's degree in economics, he joined the Air Force and was posted to Edwards Air Force Base. A year later, he stunned his family by telling them he was gay.

In 1971, Kraft was discharged from the military for undisclosed "medical reasons." Shortly thereafter, he resumed his bartending career and fully embraced the gay lifestyle. He also began taking long drives, cruising the highways of southern California.

On October 5, 1971, police found the decomposing remains of 30-year-old Wayne Dukette alongside Ortega Highway, in Orange County. Fifteen months later, on December 26, 1972, the corpse of 20-year-old Marine, Edward Daniel Moore, was found beside the 405 Freeway near Seal Beach. Moore had been strangled, bludgeoned and apparently tossed from a moving car. There were clear signs of torture on the body, including bite marks on his genitals.

Over the next year, the police discovered a succession of corpses dumped beside various freeways, all of them showing signs of horrendous torture. Several of the victims had socks forced into their rectums, a signature of the killer. In addition, there were bite marks, burn marks, and cuts inflicted with broken bottles. Some had pencils and other objects forced through their penises into their bladders. In most instances, the coroner was able to determine that the injuries had been inflicted while the victims were still alive.

23-year-old art student Vincent Cruz Mestas was found in a ravine in the San Bernardino Mountains on December 29, 1973; Malcolm Eugene Little was left propped up against a mesquite tree beside Highway 86, in Imperial County; Roger Dickerson was found near a golf club in Laguna Beach, strangled and sodomized.

August brought two more, gruesome discoveries, 25-year-old Thomas Paxton Lee, and 23-year-old Gary Wayne Cordova. Then James Dale Reeves was found in Irvine on November 29, 1974, a tree limb four feet long and three inches in diameter protruding from his anus.

In December 1974, John Leras, a 17-year-old high school student, was found floating in the surf at Sunset Beach, a wooden surveyor's stake hammered into his rectum. Three weeks later, construction workers found 21-year-old Craig Victor Jonaites strangled to death alongside the Pacific Coast Highway.

On January 24, 1975, detectives from several jurisdictions met in Santa Ana, to organize a task force. A re-examination of the various murders turned up no significant leads, but a couple of months later, they had their first break in the case, when 19-year-old Keith Crotwell turned up dead. Crotwell had last been seen getting into a black Mustang and police were able to trace the vehicle to one Randy Steven Kraft. Kraft admitted giving Crotwell a ride but said he had dropped him off at an all-night café. With no evidence to suggest otherwise, the police were forced to release Kraft without charge.

The interrogation might have unsettled Kraft because he waited nearly six months before he killed again. Then he was back with a vengeance. Larry Gene Walters, 21, was murdered in Los Angeles County on Halloween 1975, before Kraft committed his most bloody murder yet. 22-year-old Mark Hall disappeared from a New Year's Eve party, in San Juan Capistrano. His nude corpse was found on January 3, 1976, in the Cleveland National Forest. He'd been sodomized and tortured: his legs slashed with a broken bottle; his eyes, face, chest and genitals burned with a cigarette lighter; a cocktail swizzle stick jammed through his penis into his bladder; his genitals severed and stuffed into his rectum.

Nine more murders occurred during 1977, before the killings suddenly stopped. They resumed on April 16, 1978, when 19-year-old Marine Scott Michael Hughes was found beside the 91 Freeway in Orange County. He'd been strangled to death, his genitals mutilated with a knife, one of his testicles removed. Two months later, 23-year-old Roland Young was found stabbed to death, his genitals mutilated. Then another Marine, 23-year-old Richard Keith, was found dead.

As the body count continued to spiral, gay bars throughout southern California began posting warnings for their customers. It did nothing to stop the slaughter. Over a dozen male corpses, ranging in age from 13 to 24, were found littering the freeways in 1979.

Neither was Randy Kraft confining his activities to California anymore. As a freelance data-processing consultant, he traveled extensively during this period, taking in Michigan, Oregon, New York, and Florida. He also traveled to Mexico and spent time in San Diego and Lake Tahoe. And wherever he went corpses seemed to turn up.

17-year-old Michael Sean O'Fallon was killed in Oregon in 1980, his murder bearing all the hallmarks of Kraft's work. Then, on September 3, 1980, children playing near El Toro Marine Airbase found the corpse of a 19-year-old U.S. Marine, Robert Loggins.

Michael Duane Cluck, 17, was killed in April 1981, while hitchhiking from California to Oregon. Two months later, 13-year-old Raymond Davis and 16-year-old Robert Avila were found beside the freeway near Echo Park, and 17-year-old Christopher Williams was found dead beside a road in the San Bernardino Mountains.

1982 brought more murders, 26-year-old Brian Whitcher, along the I-5 near Portland on November 26; Dennis Alt and Chris Schoenborn in Grand Rapids, Michigan, on December 7, while Kraft was in town for a computer conference; two more men in Oregon in December.

By now, investigators had picked up similarities between the Oregon and California murders. They requested airline passenger records for the L.A. to Portland route. Randy Kraft's name appeared 18 times, but before the police question him, the case resolved itself in dramatic fashion.

In the early hours of May 14, 1983, two California Highway Patrolmen pulled over a suspected drunk driver on the San Diego Freeway, near Mission Viejo. The driver, 38-year-old Randy Steven Kraft, was placed under arrest for driving under the influence, but when the officers tried to rouse his passenger, they were in for a shock. The young man was dead, with obvious signs of manual strangulation on his throat. In the trunk of the car, the police found a legal pad with a coded list with 61 entries, believed to be a record of the murders Kraft had committed.

Randy Kraft eventually went on trial for murder in September 1988. Found guilty on 16 counts, he was sentenced to death. He currently awaits execution on death row at San Quentin.

52. John Muhammad & Lee Malvo

Country: United States

Confirmed Victims: 17

Suspected Victims: 17

John Muhammad was born John Allen Williams on December 31, 1960, in New Orleans, Louisiana. At the age of 18, he joined the Louisiana National Guard, serving seven years before signing up for active duty with the US Army in 1985. He trained as a truck mechanic, although he also earned the Expert Rifleman's Badge, the highest marksmanship level with the M-16 rifle. Muhammad later served in Iraq during the Gulf War before his eventual discharge in 1994, at the rank of sergeant. By then, he was deeply indoctrinated into the more extreme tenets of Islam.

Muhammad left the United States in 1999 and moved to Antigua. During his stay on the island, he befriended a young boy named Lee Boyd Malvo. After Muhammad returned to the US, in October 2001, Malvo ran away from home and joined him in Tacoma,

Washington. Soon the pair would embark on one of the bloodiest shooting sprees in US history.

Muhammad and Malvo committed their first murder on February 16, 2002, choosing a victim at random. Keenya Cook was standing in front of her house in Tacoma when the 17-year-old Malvo walked up to her and shot her in the face at point-blank range, killing her instantly.

A month later, the deadly duo was in Tucson, Arizona, where 60-year-old Jerry Ray Taylor was gunned down at the Fred Enke Golf Course. They next showed up in Clinton, Maryland, on September 5, shooting restaurateur Paul J. LaRuffa as he sat in his car, robbing him of a laptop computer and $3,500 in cash. Although seriously injured, LaRuffa survived.

Muhammad Rashid was gunned down while locking the door of the Three Roads Liquor Store on September 15. A week later, another liquor store shooting, in Montgomery, Alabama, claimed the life of Claudine Parker and left Kellie Adams severely injured.

Just two days later the shooters struck again, killing Hong Im Ballenger, in Baton Rouge, Louisiana. A young man matching Lee Malvo's description was seen running from the scene.

Five attacks had by now claimed the lives of four victims, but the shooters were only just getting started. On October 3, 2002, they carried out a spate of shootings, claiming four victims in a single day.

The carnage began just after 8 a.m. in Aspen Hill, Maryland, where Premkumar Walekar was shot and killed while fueling his taxicab at a gas station. Thirty minutes later, the killers were in Silver Springs, Maryland, where they spotted 34-year-old Sarah Ramos sitting on a bench at the Leisure World Shopping Center. Ramos was struck in the face by a bullet.

The murderous pair drove next to Kensington, Maryland, where they shot 25-year-old Lori Lewis-Rivera as she stood vacuuming her car at a Shell service station. At approximately 9 o'clock that evening, Muhammad gunned down 72-year-old Pascal Charlot. The bullet that penetrated Charlot's chest would later be matched to those from the other shootings.

The following day, October 4, Caroline Seawell was putting bags into her minivan outside a store in Fredericksburg, Virginia, when she was shot in the back. The bullet exited through her right breast, chewing through her liver on its path, but she survived, as did the next victim, 13-year-old Iran Brown.

Three days later, on October 9, 2002, Dean Meyers was fueling his car at a Sunoco station in Manassas, Virginia, when he was killed by a single shot to the head. On October 11, Muhammad carried out another gas station attack, this time killing 53-year-old Kenneth Bridges as he stood filling his car at an Exxon station in Massaponax, Virginia.

Washington D.C. and its surrounds were by now in a state of panic, with the media blasting out hourly updates on the killers dubbed the "Beltway Snipers." Yet even with the public on high alert and an FBI task force on their trail, the killers carried out a fourteenth attack. On October 14, 2002, Linda Franklin and her husband were loading their car outside the Home Depot store in Falls Church, Virginia, when she was shot in the head and killed instantly. The bullet was matched by ballistics to the same Bushmaster rifle used in the other killings.

The next day, October 15, a police dispatcher in Rockville, Maryland, received a strange telephone call. "Don't say anything, just listen," the caller said. "We are the people who are causing the killings in your area. We've called you three times before, trying to set up negotiations. We've gotten no response. People have died."

The caller hung up before the dispatcher could transfer the call to the Beltway Sniper Task Force.

On October 19, Jeffery Hopper was leaving a restaurant in Ashland, Virginia, when he was cut down by a shot to his abdomen. Hopper survived but required five surgeries to repair the damage to his pancreas, stomach, kidneys, liver, diaphragm, and intestines.

In the woods nearby, the police discovered a hunter's blind. A note left by the killers demanded that ten million dollars be placed in a Bank of America account. If the demand wasn't met, they said, the police were "going to need more body bags."

The day after the Hopper shooting, the Beltway Sniper Tip Line received a call from a man claiming to be the sniper. He again reiterated his demands, adding ominously, "Your children are not safe."

At around 6:00 a.m. on October 21, Montgomery County bus driver Conrad Johnson was shot in the chest as he got on board his bus in Aspen Hill, Maryland. Johnson died later in hospital.

On October 24, the task force finally got the break they were waiting for when a trucker spotted the suspects sitting in a Chevy Caprice at a rest area in Frederick County, Maryland. Agents descended on the scene and found Muhammad and Malvo asleep in the vehicle. They surrendered without a fight.

John Muhammad went on trial at the Prince William County Circuit Court on November 17, 2003, charged with the capital murder of Dean Meyers. Found guilty, he was sentenced to death, with subsequent trials in Maryland adding six consecutive life terms to the sentence.

Lee Malvo, meanwhile, had offered up a full confession, adding the details of seven more murders, in California, Arizona, and Texas, thus bringing the death toll to 17. He was sentenced to life in prison without the possibility of parole.

In May 2008, John Muhammad instructed his attorneys to end all legal appeals on his behalf, so that the state of Virginia could "murder this innocent black man." He was put to death by lethal injection on November 9, 2009.

51. Irina Gaidamachuk

Country: Russia

Confirmed Victims: 17

Suspected Victims: 17

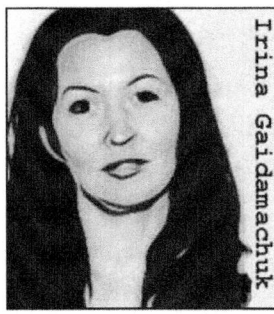

Female serial killers are rare compared to their male counterparts. Where they do exist they are most often murder-for-profit killers who target friends and relatives for inheritances or insurance payouts. Their weapon of choice is usually poison.

There are, of course, exceptions. Aileen Wournos, perhaps the most infamous female serial killer of all time, shot her male victims; Dana Sue Gray, a former fashion model with a shopping obsession, bludgeoned the elderly women she targeted; Judy Buenano even attempted to kill one of her victims with a bomb. None of them, though, compares to Irina Gaidamachuk, the brutal Russian psychopath dubbed, "Satan in a Skirt."

Irina Gaidamachuk was born in the town of Nyagan, Russia, in 1972. She suffered severe deprivation as a child, so much so that she was taken away from her parents and made a ward of the state. By then, she was already addicted to alcohol, an affliction that would plague her throughout her life and lead her eventually to serial murder.

In the early 1990s, Irina moved to the city of Krasnoufimsk, where she met and subsequently married a man named Yuri. The couple would have two children together, but the marriage was far from harmonious. Irina spent whatever housekeeping money Yuri gave her on vodka. Eventually, he cut her off, keeping a tight reign on the purse strings and forcing Irina into desperate measures.

Most addicts placed in such a situation, desperate for a fix and short of funds, turn to petty theft or prostitution. Irina Gaidamachuk came up with a far more diabolical solution. Over the next eight years, the mother-of-two committed 17 brutal murders, bludgeoning victims aged between 61 and 89 years old, to death in their homes.

Her method was simple. Once she identified a potential victim, she'd track the woman for several days, find out when she left home, who she visited and whether anyone called on her. Then, once she was ready to move, she'd knock on the victim's door and gain entrance by claiming to be a social worker. Once inside, she'd turn on the unfortunate woman, bludgeoning her to death with an axe or a hammer.

She'd then raid the apartment, before leaving with whatever cash she found. Sometimes she'd try to cover up evidence of the crime by setting a fire. The pickings were slim, only about $20 per murder, but that didn't seem to discourage Irina at all. In fact, money might well have been only a secondary motive.

The brutality of the killings actually helped Gaidamachuk avoid detection. Despite evidence to the contrary, the police refused to believe that a female could have committed such acts of cruelty. When reports came in of a well-dressed blond woman seen in the vicinity of several crime scenes they insisted that the killer was probably a man disguised as a woman. Then, after a victim survived and pointed to a female attacker, they arrested the wrong woman, 29-year-old Irina Valeyeva, and coerced her into confessing.

Gaidamachuk might have avoided detection indefinitely but like most serial killers she became overconfident in her ability to outsmart the police. She became sloppy in her planning and targeted a woman who was known to her, 81-year-old Alexandra Povaritsyna. She also varied her M.O., abandoning her social worker ruse and gaining access to Povaritsyna's home by offering to do some painting for her. When Povaritsyna turned up dead in May 2010, neighbors were quick to point the finger at Gaidamachuk. She was arrested soon after.

Sent for a barrage of psychiatric tests, Irina Gaidamachuk was declared mentally competent and committed for trial in June 2012. Found guilty, she was sentenced to 20 years in prison, just over a year for each of her victims.

As relatives of the deceased voiced their outrage at the lenient sentence, the judge explained his ruling. The maximum jail term for women in Russia is 25 years. He had given Gaidamachuk 5 years less because she is the mother of two children.

50. Donato Bilancia

Country: Italy

Confirmed Victims: 17

Suspected Victims: 17

The beautiful Italian Riviera is the last place on earth you'd expect to find a serial killer plying his deadly trade. Yet, from October 1997 to May 1998, just such a creature was working this stretch of Mediterranean coastline, gunning down 17 victims over a period of seven blood-soaked months.

The man in question was Donato "Walter" Bilancia, a habitual criminal and compulsive gambler who began his murderous career at the age of 47, old by the norm for serial killers.

Bilancia was born in Potenza, southern Italy, on July 10, 1951. At age 5, he moved with his family to Piedmont and later to Genoa in the north. He was a chronic bed wetter as a child, receiving daily beatings for this "transgression." His mother also made a habit of shaming him by placing his soiled mattress on the balcony for everyone in the neighborhood to see. He suffered endless taunts and bullying as a result.

At the age of 14, Bilancia dropped out of school and over the following years worked at a number of jobs including bartender, baker's assistant, and delivery boy. At around this time he also began insisting that friends and family call him "Walter."

By now, "Walter" Bilancia had already begun accumulating a lengthy rap sheet. While still underage, he'd been arrested for the theft of a scooter and a truck loaded with Christmas candy. He'd also been arrested and jailed after being found in possession of an unlicensed firearm. In 1974, he was committed to the Genoa General Hospital's psychiatric ward but managed to escape. Arrested soon after, he spent 18 months in prison for robbery.

Over the next two decades, Bilancia served several terms in French and Italian prisons. Notwithstanding his arrest record, he was actually an accomplished burglar who made a considerable amount of money from his criminal exploits. Unfortunately, he spent it just as quickly in Genoa's backstreet gambling dens and in Foce, the city's red light district.

Bilancia had never been convicted of a violent crime before he began his murder spree in October 1997. And as so often occurs in these cases, the first murder happened almost by accident. He had been invited to a card game by a friend, Giorgio Centenaro, and had promptly lost $25,000. Convinced that the game was rigged,

Bilancia had decided to beat the truth out of Centenaro and had waited for him with a gun. At the sight of the weapon, Centanaro had suffered a fatal heart attack.

Convinced more than ever now that he'd been the victim of a scam, Bilancia next confronted the operator of the card game, Maurizio Parenti, shooting him and his wife to death and thereafter emptying Parenti's safe. By Bilancia's later admission the murders thrilled him and fueled his taste for more killing.

Later that same month, he broke into the home of a local jeweler. Eschewing his usual stealth, he simply executed the man and his wife before robbing them. He next robbed and murdered a moneylender. Then, with his murders now beginning to cause a stir in Genoa, he went to ground.

He emerged two months later, shooting to death a security guard. Three more murders followed in quick succession. Two prostitutes, a Russian and an Albanian, were shot and killed before Bilancia gunned down and robbed another moneylender.

In March 1998, Bilancia was in Foce, engaged in a sexual act with a transsexual prostitute, when he was approached by two night-watchmen. Angered by the interruption he shot and killed both men, then fired at the prostitute, who survived to provide police with a description of the killer. Before that description had even been circulated, Bilancia struck again, killing two prostitutes and robbing a third.

On April 12, 1998, Bilancia boarded the Genoa to Venice train with the intention of killing one of the female passengers. Spotting a young woman traveling alone, he waited until she headed for the bathroom and then followed her, unlocked the door with a skeleton key, and shot her twice in the head. Six days later he committed an almost identical murder on the train to San Remo. This time, he added a repulsive variation to the crime, masturbating over the young woman's corpse.

The murders of two "respectable" women and the public outcry that followed in their wake, finally sparked the police into action. Officers were shipped in from all over northwest Italy to assist in the hunt for the killer, while a travel advisory went out to women traveling alone. Meanwhile, a task force was hastily established.

An important clue soon emerged. One of the murdered prostitutes had been seen getting into a black Mercedes Benz. A check on the vehicle turned up the name of one of Bilancia's associates. He told police that he'd lent the car to Bilancia on the night of the murder.

Bilancia was now the prime suspect in the investigation, but already he'd killed again, gunning down a gas station attendant and robbing the register of 2-million lira (about $1,000).

Over the next 10 days, task force members kept Bilancia under surveillance and collected samples of his DNA from cigarette butts and a coffee cup. Once these were matched to DNA found at the crime scenes the police moved in to arrest him.

Bilancia held out under interrogation for eight days before eventually confessing. Asked why he'd committed the murders he said that he'd been "swept by a fire" and had felt a "bite in the head."

When the matter eventually came to trial, Bilancia's plea of diminished responsibility was rejected. He was sentenced to 13 life terms with the stipulation that he must never be released.

49. Jeffrey Dahmer

Country: United States

Confirmed Victims: 17

Suspected Victims: 17+

Jeffrey Dahmer was born in West Allis, Wisconsin, on May 21, 1960, later moving with his parent's to Doylestown, Ohio, at the age of six. By then, he'd grown to be an introverted child with a macabre interest. He enjoyed picking up the carcasses of dead animals from the roadside, dissecting them and keeping the body parts in storage jars.

Jeffrey was a bright boy, but his academic performance never raised itself above average. This was due in part to an adolescent drinking problem, in part due to confusion over his sexuality. Dahmer thought he might be gay, but kept that guilty knowledge to himself.

Dahmer graduated high school in May 1978. His parent's had by then divorced and both had departed the family home, leaving the 18-year-old there by himself. It left him at liberty to do pretty much as he pleased.

On June 25, 1978, three weeks after his graduation, Dahmer brought home a 19-year-old hitchhiker named Stephen Hicks. The two spent several hours together, drinking and listening to music. But then Hicks had to leave and Dahmer didn't want him to. Picking up a 10-pound dumbbell, he bludgeoned the youth to death. He then dismembered the body and buried it in the backyard.

Over the next two years, Dahmer spent a semester at Ohio State, served in the US army and lived for a time in Florida. But by 1981, he was back in Wisconsin, living with his grandmother, and working as a phlebotomist at the Milwaukee Blood Plasma Center. On August 7, 1982, he racked up his first arrest when he was caught exposing himself to a group of children at the Wisconsin State Fair. Not long after, he lost his job.

Dahmer would remain unemployed until January 1985, when he was hired as a mixer at the Milwaukee Ambrosia Chocolate Factory. At around this time, he began frequenting gay bathhouses, trawling for sexual partners.

But the sexual encounters he found in the bathhouses frustrated Dahmer. He preferred his partners to be immobile during the act. To this extent, he began drugging his partners, then molesting them as they lay unconscious. It didn't take long for word to get out, and Dahmer found himself banned from the bathhouses.

But rather than stop his activities, Dahmer merely transferred them to a different location. He started taking his partners to hotel rooms, drugging them and then performing sexual acts on their inanimate forms. It was a short step from this "pseudo-necrophilia" to the real thing.

In November 1987, nine years after the murder of Stephen Hicks, Dahmer picked up 25-year-old Steven Tuomi in a bar and took him back to his hotel room. Once there, he drugged Tuomi and had sex with him after he passed out.

The following morning, Dahmer woke to find Tuomi dead, his chest "crushed in" and blood seeping from his mouth. Dahmer claimed that he had no recollection of killing Tuomi, but knew that he must have done it because his fists were bruised, presumably from striking the man.

Faced with the problem of disposal, Dahmer purchased a large suitcase, using it to transport the corpse to his grandmother's house. There he dissected it, first severing the head, arms, and legs, then slicing the flesh from the bones and placing the chunks in garbage bags. The bones were wrapped in sheets and pounded to splinters with a sledgehammer. All of the remains were disposed of in the trash. The entire dismemberment took two hours to complete.

The killing of Steven Tuomi seems to have wetted Dahmer's appetite for murder. He now began actively seeking out victims, luring them back to his grandmother's home, drugging and then sexually assaulting them before killing them by strangulation. Two more victims, 15-year-old James Doxtator and 25-year-old Richard Guerrero, died before another arrest temporarily halted Dahmer's murder spree. On September 26, 1988, Dahmer was arrested for drugging and sexually assaulting a 13-year-old boy. The offense earned him five years' probation.

On March 25, 1989, Dahmer picked up Anthony Sears at a gay bar and brought him back to his grandmother's house, where he and Sears engaged in oral sex. Dahmer then drugged and strangled Sears, later dissecting his body in the bathtub. This time, he kept some of the body parts, preserving Sears' skull and genitalia in acetone and storing them in his work locker.

In May 1990, Dahmer moved out of his grandmother's house and took up residence at the address that he would later make infamous: Apartment 213, 924 North 25th Street, Milwaukee. Free of the risk of discovery, he stepped up the pace of his killings, committing four more murders before the end of 1990, two more in February and April 1991, and another in May 1991.

In May 1991, Dahmer had a narrow escape when Konerak Sinthasomphone escaped from his apartment, only to be returned to him by the police. Thereafter, Dahmer's killing spree went into overdrive. He also began to conduct obscene experiments on his victims, drilling holes in their skulls and injecting hydrochloric acid into their frontal lobes in an effort to create submissive sex slaves. When these experiments failed, Dahmer simply killed the unfortunate victim, harvested whatever body parts he desired and dissolved the rest in acid. He also began to indulge in cannibalism, believing that his victims would live on inside him if he consumed their flesh.

Between June and July 1991, Dahmer claimed four victims in the space of just three weeks, murdering Matt Turner on June 30, Jeremiah Weinberger on July 5, Oliver Lacy on July 12, and Joseph Bradehoft on July 19.

It was around this time that residents of the Oxford Apartments began noticing the bumps and thumps of falling objects from Apartment 213, the occasional buzz or a power saw and, most of all, the vile smells emanating from the apartment.

But Jeffrey Dahmer's killing spree was about to be brought to an abrupt halt, his vile deeds exposed to the public.

On the evening of July 22, 1991, two Milwaukee police officers patrolling the area around Marquette University, spotted a man with a handcuff dangling from his wrist. The man identified himself as Tracy Edwards and told a bizarre tale about a "weird guy" who had tried to kill him.

Not entirely convinced by the story, the officers decided to check it out anyway.

At the address given by Edwards, a tall, blond man opened the door. He identified himself as Jeffrey Dahmer and admitted to cuffing Edwards. However, he insisted that it had all been part of a game. Edwards loudly denied it, insisting that Dahmer had hidden a knife in his bedroom. One of the officers then entered the residence to verify Edwards claims. Pinned to the wall in Dahmer's bedroom, he found dozens of photographs depicting human corpses in various stages of dissection. One showed a head in the refrigerator, another a corpse cut open from groin to sternum. Others showed corpses in erotic poses. The officer shouted for his partner to place Dahmer under arrest.

While Dahmer was taken in for questioning, an army of crime scene investigators descended on his small apartment. It didn't take long for them to discover the massive scale of the murder spree they'd uncovered. There was a human head and a heart in the refrigerator, three more heads stashed in the freezer. In the back of a bedroom closet was a metal stockpot containing decomposed hands and a penis. On the shelf above, was a kettle containing two human skulls.

On other shelves, the police found glass jars holding male genitalia preserved in formaldehyde. Then there was the barrel positioned in a corner of the room. Inside was a potent acid that Dahmer had used to dissolve the bodies of his victims into a sludge that he could later flush down the apartment's toilet.

Jeffrey Dahmer went on trial on January 30, 1992, the jury ultimately rejecting his insanity defense and finding him guilty of 15 counts of first-degree murder. He was sentenced to 15 life terms, a total of 957 years in prison.

But Dahmer would serve less than three of those years. On November 28, 1994, he was attacked and severely beaten by fellow inmate Christopher Scarver. He died in the ambulance on the way to hospital.

48. Huang Yong

Country: China

Confirmed Victims: 17

Suspected Victims: 25

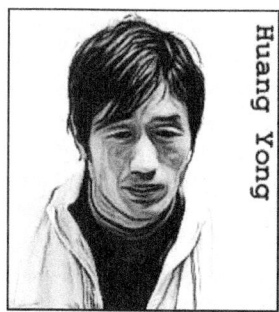

On November 11, 2003, a 16-year-old schoolboy named Zhang
Liang walked into a police station in Dahuangzhuang village,
Henan Province, China. He had an interesting tale to tell. According
to Liang, he'd been playing games at a video arcade four days
earlier, when a man approached him. The man told Liang that he
was a video game developer and had invented a new game called
"God Riding on a Wooden Horse." He invited Liang back to his
apartment to play the game. Liang, being a gaming enthusiast,
could hardly refuse.

Once they reached the apartment, the man (who identified himself
as Yong) showed him a wooden table, which he called his
"intelligent hobbyhorse." He told the boy that the game had to be
played while strapped to the table, and so Liang allowed himself to
be tied up.

What followed was a nightmare lasting four days, during which Liang was left strapped to the table, repeatedly strangled into unconsciousness and then revived. During this time, his abductor kept him alive by feeding him noodles, but he assured Liang that he would eventually die. "I've killed 25 people," he said. "You will be number 26."

One can only imagine the terror the young boy must have endured. Yet he kept his cool and made a point of engaging his captor in conversation. Eventually, he convinced Yong to let him go, by promising that he would take care of him in his old age. Once free, Liang went straight to the police.

At first, the officers seemed reluctant to believe Liang's story. They shouldn't have been. Over the previous three years, from September 2001 to November 2003, upwards of 17 young boys had gone missing from the streets of Dahuangzhuang. Most of them had last been seen alive at Internet Cafes and Gaming Arcades. And yet, despite an outcry from parents as the toll of the missing grew, the police simply refused to act, insisting they could not start an investigation without a body. The frustrated parents had eventually banded together and traveled to Beijing in order to demand action. Only then was an official inquiry launched. It had made little headway by the time Liang escaped.

On November 23, a full 12 days after Liang's escape, the police finally called on Huang Yong's home. A search of the premises turned up the table the boy had described as well as an array of leather belts and an extensive collection of violent videos. But it was the evacuation of the back yard that finally uncovered the true extent of Yong's murder spree. There, police uncovered the decomposing remains of 17 young boys and men.

Once in custody, Yong quickly confessed. He said that he had wanted to be an assassin since childhood and that the murders had allowed him to fulfill that dream. But, as he spoke, it became clear that that wasn't his only motive. Yong said that he'd strapped the boys to the table and then strangled them with a rope, sometimes reviving them several times before killing them. He then had sex with the corpses, then dissected them and buried them in the garden. The belts the police had found were souvenirs he'd kept from his victims.

Huang Yong went on trial for murder in December 2003. Found guilty, he was sentenced to death, that sentence carried out by a bullet to the back of the head on December 26.

But the well-deserved death of Huang Yong does not tell the full story. For years, the Chinese authorities have insisted that serial killers do not exist in their country, a quite ludicrous claim when you consider such recently executed monsters as Zhang Yongming, Duan Guocheng, and Yang Xinhai. In each of these cases, the investigations have been hampered by official denials, indifference, and incompetence. Still, none of these cases were as badly handled as that of Huang Yong, where despite 17 disappearances from the tiny village, despite the pleas of distraught parents, the police simply refused to act.

Five officials, including the chief of police, lost their jobs as a result of the scandal. It brought scant consolation to 17 grieving families.

Murder by Numbers: The 100 Most Prolific Serial Killers Worldwide

47. The Chicago Rippers

Country: United States

Confirmed Victims: 18

Suspected Victims: 18

On June 1, 1981, Chicago PD detectives were called to a vacant lot in Villa Park. The decomposed corpse of a young woman had been found, the handcuffs on her wrists suggesting that she had been murdered. The victim was later identified as Linda Sutton, a 21-year-old prostitute. She'd been strangled, and the killer had then hacked her breasts from her body.

On February 12, 1982, the nude body of a 35-year-old waitress was discovered on an embankment near a road. Her car was found nearby, the fuel tank empty. Detectives speculated that she had run out of gas and had sought help from the person who had killed her. What worried them, though, were the cuts to the victim's body. They were similar to those inflicted on Linda Sutton.

Just a few days later, another female corpse was discovered. The victim had been raped and strangled and, while her breasts had not been removed, they had been savagely bitten. The killer had also masturbated over the corpse.

In May 1982, Lorraine Borowski was crossing a parking lot on her way to work, when she was abducted. Her mutilated body was later found at Clarendon Hills Cemetery. She'd been raped and her breasts had been hacked from her body before her attacker bludgeoned her to death with an axe.

Given the distinctive signature of severing his victims' breasts, the police by now knew that they were dealing with a serial killer. However, they had no clues as to the perpetrator's identity, and it wasn't long before he struck again.

On May 29, 1982, Shui Mak was returning home from her family's restaurant in Streamwood. She had been riding in her brother's car, but they had gotten into an argument and he'd dropped her at the side of the road to wait for relatives who were following behind. She was never seen alive again. It would be four months before her mutilated body was discovered, buried on a construction site.

Eventually, in June 1982, the police caught a break. A young woman named Angel York was abducted off the street by two men, who bundled her into a red van. There, she was handcuffed and then subjected to repeated rapes and torture. Sometime during the ordeal, one of the men handed her a large knife and ordered her to cut her own breast. This drove him into a near frenzy, the woman later told police. He masturbated into the wound before closing it with duct-tape. Then he dumped the woman on the street. She was lucky to be alive.

The information provided by Angel York provided some solid clues, but it didn't stop the killers claiming their next victim. In August, the body of Sandra Delaware turned up in the Chicago River. Her wrists were bound with a bootlace and her bra was knotted around her neck. Like the other victims, her breast had been severed.

Within the space of the next two weeks, 42-year-old Carol Pappas went missing, as did Rose Beck Davis, a 30-year-old marketing executive. Davis was found stabbed, raped, and strangled, on September 8, 1982, her body stowed under the staircase of a North Lake apartment building.

By October, another prostitute, Beverly Washington, had been abducted, raped, mutilated, and dumped. Her attacker left her for dead, but somehow she survived and was able to give police a description of the man and his vehicle. He'd been driving a red panel van with blacked out windows, she said. He was a slender white man of about 25, with greasy brown hair and a mustache.

Three weeks after the attack on Beverley Washington, the police pulled over a red van, similar to the one she'd described. The description of the driver, though, was way off. The man said his name was Eddie Spreitzer, and that the van belonged to his boss, Robin Gecht. Officers then followed Spreitzer to Gecht's residence and had him call Gecht outside. The minute they saw him, the officers knew that he was their man. Yet Gecht denied knowing anything about the abduction and seemed genuinely unconcerned by the police questioning.

The officers next called on Beverley Washington and showed her a selection of mug shots. She unflinchingly picked out Robin Gecht as the man who had attacked her. When detectives returned to question Gecht, they found him in the company of a lawyer.

Gecht was going to be a tough nut to crack, so the investigators focused their attention on Spreitzer, who appeared to be on the verge of a breakdown. Eventually, under sustained interrogation, he admitted to seven murders and naming another member of the gang, Andrew Kokoraleis.

Brought in for questioning, Kokoraleis readily admitted to kidnapping women off the streets, raping them, then mutilating them with knives, razors, tin can lids, and can openers. He described amputating and mutilating the women's breasts with piano wire and then masturbating into the wounds. He admitted to the murders of Rose Beck Davis and Lorraine Borowski, and confessed that he had been involved in the deaths of eighteen women.

It soon emerged that there was a fourth member of Chicago's Ripper Crew, Andrew Kokoraleis's slow-witted brother, Tommy. He too was arrested and provided further details of the gang's bizarre activities.

He said that they were Satanists, who met regularly in Robin Gecht's attic, where Gecht would read verses from the Satanic Bible. He'd also hand out chunks of flesh, cut from the breasts of their victims. These the men would consume raw.

Each member of the "Ripper Crew" stood trial separately. Robin Gecht was sentenced to 120 years in prison, Tommy Kokoraleis to 70 years. Edward Spreitzer entered guilty pleas to four murders and received life terms for each. The most harshly punished was

Andrew Kokoraleis. He was sentenced to death, with the sentence eventually carried out by lethal injection on March 16, 1999.

46. Randall Woodfield

Country: United States

Confirmed Victims: 18

Suspected Victims: 44+

Randall Brent Woodfield was born on December 26, 1950, in Salem, Oregon. Unlike most serial killers, he grew up in a loving family environment, excelled academically, and was liked and respected by his teachers and peers. He was also the star player on the Newport High School football team. A bright future was predicted.

Yet, from an early age, there were signs that all was not well. Randall was just 11 when he was arrested for exposing himself to women. Released with a warning, he continued to display signs of anti-social sexual behavior leading eventually to another arrest. His high school football coaches managed to get the charge quashed so that he wouldn't be kicked off the team, but that served only to exacerbate the problem. Emboldened by his escape, Randall was soon committing more serious crimes - thefts and burglaries.

In August 1970, while attending Treasure Valley Community College in Ontario, Oregon, he was picked up again, this time for trashing his ex-girlfriend's apartment. In 1971, while enrolled at Portland State University he logged his first adult arrest on charges of indecent exposure. He received a suspended sentence.

In 1974, there was finally some good news for Woodfield, when he was picked up by the Green Bay Packers in the NFL Draft. But even on the cusp of achieving his lifelong ambition, Woodfield couldn't help himself. After a number of "flashing" incidents, the Packers gave up on the promising wide receiver and sent him home in disgrace. Woodfield was devastated, angry and depressed. Broke and without a job, he dropped out of college with just three semesters to go to graduation.

In early 1975, several Portland women were attacked by a knife-wielding man, who forced them to perform oral sex on him and then robbed them. The police set a trap, eventually arresting Woodfield when he was caught with marked currency, stolen from an undercover cop. Woodfield offered a guilty plea to reduced charges of second-degree robbery and drew a ten-year prison term. He was out in four.

Shortly after his release, a series of armed robberies began to occur along the stretch of Interstate 5 that runs through Oregon and Washington. On December 9, 1980, a young man wearing a fake beard robbed a gas station in Vancouver, Washington. Four nights later, the same man held up an ice cream parlor in Eugene, Oregon, and on December 14, a drive-in restaurant at Albany.

A week later, the bandit surfaced in Seattle, holding up another restaurant. But he wasn't content with just the money this time. He also forced one of the waitresses into a storeroom and ordered her to masturbate him. Twenty minutes later, he pulled off another hold up.

On January 8, 1981, the "I-5 Bandit" hit the same Vancouver gas station a second time, forcing a female attendant to expose her breasts after he emptied the till. Three days later, he robbed a market in Eugene. Next, he surfaced in Sutherlin, Oregon, raiding a grocery store and firing a shot that injured a female clerk. On January 14, still wearing his fake beard, he broke into a home in Corvallis and found two sisters, aged eight and ten, unattended. The girls were forced to undress and then to perform oral sex on their assailant.

Thus far, the bandit hadn't killed anyone, but the police were concerned by the escalation of violence in the robberies. Someone had been shot, several victims sexually assaulted. They feared that the attacks might turn fatal, and so it proved.

On January 18, the I-5 Bandit raided an office building in Salem, where he sexually assaulted Shari Hull and Beth Wilmot, before shooting them. Shari Hull died, but Beth Wilmot survived and was able to give a description of the assailant: white male, 25 to 30 years old, 6 foot, 175 pounds, with brown hair, a short beard and mustache.

This tallied with descriptions other witnesses had given, but brought the police no closer to catching the killer. He headed south, and between January 26 and 29, pulled off robberies in Eugene, and Medford, Oregon, plus another in Grant's Pass, where he sexually assaulted a female store clerk and a female customer.

On February 3, 1981, the bodies of Donna Eckard, 37, and her 14-year-old stepdaughter, Janell, were found together in a bed in their home at Mountain Gate, California. They'd each been shot several times in the head and forensic tests showed that the girl had also been sodomized. Also on February 3, a female clerk was kidnapped, raped and sodomized after a holdup in Redding. A near-identical crime was committed in Yreka, on February 4. That same night the bandit robbed a motel in Ashland. Five days later, he held up a fabric store in Corvallis, sexually molesting the clerk and her customer before fleeing. February 12 brought three more robberies and sexual assaults, in Vancouver, Olympia, and Bellevue, Washington.

Two weeks later, on February 15, Julie Reitz was found shot to death in her home in Beaverton, Oregon. In the course of their investigations police learned that Reitz had once dated a man named Randall Woodfield who had done time for a series of robberies and sexual assaults. They pulled Woodfield's file and realized that he was a close match to the descriptions given by several victims.

Woodfield was brought in for questioning on March 3, 1981. He was also placed into a lineup and positively identified by several of the I-5 Bandit's victims. In short order, he found himself indicted on charges of murder, rape, sodomy, kidnapping, armed robbery, and illegal possession of firearms.

Tried in June 1981 for the murder of Julie Reitz, he was sentenced to life in prison plus 90 years. An additional life sentence plus 165 years was added in October 1981, when he was convicted of the murder of Shari Hull.

Randall Woodfield is currently serving his time at the Oregon State Penitentiary in Salem. He has since been linked to at least 44 murders, but prosecutors have declined to press further charges, confident in the knowledge that he will never be free again.

45. Thierry Paulin

Country: France

Confirmed Victims: 18

Suspected Victims: 21

Between the years 1984 and 1987, a beast was loose on the streets of Paris. The fiend targeted the most vulnerable victims of all, elderly women who were robbed of their meager possessions then murdered in the most horrendous ways possible, beaten, throttled, asphyxiated, one even forced to drink drain cleaner. At least 18 victims would fall prey to one of the most depraved killers France has ever known, a man named Thierry Paulin, The Monster of Montmartre.

Thierry Paulin was born in Fort-de-France, Martinique, on November 28, 1963. His father abandoned his mother shortly after the child's birth and Thierry was raised by a paternal grandmother who seemed none too keen on the task. At age 10, the boy was reunited with his mother. But she had by now married and had other children, something that seemed to enrage young Thierry.

He took his frustrations out on his stepbrothers and sisters, beating them so frequently that his mother eventually turned to his biological father for assistance. The father, who had by now returned to France, agreed to take the boy in, but only because it meant he didn't have to pay alimony.

Paulin did not settle well in France. As a mixed-race student, he was marginalized by his peers and had few friends. He also did poorly at school, flunking out before graduation. At age 17, he volunteered for military service and was accepted into the parachute corps. But even here he was ostracized because of his race. He was also by now openly homosexual, something that did not sit well with his fellow soldiers.

In 1984, Paulin left the army and returned to his father's home in Toulouse. After learning that his mother was now living in France, he sought her out, eventually moving into her home in Nanterre, a suburb in the north of Paris.

As it had been in Martinique, Paulin's relationship with his mother and her new family was fractious. He soon found himself looking for a new place to stay.

At around this time, Paulin began working as a waiter at the Paradis Latin, a gay bar renowned for its transvestite shows. After a while, he convinced the club owners to let him take to the stage, where he performed a drag act to the tunes of his favorite artist, Eartha Kitt. He soon became a popular performer and attracted the attention of 19-year-old Jean-Thierry Mathurin.

Mathurin, who had been born in French Guyana, was a drug addict and petty criminal. It wasn't long before he and Paulin became lovers. Soon after, Paris began experiencing a spate of brutal attacks on elderly women.

The first of those attacks occurred on October 5, 1984, when 91-year-old Germaine Petitot was severely beaten. She survived but was too traumatized to give a description of her assailants. Anna Barbier-Ponthus, 83, wasn't so lucky. She was beaten and then asphyxiated with a pillow. Her killer netted 300 francs (about $50) from the murder.

Over the next two months, eight more elderly women were murdered, in and around Paris's 18th precinct. The crimes were marked by extreme overkill. Some of the victims had plastic bags pulled over their heads, others were beaten to a pulp, one had a domestic drain cleaning liquid forced down her throat. The motive in all of these cases appeared to be robbery. However, it was clear that the killer enjoyed inflicting pain and terror on his hapless victims.

Neither was he bothered by conscience. At the time the murders were being committed, Paulin and Mathurin were living an extravagant lifestyle on their ill-gotten gains. They spent their nights partying, drinking champagne, and snorting cocaine, seeking out a new victim whenever their funds ran low.

Then as suddenly as they'd begun, the murders stopped. In late November, Paulin visited his father in Toulouse, taking Mathurin with him. But his father was not prepared to accept his son's homosexuality or his gay lover. A series of violent confrontations ensued, resulting eventually in Paulin and Mathurin breaking off their relationship. Mathurin returned to Paris. Paulin stayed behind in Toulouse and tried to form a troupe of transvestite artists. When that failed, he moved back to Paris. A second wave of murders soon followed his arrival.

Between December 20, 1985 and June 14, 1986, eight more elderly women were killed. These murders were slightly different to the former series, with the victims dispatched quickly and without the torture that had accompanied the previous killings. However, the police knew that the same killer was responsible, due to fingerprint evidence left at the scenes.

In August 1986, Paulin attacked a cocaine dealer with a baseball bat and was promptly arrested and sentenced to 16 months in prison. He served a year of that sentence, emerging in autumn 1987. By then he knew that he was HIV-positive.

The Paris murders had ceased while Paulin was in jail. Now they started again in earnest. On November 25, 1987, Paulin beat 79-year-old Rachel Cohen to death. That same day, he suffocated Rose Finalteri, 87, leaving her for dead. Two days later, he strangled another elderly woman, Genevieve Germont.

On November 28, 1987, Paulin was partying hard, celebrating his 24th birthday. Unbeknownst to him, Madame Finalteri, the woman he'd suffocated, had survived the attack. She'd now regained consciousness and was able to provide a remarkably accurate description of her attacker. She said he was a mixed-race man in his early twenties, with hair "like Carl Lewis" and an earring in his left ear.

On December 1, police inspector Francis Jacob was walking along a street in Montmartre when he spotted a man fitting the description. Paulin was taken into custody. Two days later he confessed to 21 murders, including those he'd committed with Jean-Thierry Mathurin.

Paulin would never stand trial for his horrendous crimes. By early 1988, he was already showing the advanced effects of AIDS. Within a year he was afflicted with both tuberculosis and meningitis and was virtually paralyzed. He died in the hospital wing of Fresnes prison on the night of April 16, 1989.

Jean-Thierry Mathurin was left to face the music alone. Tried for the first nine murders, he was sentenced to a term of life in prison, without possibility of parole.

44. Paul John Knowles

Country: United States

Confirmed Victims: 18

Suspected Victims: 35

Paul John Knowles was born on April 17, 1946, in Orlando, Florida, the youngest of five children. Not much is known about his upbringing, but at age eight he was arrested for theft and sent to reform school. He'd spend the rest of his youth in juvenile facilities and foster homes.

Knowles logged his first adult arrest at 19, when he served time for the gunpoint abduction of a police officer. After his release, he tried to go straight for a while, but eventually fell back into a life of crime and started drifting around the country, supporting himself by burglary and petty theft.

In 1974, while serving a three-year term at Raiford Penitentiary, Knowles began corresponding with Angela Covic, a young woman from an affluent family. Convinced by Knowles's claims of unfair treatment, Covic got an expensive lawyer, Sheldon Yavitz, on the case. By May 1974, Knowles walked free.

But Covic soon regretted her intervention. Knowles frightened her, and after just four days together, she told him that their relationship wasn't going to work. Bitter at the rejection, Knowles hopped a plane to Florida, where he took out his frustration on a bartender, stabbing him during a fight.

Knowles was arrested, but he picked the lock in his cell and escaped. Shortly afterwards, he killed his first known victim, 65-year-old Alice Curtis. Knowles had bound and gagged Curtis while he ransacked her home. The gag caused her to choke on her dentures.

Knowles fled the scene in the victim's car. A week later he abducted 11-year-old Lillian Anderson and her sister Mylette, just seven. Their bodies were later found in a swamp. They'd been strangled.

One day after murdering the two girls, Knowles met 49-year-old Marjorie Howie, in Atlantic Beach, Florida. She invited him back to her apartment, where he strangled her with a nylon stocking. Soon after, he picked up and murdered a female hitchhiker.

Towards the end of August, Knowles strangled Kathie Sue Pierce to death in her home in Musella, Georgia. On September 3, he stopped at a bar near Lima, Ohio, where he got into a conversation with 32-year-old William Bates, an account executive for the Ohio Power Company. The bartender recalls them leaving together.

Bates's body would later be found in the woods nearby, strangled to death.

Knowles, meanwhile, was heading west in Bates's car. In Ely, Nevada, he shot and killed two elderly campers, Emmett and Lois Johnson. In Texas, he raped and strangled a female motorist whose car had broken down.

Next, Knowles headed for Birmingham, Alabama, where he met Ann Dawson, a 49-year-old beautician. The pair traveled together for a while, with Dawson footing the bill. She was killed towards the end of September, her body dumped in the Mississippi River.

From Alabama, Knowles headed north. On October 16, he raped and murdered Karen Wyne and her daughter, Dawn, in Marlborough, Connecticut. Three days later he forced his way into the home of 53-year-old Doris Hovey, in Woodford, Virginia, and shot her to death with her own rifle.

On November 2, Knowles abducted a pair of hitchhikers, Edward Hillard and Debbie Griffin. Hillard was found near Macon, Georgia, that same day, shot five times. His companion's body would not be discovered until August 1975.

On November 6, Mandy Carr arrived home from her job as a nightshift nurse and found her husband, Carswell, stabbed to death and her 15-year-old daughter, Mandy, raped and strangled. It would later emerge that Carr had met Knowles at a bar and invited him home. A number of items were reported missing from the home, including most of Mr. Carr's clothing, his credit cards, and a Mickey Mouse watch that Mandy had worn.

Soon after the double homicide, Knowles showed up in Atlanta, Georgia, where he met British journalist, Sandy Fawkes at the bar of a Holiday Inn. Knowles introduced himself as Lester Daryl Golden. The two soon struck up a conversation and ended the evening in bed together.

Fawkes enjoyed his company and as she had to visit several locations and Knowles offered to drive her, she decided to let him hang around. Over the next few days, Fawkes got to know her companion better. She found him to be sensitive and considerate. He dressed well and drove a brand new Chevy Impala. She believed him to be rich.

But there was something strange about him too. On one occasion she watched him while he slept and recalled how his lips were curled back in a snarl. Fawkes joked with him that he might be a serial killer, but she never had reason to believe that he was.

After parting company with Fawkes, Knowles broke into the home of Beverly Mabee, an invalid suffering from cerebral palsy. Tying Beverley to the bed, he kidnapped her twin sister, Barbara Tucker, then drove away in their beige Volkswagen. Beverly managed to get free of her bonds and called the police, who broadcast Knowles picture on television and put out an all-points bulletin.

Knowles, by this time, had reached Fort Pierce, Florida, where he released Barbara Tucker. On November 16, State Trooper Charles

Campbell recognized the stolen Volkswagen and pulled Knowles over in Perry, Florida. But Knowles overpowered the officer and kidnapped him in his own cruiser. He then used the siren to pull over a motorist, James Meyer. Forcing both Campbell and Meyer into the back seat, he headed north, towards Georgia.

But time was running out for Knowles. On November 17, he tried to run a police roadblock in Stockbridge, Georgia, but he lost control of the car and struck a tree. He escaped into Henry County woods and managed to evade the subsequent police search before being apprehended by a civilian armed with a shotgun. Knowles's two hostages were found four days later. They'd been shackled to a tree, then shot execution-style in the back of the head.

Once in custody, Knowles played the media attention to the hilt and seemed to revel in his notoriety. He gave several interviews and said that he fully expected to be executed. The only thing he'd miss, he said, was seeing the police make fools of themselves.

On December 18, 1974, while being transferred to a maximum-security prison, Knowles managed to get free of his handcuffs and made a grab for a deputy's gun. He got off a single shot before Georgia Bureau of Investigation agent, Ron Angel, shot him three times. Knowles died at the scene.

43. Sergei Ryakhovsky

Country: Russia

Confirmed Victims: 19

Suspected Victims: 19+

By any definition, Sergei Vasilyevich Ryakhovsky was an intimating man. Standing six-feet-six-inches tall and weighing in at 280 pounds, with a pasty complexion, bull-neck, and ham-sized fists, Ryakhovsky was not the sort of man you'd want to encounter in a dark alley. Or in a crowded room, in broad daylight, for that matter. Add in the fact that this behemoth was also one of Russia's most depraved serial killers and he becomes the stuff of nightmares, a terrifying creature on a par with the fictional monster, Hannibal Lecter.

Ryakhovsky (known as "The Hippopotamus" because of his bulk) was born in Moscow, Russia, on December 29, 1962. He first appeared on police radars in 1989, when an elderly woman was found strangled to death and severely mutilated. Over the next four years, he'd claim at least 19 victims, all of them found in and around the Russian capital.

Unlike most serial killers, Ryakhovsky was not particular about his choice of prey. His victims included young and old, male and female, gay and straight; they ranged in age from 14 to 78 and included 12 men, 4 women, and 3 boys. Six others were attacked but managed to escape.

The killer's modus operandi was as varied as his choice of victim. Selecting targets of opportunity, he'd either strangle, stab or bludgeon them to death. Sometimes strangulation was carried out with a rope, in other instances with his massive hands. When he decided to use a bludgeon, it was generally a claw hammer; for stabbing, he used a long bladed knife or a screwdriver.

One thing, though, was consistent. Ryakhovsky was a necrophile and had more interest in the dead body than the living person. All of his victims, regardless of age or gender, were raped and sodomized postmortem. He also carried out bizarre mutilations to the bodies, escalating with each murder.

In January 1993, Ryakhovsky murdered a 78-year-old man, cut off his head with a hunting knife, and carried it away from the scene. His bloodlust unsated, he returned the next day to saw a leg from the corpse. With his next murder, he pushed a homemade bomb into his 65-year-old victim's vagina, then detonated it to rupture her abdomen. Seeking to outdo that atrocity, he hung a 16-year-old boy from a rafter, ripped open his abdomen with a knife and pulled out his guts and internal organs.

Needless to say, Ryakhovsky's murder spree caused alarm among Moscow's Militsiya, even if the public was kept largely in the dark about his activities. A concerted effort was made to capture him, but it was getting nowhere until a chance discovery effectively solved the case.

On April 9, 1993, Militsiya officers were carrying out a grid search on a tract of forest where a body had been found. During the operation, they chanced upon a shack, concealed in dense woodland. Inside they found a rope looped through the rafters and terminating in a noose. Believing that the rope had been left there in preparation for Ryakhovsky's next murder, they staked the place out. Four days later they hit paydirt when the Hippopotamus came wading through the forest.

The officers waited until he entered the cabin before moving in. Given Ryakhovsky's huge size and his obvious propensity for violence, they approached cautiously and shouted out for him to surrender. They needn't have worried. Ryakhovsky gave himself up without a fight. When the officers entered the shack he was down on his knees, shivering like a frightened puppy.

Once in custody, Ryakhovsky regained some of his composure. He described his crimes with relish, willingly leading investigators to the various crime scenes and describing his methods of mayhem. He said that the murders were not planned but that he'd been on a mission to clear the world of homosexuals and prostitutes. When it was pointed out to him that many of his victims (including a 70-year-old woman and a 78-year-old man) were neither, he simply shrugged, as though such trivialities were unimportant.

Ryakhovsky was next examined by psychiatrists from Moscow's Serbsky Institute, who declared him sane and fully responsible for his actions. He went on trial in July 1995 and was found guilty of murder. The sentence of the court was death by firing squad, to which Ryakhovsky responded with a Terminator-esque: "I'll be back."

Sergei Ryakhovsky would not keep his date with the executioner. In 1996, Russia declared a moratorium on executions and his death sentence was commuted to lifetime imprisonment. He served that time in the maximum-security penal colony IK1, dying there in 2005 from tuberculosis.

42. Larry Eyler

Country: United States

Confirmed Victims: 19

Suspected Victims: 23+

For a period of two years, from late 1982 to 1984, a killer cruised the roads of the American Midwest from Wisconsin to Kansas, picking up hitchhikers and male prostitutes. His attacks were frenzied - hacking and stabbing and then mutilating the bodies before dumping them in rural locations. At least ten victims met horrendous deaths before the police realized that they had a serial killer on their hands.

The first Highway Killer victim was discovered on October 23, 1982, in a cornfield outside Kankakee, Illinois. A couple of months later, on Christmas Day, a second corpse, that of 25-year-old John R. Johnson, was found in Lowell, Indiana. He'd been stabbed to death, his body severely mutilated.

December 28 brought the discovery of two more corpses. Twenty-three-year-old Steven Agan was found near Newport, Indiana;

John Roach, a 21-year-old from Indianapolis was dumped along Interstate Highway 70 in Putnam County. Both had been stabbed and mutilated. Pathologist Dr. John Pless, who examined the bodies, suggested that a serial killer might have killed the men. Senior police officers accused him of being "alarmist."

While the police continued to drag their heels, two bodies showed up in March 1983, two more in April. Eventually, after the Highway Killer claimed his tenth victim, 21-year-old Daniel McNeive, the authorities paid attention to Dr. Pless's warning.

On May 15, 1983, law enforcement officers from several Indiana jurisdictions gathered in Indianapolis to discuss the Highway Murders. As a result of those discussions, a task force was set up, with fifty officers from eight jurisdictions assigned to the case.

And the task force soon had their first solid lead, after an anonymous tipster suggested that they take a look at a 31-year-old Terre Haute resident named Larry Eyler.

Eyler was already known to the police. In August 1978, he'd been involved in a sexually motivated knife attack on a hitchhiker. Three years later, he'd been arrested for drugging a 14-year-old boy and dumping him in some woods outside of Greencastle, Indiana. Both victims had survived and Eyler had walked when they'd declined to press charges.

With nowhere else to take their investigation, the task force focused their attention on Eyler, placing him under surveillance. It wasn't enough to save the next victim. On August 30, 1983, 28-year-old Ralph Calise left his apartment in Oak Park, Illinois, and disappeared. Three days later, a tree-cutting crew found his mutilated corpse in Lake Forest. The police were able to lift their first forensic evidence from the scene, boot and tire tracks.

A month later, on September 30, Chicago police spotted Eyler picking up a male prostitute named Darl Hayward. They followed as Eyler drove south along I-90, but had to give up the chase when he crossed into Lake County, Indiana. Amazingly, none of the Chicago cops had thought to alert their Indiana counterparts.

A short while later, Indiana State Trooper Kenneth Buehrle drove by and spotted Eyler's pick-up parked illegally at the side of the highway. Then he saw Eyler and Hayward coming out of the woods and walking across a field.

Buehrle asked Eyler for his driver's license and radioed in to check for outstanding warrants. He had no idea who Eyler was, but members of the Highway Killer task team, working the night shift, picked up the broadcast and immediately rushed to the scene.

Eyler was taken to the Lowell barracks, where he surrendered his boots for examination and consented to a search of his truck. The search turned up a bloodstained knife, but as police had no evidence of a crime having been committed, they were forced to let Eyler go.

Shortly after that incident, a dismembered torso was found in a trash bag near Highway 31, in Kenosha County, Wisconsin. The victim would later be identified as Eric Hansen, an 18-year-old male prostitute from St. Francis, Wisconsin.

On October 15, the skeletal remains of an unknown victim were found in Jasper County, Indiana, the bones notched by knife wounds, indicating death by stabbing. Four days later, mushroom hunters found four decomposing bodies on a farm outside Lake Village, Indiana. Two of the victims would never be identified; the other two were 22-year-old Michael Bauer and 19-year-old John Bartlett.

In the meanwhile, investigators were gathering and collating evidence against Eyler. They had human blood on the knife taken from his truck, distinctive nicks on the soles of his boots that matched footprints found at the Calise murder scene, and type A+ blood found on the inner lining of his boots. They had handcuffs seized from Eyler's home, which were found to be consistent with marks left on Calise's wrists. Likewise, the tire tracks from Eyler's truck matched tracks found at the scene.

However, prosecutors were in for a shock when they brought the matter to court. All of their forensic evidence, with the exception of the tire tracks, was ruled inadmissible.

On February 2, 1984, Larry Eyler walked from the court a free man. He immediately departed Indiana for Chicago, leaving the police to wonder whether he'd just gotten away with murder.

And Eyler might well have escaped justice were it not for his own arrogance in committing a crime so reckless, it was almost as though he was asking to be caught.

On August 21, 1984, the janitor of an apartment building on West Sherman Street, Chicago, found a number of plastic trash bags overflowing from a dumpster. He began moving them, but as he lifted one of the bags, it split open disgorging a severed human leg.

The police were called and discovered the remains of a white male, cut into eight pieces and split among various bags. Witnesses described seeing a tenant from the building next door throwing the bags into the dumpster. Officers went to question the man. It was Larry Eyler.

Eyler was taken into custody while police searched his apartment. They found a number of bloody hacksaw blades, numerous bloodstains, trash bags matching those the body had been placed in, and a t-shirt belonging to the victim, 16-year-old Danny Bridges.

Larry Eyler eventually went on trial in July 1986. Found guilty, he was sentenced to death, but it was a sentence that would never be carried out. Eyler died of AIDS on March 6, 1994. He was 41 years old.

41. Surender Koli & Moninder Singh Pandher

Country: India

Confirmed Victims: 19

Suspected Victims: 31+

For two years, residents of Nithari, on the outskirts of the Indian capital of New Delhi, had streamed to the local police station with complaints of missing children. Their complaints had been met with indifference, derision, even hostility. Not even the discovery of human bones or reports of a vile smell emanating from a drain in the area would spur the police into action.

On December 29, 2006, two men who had lost daughters eventually took their frustrations to former Resident Welfare Association President S. C. Mishra. The men claimed that they knew the location of the remains of several missing children. They'd been disposed of in the drains behind the palatial home at number D5.

At first, Mishra was skeptical. The house the men were referring to belonged to Moninder Singh Pandher, a millionaire businessman with political connections. Eventually, though, he was persuaded to join the two men in searching the drain. Almost immediately, they discovered a decomposing hand. Within a short while, three incomplete skeletons were recovered and the police were called.

As news of the discovery leaked out, anxious parents descended on the residence. Soon a full-scale riot was in progress, with police struggling to contain angry locals. As much for their own protection as for any other reason, Moninder Singh Pandher and his manservant, Surinder Koli, were taken into custody. Soon Koli would begin talking, revealing one of the most horrendous cases of child serial murder in India's history.

Moninder Singh Pandher was born into a wealthy family in Punjab, graduated from Delhi's prestigious St. Stephen's College, and inherited a successful family business with interests in transport, real estate, and agriculture. He grew up with a love of luxury, a taste for fine wine and single-malt whiskey, a fondness for golf and a yearning for international travel. In the years leading up to his arrest, he'd visited the United States, Switzerland, Dubai, Canada and China.

But not everything about Pandher's life was as idyllic as it seemed. He was estranged from his wife and lived apart from his family, barely seeing them. In lieu of familial companionship, he spent his free time with prostitutes, usually procured by his servant, Koli. As would later emerge, not all of his sexual partners were of age, or willing.

Surender Koli followed a quite different path to serial murder than his employer.

Born in Almora, Uttarakhand, Koli was a high school dropout who skinned animals for a living before abandoning his wife and child to move to Delhi. There, he did various odd jobs as a cook and dishwasher before finding employment as a manservant to a retired army brigadier. The officer later introduced him to Moninder Singh Pandher. Not long after, he left his employer to work for Pandher. Now, both of them were in custody, charged with murder.

While the search of the drain at Pandher's house continued to uncover more and more human remains, Pandher and Koli were sent to Gandhinagar for extensive narco-analysis. These procedures, involving polygraphs, truth serums, and brain monitoring, are inadmissible in court. However, they are used to aid police in their investigation. In this case, they produced some interesting results.

Only Koli was subjected to the truth serum, Pandher being excused on health grounds. Under its effects, Koli provided contradictory statements. At first, he said that Pandher was unaware of the killings and that he had committed the murders while Pandher was abroad.

Explaining his motive, Koli said that he had often acted as a procurer of prostitutes for his master, and that seeing Pandher and his guests engaged in sexual acts with prostitutes had led to him becoming increasingly sexually frustrated. He also said that he was a necrophile, and craved erotic contact with dead bodies.

His first victim was 14-year-old Rimpa Halder who he strangled to death before having sex with her corpse. He then tried to eat the child's liver but was immediately ill. Later, he dismembered the body with a saw, dumped the larger pieces in the drain behind the house and flushed the innards and smaller pieces down the toilet.

So far, Koli appeared to absolve Pandher of blame, but his later testimony contradicted this. He now said that after he lured a victim into the house with candy, he would rape the child before handing her over to Pandher. When Pandher was done sexually assaulting the victim, he (Koli) would strangle her before dismembering the body and disposing of it.

He denied that the murders were part of an organ trafficking scam (as had at one time being suspected), although he confessed to cannibalizing the corpses. He also denied that the victims were used in child pornography, even though the police found nude pictures of Pandher with several children on his computer.

Pandher and Koli eventually went on trial in February 2009, by which time 38 victims (all but one aged between 3 and 11 years) had been identified from the remains pulled out of the drains at the Pandher residence. Both men were found guilty and both sentenced to death.

The case had far-reaching consequences, with an inquiry by the National Human Rights Commission that led to the dismissal of several police officers, for dereliction of duty. In addition, the trial judge severely criticized India's CBI (Central Bureau of Investigation) who had taken over the case during its early stages. The CBI had sought to downplay Pandher's role in the murders, placing all of the blame on Koli.

40. Alexander Spesivtsev

Country: Russia

Confirmed Victims: 19

Suspected Victims: 80+

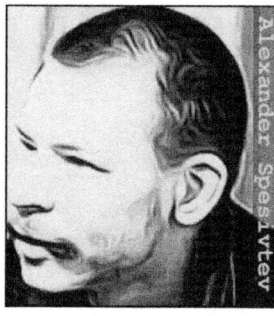

Novokuznetsk is a gloomy industrial town in south central Siberia, home to some of Russia's largest aluminum smelters and collieries. In the early nineties, is was also home to a large population of street children, a fact that greatly annoyed one citizen, in particular, a man named Alexander Spesivtsev, but known to all as Sasha.

Spesivtev was an interesting specimen. Possessed of a genius level IQ, he was a poet and philosopher who boasted a body of published work, most of it bemoaning the evils of democracy. That was Spesivtsev the intellectual. But there was another side to Sasha. He was a convicted murderer who had strangled his former girlfriend and spent years in mental institutions before being released as "cured." Now he found himself back in his hometown, cruising the streets and the railway station with his vicious Doberman, hocking black market cigarettes.

The police were well aware of Sasha's illicit commercial activities, but a carton or two of Marlboros kept them at bay. That too was perhaps the reason they ignored a plethora of complaints from Sasha's neighbors.

'Spesivtev plays ear-splitting rock music at all hours of the day and night,' they said. 'And the stench from the apartment he shares with his mother, Ludmilla, is quite overwhelming.'

The police took not a modicum of notice. They had neither the manpower nor the resources to deal with public order offenses. Besides, they had more urgent matters demanding their attention, like the human remains that kept washing up on the banks of the river Aba. Granted, they were the bodies of street children and therefore not high priority, but a number of prominent citizens were beginning to kick up a fuss and were demanding answers.

So Sasha Spesivtev's neighbors grudgingly kept their peace about his loud music and smelly apartment. However, in August 1996, there was a new problem, one that couldn't be ignored. The toilet in Sasha's apartment was overflowing and foul-smelling water was seeping under his door into the corridor. This time, the neighbors called not the police, but a plumber.

When no one in the Spesivtsev apartment answered the plumber's knock, he was forced to pry the door open. He'd soon wish that he hadn't.

Lying on the floor of the living room was a human ribcage; in the kitchen were bowls with chunks of pale flesh; in the bathtub lay a child's mutilated, headless corpse; on virtually every surface were blood spatters, some fresh, some brown with age.

Amazingly, among all this carnage, there was a living victim. Fifteen-year-old Olga Galtseva lay on a couch in a pool of congealed blood, multiple deep stab wounds to her chest and stomach. She was rushed to hospital, where doctors fought in vain to save her. She died seventeen hours later.

But Olga had at least lived long enough to point the finger at her killer. She said that Ludmilla Spesivtsev had lured her and two younger girls to her flat with the promise of a meal. Once inside Sasha had set his dog on them, menacing them until they agreed to do what he said. He'd then raped the girls before killing one of them. Then he'd forced the other two to cut up the body in the bathtub.

Spesivtev's mother had cooked a meal, using flesh from the victim. When the other girl had refused to eat it, Spesivtev had set the Doberman on her and the dog had killed her. He had been stabbing Olga when the plumber forced the door. He'd then fled through a window.

As police patrols began searching for Spesivtev and his mother, detectives continued rummaging through his filthy apartment. Among the gory artifacts they found a diary detailing the murders of nineteen young girls. 'I am cleaning the streets,' Spesivtsev had written, 'ridding society of this detritus.'

Sasha was taken into custody soon after, his mother arrested at the school where she worked. Despite her protestations of innocence, Ludmilla Spesivtseva was found guilty of murder and sentenced to life in prison. Sasha, meanwhile, was declared insane and packed off to a psychiatric facility where he will hopefully see out the rest of his days.

39. Mohan Kumar

Country: India

Confirmed Victims: 20

Suspected Victims: 20+

From India comes the chilling story of Mohan Kumar, a one-time primary school teacher turned Bluebeard serial killer. This astonishing case first came to the attention of the Indian authorities in 2009, with the disappearance of a young woman named Anitha from the village of Bantwal Taluk.

The Indian police deal with countless missing persons cases every year, and when the victims are poor and without influence or connections, they seldom receive the attention they deserve. In this instance, however, the girl's parents were so sure that she'd met with foul play, that they approached a local Hindu organization for help. They, in turn, put pressure on the police to take action. Soon they'd discovered an incredible web of deceit that had claimed the lives of at least 20 women between 2005 and 2009.

The Bantwal police began their investigation in the obvious place. They subpoenaed Anitha's cell phone records and started working through the list. Still convinced that the girl had run off with a lover, they were astonished to find that one of the numbers Anitha had called belonged to a girl who'd recently been found dead in a toilet at a Mysore bus station. When Anitha's parents failed to recognize the girl's name and insisted that Anitha hadn't known her, the police had the first inkling that they might be onto something bigger than a mere missing persons case.

Obtaining the dead girl's cell phone records, they compared them to Anitha's and picked up one common number. It belonged to a 46-year-old former schoolteacher named Mohan Kumar.

Kumar was pulled in for questioning and with hardly any prompting began reeling off an incredible tale of murder, lust, and betrayal. He said that he'd lost his teaching job in 2003 and, unable to find other employment, he'd hit on the idea of robbing and killing young women.

His modus operandi was simplicity itself. He targeted only victims from a lowly socio-economic background, whose disappearances or deaths were unlikely to cause a stir. He also focused on women in their late twenties or early thirties who he believed would be desperate to find a husband.

Once the smooth talking Kumar spotted a likely target, he'd approach her in a public place, usually with the line, "Do I know you? I'm sure I've seen you somewhere before."

He'd then strike up a conversation with the woman, presenting himself as an eligible bachelor (even though he already had two wives and was divorced from a third). If the woman appeared susceptible to his charms, he'd set up another meeting, eventually broaching the subject of marriage.

In India, the bride's family is usually required to pay a dowry consisting of cash, jewelry, and household goods, but the gallant Mohan said that he was prepared to forfeit this, although it would mean the couple would have to elope. Secrecy was therefore of the utmost importance.

A few of the women were wary enough to reject Kumar's proposal. Most, though, were easily duped. He'd then arrange to meet the woman at a temple in a nearby town, where the marriage ritual would be completed. Afterwards, he'd take his new bride to a lodge where they'd spend the night and the union would be consummated.

The following morning, Kumar would ask the woman to accompany him to the bus station in order to get a ride to a local temple. He'd instruct her to remove all her jewelry and valuables and give them to him for safekeeping.

(Although Kumar's victims were poor, they'd wear their best jewelry for the wedding, often borrowing additional items from friends and neighbors. Others, at Kumar's urging, cleared out their life's savings before meeting up with him for the ceremony.)

On reaching the bus station, Kumar would hand the woman a powder, insisting that she take it. It was a contraceptive, he'd say, which she needed to take because they'd had unprotected sex the night before. Trustingly, the woman would retire to the public bathroom to swallow the powder, not knowing that it was cyanide. Within minutes, she'd be dead and Kumar would ride out on the next bus carrying her cash and jewelry with him.

He'd killed women by this method at the Mysore, Madikeri, Bangalore and Hassan bus stands as well as at the Kollur temple. The deaths were usually put down as suicides, the young women believed to have taken their own lives over the breakup of a relationship.

Mohan Kumar eventually went on trial in 2013. Found guilty on three counts of murder he was sentenced to death on December 21. He currently awaits execution.

38. Viktor Sayenko & Igor Suprunyuck

Country: Ukraine

Confirmed Victims: 21

Suspected Victims: 21+

The Eastern European nation of Ukraine has produced some of the world's most depraved killers, not least the 'Rostov Ripper,' Andrei Chikatilo, a necrophile and cannibal who murdered at least 50 women and children in a reign of terror lasting from 1978 to 1990. But not even Chikatilo can match the sheer ferociousness of the murder spree perpetrated by Viktor Sayenko and Igor Suprunyuck. In the space of just three weeks, from June 25 to July 16, 2007, these teenaged psychopaths claimed 18 victims, bludgeoning them so brutally that the corpses were rendered unrecognizable. And to add an extra level of depravity, they videotaped some of the murders, even posting one on the Internet.

Sayenko and Suprunyuck first became friends in the third grade. They had a lot in common, both of them from wealthy and influential families. Suprunyuck's father was a test pilot and later the personal pilot of Ukrainian President Leonid Kuchmatwo; Sayenko's father was a lawyer, and would later represent his son during his murder trial.

How then did these two privileged, rich kids veer towards serial murder? It is difficult to say. Tracing their friendship to its earliest days we find that Sayenko was a diligent student, while Suprunyuck was shy and withdrawn, but was often in trouble.

Their first brush with the law came when they were in the fifth grade. They were arrested for throwing rocks at passing trains but were released with a warning. By the eighth grade, they'd gravitated to torturing animals, recording their horrendously cruel acts on video.

At 17, Suprunyuck was arrested after he beat up another boy and stole his bicycle, which he later gave to Sayenko. Again, he was released with nothing more than a few stern words.

Suprunyuck had never been much of a student and under his influence, Sayenko's academic performance had also dropped off significantly. However, the pair somehow managed to graduate high school and thereafter drifted into menial jobs. Sayenko became a security guard; Suprunyuck used the Daewoo Lanos his parents had bought for him, as an unlicensed taxi. He also earned extra income by beating and robbing some of his passengers. Soon he'd gravitate to more serious crimes.

Late on the evening of June 25, 2007, Sayenko and Suprunyuck were prowling the streets when they encountered 33-year-old Ekaterina Ilchenko, returning home after visiting a friend. Suprunyuck was carrying a hammer and as the woman passed he struck her on the side of the head, then bludgeoned her face into a bloody pulp.

Just an hour later, the two men found Roman Tatarevich asleep on a bench across the road from the Public Prosecutor's office. Tatarevich was beaten to death before he'd even had a chance to rise, his features rendered unrecognizable under the vicious onslaught.

The psychopathic duo waited just six days before committing their next murder. On July 1, they traveled to the nearby town of Novomoskovsk, leaving two more victims, Evgeniya Grischenko and Nikolai Serchuk, dead.

On the night of July 6, Sayenko and Suprunyuck were back in their hometown of Dnepropetrovsk, trawling for victims. In the early morning hours they encountered Egor Nechvoloda, walking home from a nightclub. They battered him to death, then set off in search of another victim.

Twenty-eight-year-old Elena Shram was working the night shift in her job as a security guard. She was no match for the murderous twosome. And they weren't done yet. That same night they beat to death Valentina Hanzha, a mother of three young children.

The next day, July 7, Sayenko and Suprunyuck encountered two 14-year-old boys on their way to a fishing hole in the village of Podgorodnoye. They attacked the children, killing Andrei Sidyuck. The other boy, Vadim Lyakhov, managed to escape and provided the police with their first description of the Dnepropetrovsk Maniacs.

On July 12, 48-year-old Sergei Yatzenko went missing while riding his motorcycle near Dnepropetrovsk. His body was found four days later, rendered unrecognizable by a savage attack.

Unlikely though it seems, given the ferocity of their initial spree, Sayenko and Suprunyuck now upped the tempo, committing thirteen more murders over the next four days. Their victims appear to have been chosen at random and included women and children, the elderly, vagrants, and people who were under the influence of alcohol and therefore easy to subdue. The ferociousness of the attacks also increased. Many of the victims were mutilated and tortured, some had their eyes gouged out while they were still alive, a pregnant woman had the fetus ripped from her womb. Many of the attacks were filmed on video.

But Sayenko and Suprunyuck were already making a number of reckless mistakes, one of which would lead directly to their capture. With the later murders, they'd taken to robbing their victims of cash, cell phones, and other valuables. On July 23, 2007, Suprunyuck attempted to sell a stolen phone at a local pawnshop. The pawnbroker insisted that he turn the phone on, to prove that it worked. Suprunyuck gladly agreed.

Unbeknownst to him, the police were monitoring the phone and once it was turned on they were able to pinpoint its location. Officers raced to the scene and arrested Suprunyuck on site. He soon gave up his accomplice.

Under questioning both Sayenko and Suprunyuck quickly confessed, although Suprunyuck later withdrew his confession. At their trial, beginning in June 2008, Suprunyuck pleaded not guilty, while Sayenko entered guilty pleas to all charges.

Much was made of the motive behind the killings. It was suggested that Sayenko and Suprunyuck had struck a deal with a wealthy snuff movie collector, whereby they agreed to carry out and film 40 murders in exchange for a large sum of money. Lead investigator Bogdan Vlasenko rejected this idea. "We believe they did it as a hobby," he said. "To have a collection of memories for when they get old."

Whatever the motive, there was little doubt as to the outcome of the trial. On February 11, 2009, both Viktor Sayenko and Igor Suprunyuck were found guilty on multiple counts of murder. As Ukraine has no death penalty they were sentenced to life in prison.

37. William Bonin

Country: United States

Confirmed Victims: 21

Suspected Victims: 36+

William Bonin did not have the best start in life. Born to alcoholic parents, the boy and his two brothers suffered severe neglect and abuse. He got an early start to his criminal career too, racking up his first arrest in 1957, at the age of just 10. That saw him shipped off to a reformatory where he suffered yet more maltreatment, as well as knifepoint rapes by other inmates. By his teens he had become an abuser himself, preying on neighborhood children and even his own brother.

Despite, this insalubrious start, Bonin graduated high school in 1965 and shortly thereafter joined the U.S. Air Force. He served in Vietnam as an aerial gunner and was awarded a Good Conduct medal.

Back in the States, Bonin lived for a short while with his mother in Connecticut before moving to California. There he began accumulating a lengthy rap sheet for sexual assaults on young boys and serving a succession of short prison terms. Eventually, after yet another period of incarceration in 1979, he announced to a friend: "This is never going to happen to me again." Shortly after, the series of murders, attributed to the "Freeway Killer," began.

Bonin's first murder was carried out with the help of an accomplice, Vernon Butts, a low-life drifter with a lengthy rap sheet. On the morning of May 28, 1979, 13-year-old Thomas Glen Lundgren left his parents' home in Reseda in order to visit a friend. His mutilated corpse was found the next day in Agoura. He'd been emasculated, and an autopsy would reveal that he'd been slashed, stabbed, and bludgeoned before being strangled to death.

Two months later, on August 4, 1979, Bonin and Butts abducted 17-year-old Mark Shelton in Westminster. Shelton was sodomized with foreign objects, which caused his body to go into shock that proved fatal. He was discarded alongside a freeway in San Bernardino County.

The following day, Bonin and Butts picked up 17-year-old German student, Markus Grabs, on the Pacific Coast Highway. Grabs was bound and taken to Bonin's home where he was sodomized, beaten and stabbed over 70 times. His nude body was discarded in Malibu Canyon.

Three weeks later, on August 27, the mutilated corpse of 15-year-old Donald Hyden was discovered in a dumpster near the Ventura

Freeway. He had been raped and strangled and his throat had been cut. An attempt had also been made to castrate him.

On September 9, 1979, Bonin and Butts lured 17-year-old David Murillo into Bonin's van where he was bound, raped, bludgeoned and strangled before his body was discarded alongside Highway 101. Eight days later, they abducted 18-year-old Robert Wirostek as he cycled to work. His ravaged body was discovered on September 19 beside Interstate 10.

After this murder, the Freeway killer dropped out of sight for three months. Then, in late November, he was back, taking three victims in under a fortnight.

The first victim was an unidentified youth whose savagely beaten body was discovered in Kern County. The following day, Bonin abducted and strangled 17-year-old Frank Fox, leaving his body on a stretch of highway near San Diego. Ten days later, he murdered 15-year-old John Kilpatrick, leaving body alongside a road in Rialto.

On New Year's Day, 1980, Bonin brutalized and strangled 16-year-old Michael Francis McDonald, dumping his corpse in San Bernardino County, where it was found two days later.

On February 3, 1980, Bonin brought in a new accomplice, another sexual psychopath, named Gregory Matthew Miley. The pair picked up 15-year-old Charles Miranda in West Hollywood then drove him to an isolated spot where they sodomized and then violated the teen with a blunt object. A few hours later, they abducted 12-year-old James McCabe from a bus stop. McCabe's naked body was found three days later, alongside a dumpster in the city of Walnut. Bonin and Miley used the $6 found in the boy's wallet to buy lunch.

A rapid spree of murders followed. Ronald Gatlin, 18, disappeared from North Hollywood on March 14. His body was discovered the next day in Duarte, beaten, strangled and stabbed with an ice pick. Harry Todd Turner, 14, disappeared from Hollywood on March 20. Discovered five days later near the Santa Monica Freeway, his body was marked with bites and cigarette burns. Glen Norman Barker, 14, was sexually assaulted and strangled, his corpse found March 22, beside the Ortega Highway with another body in close proximity, that of 15-year-old Russell Duane Rugh.

And still, the killings continued. Steven Wood, 16, went missing on his way to school on April 10, 1980. The same day, Lawrence Eugene Sharp, 18, of Long Beach disappeared. His corpse showed up on May 18, 1980, in a trash bin behind a Westminster service station.

On April 29, 1980, Bonin and Butts abducted Darin Lee Kendrick, 19, from a Stanton store where he worked. In a particularly brutal murder, even by their standards, Kendrick was forced to swallow hydrochloric acid and an ice pick was pushed into his ear causing a fatal wound to the upper cervical spinal cord. His corpse was found the next morning.

On May 19, Bonin abducted 14-year-old Sean King from a bus stop in Downey. The boy's raped and strangled body was discarded in Yucaipa.

But unbeknownst to William Bonin, time was running out on his murder spree.

On May 29, 1980, William Pugh, who had assisted Bonin in the murder of Harry Todd Turner, was picked up on an auto theft charge. Pugh confided to a counselor that he believed William Bonin to be the Freeway Killer. The counselor passed this information on to the LAPD.

On June 2, 1980, Bonin was placed under surveillance. By then, he'd already committed another murder – that of 19-year-old Steven Wells, killed with the help of accomplice, James Munro.

On June 11, the surveillance team watched Bonin try to pick up five separate teenage boys before he succeeded in luring a youth into his van. The police followed him to a deserted beach parking lot. By the time they approached the van and threw the doors open, Bonin had the boy bound and was in the process of sodomizing him. The Freeway Killer was caught at last.

Once in custody, Bonin confessed to 21 murders. He went on trial in November 1981 and was found guilty of murder three months later, the jury recommending that he be put to death. That sentence was eventually carried out 14 years later, on February 23, 1996, when William Bonin became the first person to be executed by lethal injection in the state of California.

36. Patrick Kearney

Country: United States

Confirmed Victims: 21

Suspected Victims: 43+

Patrick Wayne Kearney was born in Los Angeles in 1940, the youngest of three sons. His childhood appears to have been relatively stable, at least as far as his home life was concerned. At school, though, he was an easy target for bullies – a thin, sickly and diminutive child who was painfully shy.

Unable to strike back against his bigger and stronger tormentors, Patrick began to develop violent revenge fantasies, keenly detailed visions of murder. He'd later admit that, by age eight, he knew that he was going to be a killer.

Yet, nothing in Kearney's life suggested the serial murderer he would become. He was an intelligent boy, who did well at school. After graduating, he served in the military, married and moved with his wife to Texas. Then, after the marriage failed, he met and fell in love with David Douglas Hill, a 6'2" high school dropout from Lubbock, Texas.

In 1967, the pair moved back to California and set up house together. Kearney found work as an aeronautics engineer with the Hughes Aircraft Corporation, while Hill stayed home and looked after domestic affairs. Their relationship, which would last ten years, was frequently stormy. Hill would often leave in a huff and spend the night with friends or pick up a one-night stand out of revenge. Occasionally, he even went back home to Lubbock, remaining there for days at a time.

It was on these occasions, with Hill out of the picture, that Kearney's repressed rage would simmer to the surface. That was when he'd hit the streets, cruising the interstate or trawling gay bars, picking out victims who reminded him of those who had bullied him during his childhood.

Kearney's M.O. was simple, efficient and consistent. He was primarily a necrophile, meaning he had no interest in keeping his victim alive for torture or any other purpose. Also, he was a slight man, just 5'5" tall, unable to physically subdue victims who tended to be bigger and physically stronger than him. The method he developed compensated for both these factors

After picking up a man, Kearney would drive to a quiet stretch of road, then produce his Derringer .22 and shoot the victim in the head. He'd do this while driving the car in order to catch his victim by surprise, and was particularly adept at steering the vehicle with his left hand while firing with his right. Kearney would then drive to a secluded spot where he'd have sex with the corpse. Then he'd dismember the body with a hacksaw, place the sections in trash bags and dispose of them in various locations along the freeways, or out in the desert, where coyotes and insects would consume the remains.

On the occasions that he killed people in his own home, he would dissect the body in the bathtub, drain it of blood and wash the body parts carefully. Then he'd pack the pieces in bags secured with duct tape. He was very careful not to leave any trace evidence, something he'd learned by studying various books on serial killers.

The Trash Bag Murders first came to the attention of police on April 13, 1975, when the body of Albert Rivera, 21, was found packed in a heavy-duty trash bag, along Highway 74, east of San Juan Capistrano. Soon police were inundated with gruesome new discoveries, each of them bearing the killer's unique signature, bodies neatly dismembered and packaged, none of them bearing any viable clues. The killer was elusive, the case complicated by other serial killers working the same turf at that time. It seemed that police were never going to catch a break in the case.

But then, on Sunday, March 13, 1977, Kearney made a mistake. 17-year-old, John LaMay had been invited by Dave Hill to visit him at his home in Redondo Beach. Except, when LaMay arrived, Hill wasn't there, Kearney was. He invited LaMay inside to wait for Dave. Then, while LaMay watched TV, Kearney snuck up behind him and shot him in the head. Kearney then had sex with the corpse before dismembering it and disposing of it along the highway.

Unbeknownst to Kearney, LaMay had told a neighbor that he was going to Redondo Beach to see a guy by the name of Dave. When LaMay's remains were found five days later, the neighbor passed this information on to the police and it didn't take them long to track down the house. In fact, they'd called there just days before, doing routine questioning about a missing 8-year-old named Merle Chance (another of Kearney's victims).

When they called at the house again, Kearney and Hill assured them that they knew nothing about the missing teen. But the detectives were not entirely convinced. One of them secretly pulled a few fibers from the carpet. Kearney, usually so careful not to leave trace evidence, had slipped up in the LaMay murder. The tape used to bind the bags had some fibers caught up on it.

Although this evidence would be inadmissible in court, the police ran tests on the fibers – and got a match. Kearney meanwhile, was destroying all of the cuttings he'd collected on the Trash Bag Killer Case. When the police called again and asked him and Hill to supply samples of their pubic hair, he decided it was time to run. By the time police returned with a search warrant, he and Hill were long gone.

Police nonetheless searched the apartment and turned up a hacksaw with traces of human blood and tissue, rolls of duct tape similar to that used in the Trash Bag Murders, and traces of blood in the bathroom.

Kearney and Hill had meanwhile fled to El Paso, Texas, but Kearney soon decided that he wasn't suited to the life of a fugitive. On July 1, 1977, he gave himself up to the Riverside County Sheriff.

Patrick Kearney was eventually charged with 21 counts of murder and received 21 life sentences. David Hill was cleared of any involvement in the Trash Bag killings.

35. Earle Nelson

Country: United States

Confirmed Victims: 22

Suspected Victims: 25+

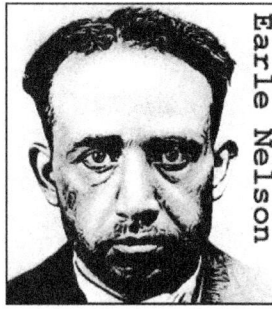

Earle Leonard Nelson was born with a number of strikes against his name. He never knew his mother for one thing - she died of syphilis in 1898, when Earle was just nine months old. And he didn't get to know his father either – he died just six months later, of the same disease.

Earle was raised in San Francisco by his grandmother, a widow, with two young children of her own. She genuinely cared for her grandson, but he was a difficult child, hyperactive at times, and at others, depressed and obstinate.

From a young age, Earle was obsessed with the Bible, although he seemed to have difficulty abiding by its teachings. At the age of just seven, he was expelled from school because of his waywardness.

He was a loner, a persistent shoplifter, a daydreamer - with a fierce temper and a propensity for violence when annoyed.

At age eleven, he suffered a serious head injury when he was struck by a streetcar. He was knocked unconscious and remained so for the next week. And there was an even more traumatic event three years later - his grandmother died. The 14-year-old Earle was shipped off to his Aunt Lillian.

Not long after, Earle dropped out of school for the final time. He took menial jobs, but they never lasted, due to his eccentric behavior and inherent laziness. Often, he just wandered away from a work site and never went back.

At the age of just 15, he began regularly visiting prostitutes, spending the bulk of his meager earnings on them. The rest of his money went on booze and lurid magazines. He also started wandering, disappearing for days on end, returning home battered and bruised from brawling. Even more worryingly, he'd taken to creating imaginary acquaintances, carrying on lengthy conversations and arguments with them.

In 1915, Earle got into trouble with the law for the first time when he received a two-year sentence for burglary. In 1918, he enlisted in the Navy, but his outlandish behavior saw him committed to Napa State Mental Hospital, where he remained for the next thirteen months. He thereafter returned to live with his Aunt Lillian and began work as a janitor at St. Mary's Hospital, near San Francisco. There, the 21-year-old Earle fell in love with 58-year-old Mary Martin. He asked her to Mary him, and Mary said yes.

Mary Martin would soon have cause to regret her decision. Her new husband refused to bathe, had appalling table manners, and had an insatiable sex drive. He was also extremely possessive, reacting furiously if Mary so much as talked to another man, even her own brother.

The next significant event in Earle Nelson's descent towards serial murder was a second serious head injury, suffered when he fell from a ladder at work. After that, he began speaking of hearing voices and seeing visions. When he announced that he was leaving for Palo Alto, Mary refused to go with him. It was probably a wise decision.

Nelson attempted his first murder on May 19, 1921, strangling 12-year-old Mary Summers. However, the girl fought so vigorously that he let her go, then fled when she started screaming. Arrested soon after, Nelson was ruled incompetent to stand trial and was sent instead to Napa State Hospital – a place he'd escaped from three times in the past.

Nelson's second stretch at Napa would last four years. After his release, he persuaded Mary to take him back. But he stayed just a few weeks before hitting the road. Earle Nelson was about to make the transition from petty criminal to serial murderer.

His first victim was Clara Newmann, a 62-year-old widow, who ran a boarding house in San Francisco. Newmann's body was found by her nephew, in a vacant attic bedroom. She'd been strangled, and an autopsy would reveal that she had been raped after death.

A little over two weeks later, another landlady was murdered, in nearby San Jose. The circumstances of Laura Beal's death were almost identical to those of Clara Newmann and the papers immediately began reporting that it was the work of the same man. The police received hundreds of tips, none of which got them any closer to finding the murderer. Then, on June 16, 1926, the killer struck again, strangling and violating Mrs. Lillian St. Mary at the boarding house she ran.

With the city of San Francisco gripped by panic, Nelson made his way to Santa Barbara, where he strangled and sexually assaulted landlady, Ollie Russell. He next appeared in Oakland, where he throttled 50-year-old Mary Nisbet, then in Portland, Oregon where he killed 30-year-old Beata Whithers. Just two days later, Virginia Grant was murdered, raped and robbed in her home. Then Mabel Fluke was found strangled and sexually assaulted, her body concealed in an attic crawl space.

Over the next 16 months, Nelson visited San Francisco, Oakland, Stockton, and Portland, Oregon, leaving a string of corpses in his wake. By the end of 1926, he had killed 14 women and an eight-month-old baby. He next headed east, stopping in Iowa, Kansas City, and Philadelphia, where he killed a 60-year-old woman. He then made his way to Buffalo, New York, Detroit and Chicago before turning north. He'd already killed 20 women in the United States - now he was heading for Canada.

Nelson crossed the border and made his way to Winnipeg, where he found lodgings with Mrs. Catherine Hill on Smith Street. Not long after his arrival a 14-year-old schoolgirl named Lola Cowan went missing. Then a housewife named Emily Patterson was murdered and the police conducted a search of all boarding houses in the area. In Nelson's room on Smith Street, they discovered the decomposing body of Lola Cowan, hidden under the bed.

But Nelson had already left town and was heading back towards the border when a store owner in Wakopa recognized him and alerted the authorities. When an armed constable arrived, Nelson immediately surrendered.

Within weeks of his capture, Nelson was charged with murders in San Francisco, Portland, Detroit, Philadelphia, and Buffalo, but it was clear that he'd never see the inside of an American courtroom. The Canadian authorities were determined to punish him for the crimes he had committed there.

Nelson was duly tried for the murders of Lola Cowan and Emily Patterson, but there was never any doubt as to the outcome. He went to the gallows on January 13, 1928, protesting his innocence to the end.

34. Gerald Stano

Country: United States

Confirmed Victims: 22

Suspected Victims: 41

Gerald Stano was born in Schenectady, New York, on September 12, 1951. His birth name was Paul Zeininger and his natural mother inflicted such extreme emotional and physical abuse on him, that he was removed from her care when he was just six months old.

When Norma Stano, a social worker, heard of the young boy, so cruelly mistreated, she became determined to adopt him. Against the advice of colleagues, she and her husband Eugene eventually did, six months later. They named the boy, now almost two years old, Gerald Eugene Stano.

By all accounts, the Stanos were loving, caring parents, but from an early age their adopted son was plagued by problems. He was an

emotionally distant child, a frequent bed-wetter who suffered
from a lack of co-ordination, which often made him fall down
without cause. He did poorly at school and was a target for bullies.
He was also constantly in trouble, once for dropping rocks onto
passing cars from a highway overpass, on other occasions for
stealing. He eventually graduated high school at 21, having
repeated three grades.

Soon after graduation, Stano enrolled on a computer course, and to
the delight of his parents, he excelled. He got a job at a local
hospital but was fired within weeks for stealing. Thereafter, he
bounced from one short-term job to the next.

In 1973, Stano's parents moved to Ormond Beach, Florida, taking
Stano with them. Then, in 1975, there was good news at last. Stano
met a pretty, 22-year-old hair stylist and married her on June 21.
He made a serious effort at going straight but it didn't last. Within
weeks he was drinking and drugging and physically abusing his
wife. Six months later, the marriage was over. Stano moved back in
with his parents and began taking long, nighttime drives. Over the
next five years, 33 young women would die horrible deaths at his
hands.

On Sunday, February 17, 1980, Daytona Beach detectives were
called to the site of a decomposing body in a field near the airport.
The victim was a 20-year-old student named Mary Carol Maher.
She'd been stabbed to death in a frenzied attack, the blows
directed mainly at her head. The killer had then covered her body
with tree branches. Given the paucity of forensic evidence at the
scene, the police did not hold out much hope of solving the
murder. But they soon had a very workable lead.

On the morning of March 25, a woman walked into the Daytona Beach police station and lodged a complaint against a man who'd slashed her thigh with a knife, leaving her with a wound that required 27 stitches. She knew where police could find the man, she said. She'd just seen his car parked outside a nearby apartment building. The vehicle turned out to belong to 28-year-old Gerald Eugene Stano.

Stano was brought in for questioning on April 1, 1980. Asked about Mary Carol Maher, he admitted that he'd once given her a ride in his car, but denied having anything to do with her death. The officers were unconvinced. They continued probing until Stano eventually admitted that he'd killed Maher and then agreed to drive officers out to where he'd dumped the body.

As news of Stano's arrest circulated through the precinct building, another detective came forward and asked Stano about a missing 26-year-old prostitute named Toni Van Haddocks. Stano said he didn't know her, although the detectives were sure he was lying. Still, without evidence of wrongdoing, they didn't press the matter. Stano was charged with the murder of Mary Carol Maher and remanded to the county jail.

On April 15, 1980, a 12-year-old boy discovered skeletal human remains in the woods near Holly Hill, concealed under tree branches. It turned out to be Toni Van Haddocks. Cause of death was determined to be multiple stab wounds to the head.

Brought back in for questioning, Stano initially denied killing Toni Van Haddocks, but after hours of interrogation, he eventually broke down and confessed.

Which left detectives to wonder; just how many murders had Gerald Stano committed? They began looking into unsolved homicides in Daytona Beach and beyond, turning up a number that matched Stano's unique M.O. and signature. In each case, the victims had suffered multiple stab wounds to the head and been left concealed under tree branches.

Stano was eventually offered a deal, immunity from execution if he pled guilty to the murders of Maher, Van Haddocks and one other, and had his confessions in other cases read into the court record. He agreed. On September 2, 1981, Judge S. James Foxman accepted his plea bargain and imposed three life sentences.

Stano was taken to the Florida State Prison to begin his sentence. But less than a year later, he contacted detectives and said there were other murders he wanted to confess to. Warned that these murders were not covered by the plea deal and might land him on death row, Stano pressed on nonetheless, providing sworn confessions to at least 20 more murders. They eventually landed him with three death sentences.

Stano would spend 14 years on death row, during which he became a serial confessor, admitting to any crime that he was even vaguely aware of. After a number of stays, he was eventually put to death on March 23, 1998.

But that was not the end of the story. After Stano's death, questions began to be raised about several of his confessions. In at least one case, there was evidence to suggest that someone other than Stano was responsible. In other cases, though, Stano shared details that only the killer would have known. And by linking the murders via M.O., the police are confident that they can connect Gerald Stano to at least 41 victims.

33. Arnfinn Nesset

Country: Norway

Confirmed Victims: 22

Suspected Victims: 130+

He made the unlikeliest of serial killers, a balding, bespectacled and mild-mannered nursing home administrator, who was well liked by his patients and valued by his employers. And yet, Arnfinn Nesset enters the record book as the deadliest Scandinavian killer of all time. Suspected of 138 murders, he was eventually convicted of 22.

Nesset had already enjoyed a 20-year nursing career when he arrived at the Orkdale Valley Nursing Home in 1977. The hospital is a geriatric care facility, so deaths are frequent and expected. Still, there appeared to be an escalation in the number of deaths shortly after Nesset took up his post. This higher rate continued over the next three years and was eventually accepted by hospital staff as the norm. Nobody imagined that a killer might be at work.

Then, in early 1981, an employee at the clinic noticed that administrator Nesset had placed an unusually large order for Curacit, a muscle relaxant that is derived from curare, the poison used by indigenous South American tribes on the tips of their hunting arrows.

Uncertain what to do with the information, the staff member passed it on to a local journalist, who informed the police.

Nesset, 46 years old at the time, was brought in for questioning. Initially, he protested his innocence, claiming he'd ordered the drug to poison a pack of feral dogs that had been hanging around the nursing home. Then, inexplicably, he started confessing, telling stunned investigators, "I've killed so many I'm unable to remember them all."

He then began a rambling confession, in which he claimed that he'd started killing soon after beginning his nursing career in 1962. He'd killed patients in three other institutions, he said, always using the same method, curare poisoning. Asked about his motive, Nesset first said they were mercy killings, then blamed his schizophrenia, and finally admitted that he killed for the morbid pleasure it gave him.

With officers now scrambling to verify the details of Nesset's earlier murders, Nesset was sent for psychiatric evaluation and found fit to stand trial.

Meanwhile, the police turned up 68 suspicious deaths at the institutions where he'd previously been employed. They soon dismissed the possibility of charging Nesset for any of those crimes. Curare breaks down quickly in the human body and the presence of the poison becomes increasingly difficult to trace over time. When the charge sheet was eventually drawn up, it included the 27 murders Nesset had confessed to, all of them having occurred at Orkdale Valley. He was also charged with forgery and embezzlement, relating to money misappropriated from his victims.

Nessett went on trial in October 1982, but the day before court proceedings were due to start, he threw prosecutors a curveball by suddenly retracting his confessions. That left the prosecution having to prove murder, no easy task despite the presence of Curacit in the victims' bodies, and Nesset's signature on the purchase orders.

In the end, Nesset was found guilty of 22 counts of murder after a five-month trial. He was sentenced to 21 years in prison, the maximum possible under Norwegian law.

Nesset was released in 2004, and promptly disappeared. He is believed to be living under an assumed name, somewhere in Norway.

32. Ronald Dominique

Country: United States

Confirmed Victims: 23

Suspected Victims: 23+

Houma is a small, sleepy town in Terrebonne Parish in the southeastern part of Louisiana. Nothing much happens here, although the town does have a close-knit gay community and a number of nightspots catering to them. For almost a decade, from 1997 to 2006, a member of that community, a pudgy, non-threatening man who walked with a limp, operated as a serial killer. His name was Ronald Dominique, and he is responsible for at least 23 murders.

Typical of most serial killers, Dominique had a predator's eye for the weak, the vulnerable, and the easily led. He targeted hustlers, drug addicts and the homeless, luring them back to his trailer on Blue Bayou Road with promises of cash for sex, or (if the victim was straight) with the prospect of sex with Dominique's fictitious wife. Once they reached the trailer, Dominique would ask the potential victim if he could tie him up. If the man refused, he was allowed to walk away unharmed. If however, he relented, Dominique would bind and then rape him, before strangling him to death. The body would then be dumped in a sugarcane field, a ditch or a bayou in any of six southeast Louisiana parishes.

The first body – that of 19-year-old David Levron Mitchell – turned up near Hahnville in early 1997. Six months later, the strangled corpse of 20-year-old Gary Pierre was found in St. Charles Parish, and in July 1998, the body of 38-year-old Larry Ranson was discovered, also in St. Charles Parish.

The Ranson murder confirmed investigators' fears that a serial killer was at work in the area. Still, the killings of vagrants, addicts, and hustlers did not raise much public ire. Despite a lack of progress in the case, it was not until March 2005 that the Louisiana State Police, the FBI, and several parish Sheriff's departments came together to form a task force. By then, 23 men were dead.

When the case eventually resolved itself in November 2006, it was a tip from a parolee, rather than investigative effort, that cracked it. The ex-con told his parole officer about an encounter with a man named Ron, who he'd met in a bar. Ron, he said, had propositioned him to go back to his camper with the offer of having sex with his wife. Once they got there, however, Ron insisted on tying him up, claiming that his wife was "shy." The ex-con refused and Ron did not push the issue, allowing him to leave unharmed. However, the encounter had spooked him. He was certain that if he'd allowed himself to be tied up, he'd have been killed.

The parole officer passed the information on to the task force and although the ex-con did not know Ron's address he was able to lead investigators back to the trailer.

"Ron" turned out to be Ronald Dominique. Brought in for questioning in November 2006, Dominique voluntarily provided a DNA swab, which would link him to the murders of 19-year-old Manuel Reed and 27-year-old Oliver Lebanks.

Dominique had in the interim moved from his trailer to the Bunkhouse homeless shelter in Houma, and it was there that he was taken into custody on December 1, 2006. Soon after his arrest, he confessed to 23 murders. He would eventually be tried for eight.

On September 23, 2008, Ronald Dominique was sentenced to eight life terms after pleading guilty in order to avoid the death penalty. He is currently incarcerated at the Louisiana State Penitentiary in Angola.

30. Bela Kiss

Country: Hungary

Confirmed Victims: 24

Suspected Victims: 24+

The story of Bela Kiss is one of the great, unsolved mysteries in the annals of true crime. Kiss was a handsome man with blond hair and striking blue eyes. A tinsmith by trade, he arrived in the village of Czinkota, Hungary, in February 1912, bringing with him his young wife, Marie.

Within weeks of the couple's arrival, Marie Kiss had taken a lover, a local man named Paul Bikari. In December 1912, a saddened Kiss told neighbors that Marie had deserted him and run away with her new love.

Bela Kiss was a popular man in the village, considered by his neighbors to be amiable, hardworking and generous. In typically stoic fashion, he made a brave face of his wife's desertion, hiring an elderly housemaid named Mrs. Jakubec to pick up domestic duties.

Not long after the adulterous Mrs. Kiss disappeared, town gossips began noting the number of lovely young women that were visiting Kiss' home. None of them stayed very long and none were introduced to anyone in the town, not even Mrs. Jakubec. Still, no one begrudged Bela a bit of happiness after his wife's desertion.

Another item that fueled village gossip was Kiss's habit of collecting large steel drums. The local constable, suspecting that Kiss might be using them for brewing illegal vodka, called on the Kiss residence and counted 21 of the barrels lined up in a shed. Questioned about them, Kiss assured the policeman that they were for storing gasoline, which would soon be in short supply, with a war coming.

In November 1914, Kiss was conscripted into the Hungarian army and left Czinkota to take up his patriotic duty. Some 18 months later, villagers were saddened to hear that he'd fallen on the field of battle.

In July 1916, Superintendant Charles Nagy of the Budapest Police Department received a disturbing phone call. The caller was from Czinkota and said that he'd uncovered evidence of murder on a property he'd been renting to a man named Kiss.

The landlord explained that he had gone to the house to carry out repairs in anticipation of letting the property to a new tenant. He'd found several steel drums in a shed and had punctured one of them in order to determine its contents. The liquid that had seeped out smelled so horrible that the landlord was convinced the barrel contained decomposing human remains. He begged Nagy to investigate as soon as possible, as he could not rent out the house until the matter was resolved.

Certain that the landlord was exaggerating, but nonetheless intrigued,

Nagy grabbed two detectives and set off for Czinkota. He was met at the house by an irate Mrs. Jakubec. Her employer had instructed her to safeguard his property, she said, and she forbade the officers from opening the barrels.

Over the protests of the elderly woman, Nagy instructed his men to pop the lid on one of the drums. The contents confirmed the landlord's worst fears. Inside was the body of a young woman preserved in wood alcohol. When the other six barrels were opened, they too were found to each contain a naked female corpse. All of the victims had been strangled.

Nagy got to work immediately. After the local constable informed him that Kiss had, in fact, kept 21 barrels on the property, he ordered a search. When the barrels were found, each of them contained preserved human remains, all but one of them female. The male victim was Paul Bikari, erstwhile lover of Kiss' wife. Marie Kiss was also among the corpses found.

Next, Nagy contacted the military to ascertain that Bela Kiss had indeed been killed. While he waited on a reply, he began interrogating the frightened housekeeper. Mrs. Jakubec insisted that she knew nothing about Kiss's affairs, but that her employer was a good man who treated her well and paid her a fair wage.

The police then conducted a search of the home. In Kiss's bedroom, they found a locked door to another room. Quizzed about it, Mrs. Jakubec said that her employer forbade her from ever entering the room. She did, however, have a key, which she handed over.

The room was unremarkable, lined by overflowing bookshelves and devoid of furniture but for a large desk and chair. However, on searching the desk, Nagy was given a whole new perspective on Bela Kiss.

Kiss, it appeared, had been keeping up correspondence with dozens of women. Nagy found hundreds of letters, all of them in response to advertisements that Kiss had placed in the matrimonial pages of the Budapest newspapers. All in all, Kiss had received 174 proposals of marriage. He'd accepted 74 of them. Also in the desk, Nagy found a photo album with pictures of over 100 women.

It soon became clear that Kiss had been running some kind of matrimonial scam, wooing lonely women, relieving them of their cash and killing those who protested too loudly or asked too many questions.

On October 4, 1916, Nagy received a surprising message from the administrator of a Serbian hospital. According to the message, Bela

Kiss was a patient at the hospital, currently recuperating from war injuries.

Nagy departed Budapest immediately, confident of making an arrest. But, by the time he arrived, Kiss had flown the coop, having apparently been tipped off about Nagy's arrival.

Confident now that Kiss was still alive, Nagy sent bulletins to every precinct in Hungary. Tips immediately began pouring in from all corners of the country and from beyond its borders. One promising sighting was reported near the Margaret Bridge in Budapest in 1919, but Kiss remained frustratingly elusive.

Sightings of Bela Kiss would continue to come in over the years that followed. In 1920, a Legionnaire of the French Foreign Legion reported to police that one of his colleagues might be Kiss. By the time investigators arrived to interrogate the man, he had deserted. Kiss was also "spotted" in Romania, Turkey, and the United States, although none of these reports led to the capture of the fugitive.

We will likely never know what really happened to Bella Kiss. Perhaps he really was killed in the war as originally reported. Or maybe he died an old man in some foreign land. Either way, he got away with murder.

30. Fritz Haarmann

Country: Germany

Confirmed Victims: 27

Suspected Victims: 70

Friedrich "Fritz" Haarmann was born on October 25, 1879, the sixth child of an impoverished family. He was a quiet and somewhat effeminate boy, who eschewed the rough and tumble games of his male counterparts and preferred playing with dolls.

At 16, despite his poor academic record, he enrolled in military college and surprised his family by proving to be an excellent cadet. But his military career was short-lived and he was discharged within a year for medical reasons.

Back in Hannover, Haarmann found work in a cigar factory and also came to the attention of the police as a child molester. Arrested on molestation charges he was confined to an asylum but escaped and fled to Switzerland.

Haarmann returned to Germany two years later and over the next decade made his living as a petty thief and conman. He was a less than capable criminal and was arrested on numerous occasions, spending several short terms in prison. Through these arrests, Haarmann came to establish a relationship with members of the Hannover constabulary and began supplementing his income by providing the police with information on other criminals.

This arrangement shielded Haarmann from prosecution until 1914, when he was convicted on fraud and theft charges and sent to prison. No bad thing as it turned out, World War I erupted soon after, and Haarmann was spared conscription. He'd spend the entire duration of the war in jail, before his release in 1918.

Haarmann emerged to a country in financial ruin, but also one with boundless opportunities for the sharp-eyed criminal. He soon resumed his work as a police informant, while also picking up the threads of his illicit activities. Soon his catalog of offenses would include murder.

Haarmann's first known victim was 17-year-old Friedel Rothe, reported missing on September 25, 1918. Friends of Rothe told the police that they had seen the youth in the company of Fritz Haarmann shortly before his disappearance, but investigators dismissed these allegations. It was only at the insistence of Rothe's family, that they eventually raided Haarmann's apartment. They found their star informant in bed with a naked boy.

Charged with sexual assault, Haarmann was sent to prison for nine months. But the police had missed a trick. Had they searched Haarmann's apartment, they would have found Friedel Rothe's head, hidden behind a stove.

Haarmann's latest conviction did nothing to damage his arrangement with the police. Back on the streets he resumed his career as an informant and also returned to his murderous activities. Over the next five years he would claim at least 26 victims, most of them young runaways or male prostitutes who he picked up at Hannover's central railway station.

Haarmann's M.O. was simple. He'd lure his young victims back to his apartment with promises of work or food or cigarettes. Once there, he'd overpower them, then rape and strangle them, usually biting through their throats as he was committing sodomy. The victim would then be dismembered, choice cuts held back for sale as pork on the black market, the rest of the corpse tossed carelessly into the River Leine.

The clothes and other possessions of the victims were either sold or kept by Haarmann or his lover, Hans Grans. Although not actively involved in the killings, Grans was well aware of them and even on occasion pointed out potential victims to Haarmann. Grans, Haarmann later confessed, urged him to kill only the "prettiest" boys.

By 1924, Haarmann was claiming on average two victims a month, and even in those uncertain times, such a spate of disappearances inevitably drew the attention of the police. Then, after human bones and other body parts started showing up in the Leine, outraged citizens demanded action.

In June 1924, the police dragged the river and found over 500 human bones, later determined to have come from at least 22 separate individuals.

Suspicion quickly fell upon Haarmann, who was often observed talking to young men at the Hannover rail station and who, as well as being a convicted child molester, had been a suspect in the 1918 disappearance of Friedel Rothe.

Haarmann was placed under surveillance and, on the night of June 22, was observed prowling the railway station. He was arrested after trying to lure a boy to his apartment. A search of his premises turned up bloodstains on virtually every surface. After the police discovered trunks full of clothes and other items, Haarmann was placed under arrest.

But the evidence was not quite as conclusive as it seemed. Haarmann explained away the blood by insisting that it came from his illegal trade as a butcher. He said the clothes were second-hand items that he had purchased for resale. As he was a trader in both meat and used clothing, the explanations seemed plausible.

But here luck finally turned against Fritz Haarmann. While he was being interrogated, a family named Witzel arrived at the police station to enquire about their missing son, Robert. While they waited, a man walked past wearing a jacket that Mrs. Witzel recognized. When she confronted the man, he said that he'd bought the jacket from Fritz Haarmann. The garment turned out to have a label inside bearing the name Robert Witzel.

Faced with this new evidence, Haarmann eventually admitted to murdering Witzel, and numerous other boys. Asked how many, he stunned investigators by answering nonchalantly, "somewhere between 50 and 70."

Haarmann went on trial in December 1924, charged with 27 murders. The trial was a sensation throughout Germany, with Haarmann dubbed a 'vampire' and a 'werewolf' by the press. He certainly lived up to that billing, taking the stand to describe his modus operandi as follows:

"I would throw myself on top of those boys and bite through the Adam's apple, throttling them at the same time.

"Afterwards, I'd make two cuts in the abdomen and put the intestines in a bucket, then soak up the blood and crush the bones until the shoulders broke. Now I could get the heart, lungs and kidneys and chop them up and put them in my bucket. I'd take the flesh off the bones and put it in my waxcloth bag. It would take me five or six trips to take everything and throw it down the toilet or into the river. I always hated doing this, but I couldn't help it - my passion was so much stronger than the horror of the cutting and chopping."

Haarmannn was found guilty on 24 of the 27 charges against him. Condemned to death on December 19, 1924, he requested a public execution. He also asked that his headstone bear the inscription,

"Here Lies Mass Murderer Haarmann." Neither request was granted. He was guillotined within the walls of Hannover Prison on April 25, 1925.

29. Mikhail Popkov

Country: Russia

Confirmed Victims: 24

Suspected Victims: 29+

Mikhail Popkov is not the first policeman to lead a double life as a serial killer, neither is he likely to be the last. When you think about it, the job provides the perfect cover. What better way to coax or coerce a victim than to present a badge of authority?

Popkov was born in March 1964, and was raised by an abusive, alcoholic mother. Nonetheless, the boy showed no signs of aberrant behavior or psychology and grew up to be an apparently well-adjusted young man. He eventually joined the police force in Angarsk, Russia, married a fellow police officer and fathered a child. The only blot on his record was the shooting death of a suspected rapist, although a tribunal would later rule the use of force justified. Those who knew Popkov said that he was a pleasant, sociable man who always had a story to tell or a joke to share. He was also a keen athlete, who enjoyed participating in biathlons. Nobody, not his wife or his police colleagues, detected any hint of the monster that lurked just below the surface of that amiable façade.

Between the years 1992 and 2000, a serial killer was preying on the women of Angarsk, a remote town in the Irkutsk Oblast, Siberia. The fiend preferred a particular type of victim, short and full-figured. He also tended to prey on women who were leaving bars or taverns and even had a preferred day of the week for carrying out his attacks. Many of his victims were found on a Wednesday, earning him the sobriquet, the "Wednesday Killer." He had another nickname too, "Werewolf," such were the horrendous injuries he inflicted on his victims.

At least 24 women fell to this depraved fiend during his eight-year spree. The victims were picked up in town, then driven into the surrounding forest where they were forced to strip. The killer then attacked them with an array of weapons including an axe, an awl, screwdrivers, a slipknot and various knives. Several victims were decapitated. One had her heart ripped out. But the monster still wasn't done. Having mutilated the bodies he then had sex with the bloody remains, before leaving them to be found on the forest floor.

On 26 January 1998, the ineffective police inquiry into the series of murders eventually had its first solid lead, when a 15-year-old girl named Svetlana was found wandering naked and dazed in sub-zero temperatures near the village of Baikalsk. The girl was rushed to a nearby hospital where she eventually recovered enough to tell her harrowing story.

Svetlana said that she'd been walking along a road when a man in a police car stopped to give her a lift, insisting that it was dangerous for her to be alone outside after dark. Svetlana accepted the ride, but instead of driving her home as he'd promised, the officer took her to some woodland, where he forced her from the car at gunpoint and instructed her to strip. Once she was naked, the man grabbed her by the hair and began smashing her head against a tree. Somehow she'd gotten loose and made a run for it, although she couldn't remember exactly how she had escaped.

The detectives who listened to the girl's story were at first skeptical, unprepared to accept that one of their own was responsible for the attack. Nonetheless, they provided her with an array of photos. Unerringly, Svetlana picked out Mikhail Popkov.

Now the detectives really were incredulous. Mikhail Popkov, the jovial, happily married family man had done this? Surely there must be some mistake. Perhaps the blows to the girl's head had left her confused. And those beliefs appeared to be vindicated when they spoke to Popkov's wife. He'd been at home with her all night, she insisted.

The Popkov lead was apparently a dead end, and although the Wednesday Murderer would go on to claim several more victims over the next two years, the police were never close to catching him. Then, after 2000, the murder spree stopped, leading police to believe that the killer had died, or been jailed on another charge.

In 2012, cold case investigators looking over the statement given by Svetlana, decided to pursue the possibility that a cop might have been responsible. They requested blood samples from 3,500 current and former Angarsk police officers, to be sent for DNA comparison against sperm lifted from the victims. Mikhail Popkov, who had since left the police force and was working as a security guard, was one of those subpoenaed. His sample provided a match.

Popkov was arrested on June 23, 2012, and quickly confessed. He gave no motive for the murders, saying only that he felt compelled to kill. He did, however, clear up the mystery of why he'd stopped. He said that he'd contracted syphilis from one of his victims, rendering him impotent.

Mikhail Popkov is currently awaiting trial for murder.

28. Wayne Williams

Country: United States

Confirmed Victims: 24

Suspected Victims: 31

Between July 1979 and May 1981, twenty-nine African American children, teenagers, and young men were murdered in Atlanta, Georgia. These were by no means the only murders in Atlanta during that period, but police would link these twenty-nine to a single perpetrator, Wayne Bertram Williams. He'd eventually be convicted of only two murders, although investigators believe they can link him to at least twenty-three. Others believe that Williams is innocent, and didn't kill anyone at all.

The first two murders occurred in July 1979, when two 14-year-old boys, Edward Hope Smith and Alfred Evans, disappeared from different parts of Atlanta. They were found together, on July 28, in a wooded area to the southwestern of the city. Edward had been killed by a .22 caliber pistol, Alfred had been strangled.

The next victim, 14-year-old Milton Harvey, went missing on September 4, 1979, while cycling to the bank to pay a bill for his mother. His badly decomposed body would be found in mid-November, discarded on a garbage dump. By then, 9-year-old Yusef Bell was missing. He was found on November 8, his body wedged into a gap in a concrete floor. He'd been strangled to death.

No further murders occurred between November 1979 and February 1980. But just as Atlanta's citizens were beginning to think the nightmare might be over, the killer was back. Twelve-year-old Angel Lenair disappeared on March 4, her body discovered a week later. Jefferey Mathis, aged ten, went missing on March 11. A week later, 14-year-old, Eric Middlebrooks was found bludgeoned to death. Less than a month later, on June 9, 12-year-old Christopher Richardson went to a local swimming pool in Decatur. He never got there.

Ten-year-old Aaron Wyche was the next to die. His body was found beneath a highway bridge, the medical examiner insisting that death was caused by a fall, even though the boy had died of asphyxia. Soon after, 9-year-old Anthony Carter was found stabbed to death behind a warehouse. Then, on July 30, 1980, eleven-year-old Earl Terrell was abducted from outside the South Bend Park swimming pool, bringing the FBI into the case.

As the "Summer of Death" wound to its conclusion, there was another murder. Thirteen-year-old Clifford Jones was found strangled, his body discarded in a dumpster behind a Laundromat known to be a gay pick up spot.

The task force was now up and running, working on the assumption that at least some of the murders were connected. But what baffled the police was that while some of the crimes seemed to fit a pattern, others clearly didn't. In an attempt to make sense of this anomaly, the task force began drawing up a list of the crimes that they believed were part of the series. That list was soon mired in controversy, as the criteria for inclusion kept changing. Many murders that seemed to fit the criteria didn't make the cut, others that bore little resemblance to the pattern were included.

During the fall of 1980, the mayor of Atlanta issued a citywide curfew, while police patrols were also stepped up. It did nothing to stop the killings. Twelve-year-old Charles Stephens was found strangled to death on October 10. And by the beginning of November, another child, 9-year-old Aaron Jackson, had been murdered.

The next to go missing was 16-year-old Patrick "Pat Man" Rogers. He turned up in the Chattahoochee River on December 21, 1980, dead from a blow to the head. Then the killer seemed to change location, moving his killing ground from central Atlanta to the outer suburbs.

Lubie Geter, 14, disappeared in January 1981, his badly decomposed body found a month later. Terry Pue also disappeared in January, an anonymous tipster leading police to the site of his body a day later. He'd been strangled. Eleven-year-old Patrick Baltazar went missing on February 6, 1981, and was found a week later. That same month, thirteen-year-old Curtis Walker disappeared. Then 15-year-old Joseph "Jojo" Bell was missing, then Jojo's best friend, Timothy Hill.

Timothy Hill would be the last child victim. From now on the killer targeted young men.

Eddie "Bubba" Duncan was the first adult to make it onto the task force's list. Duncan was 21 years old when he disappeared on March 20, 1981. He was found dead on April 8.

The second adult victim was 21-year-old Larry Rogers. His body was found in an abandoned apartment two weeks after his disappearance. Michael McIntosh, a 23-year-old ex-convict, was last seen on March 25. His body was fished out of the Chattahoochee River in April. That same month, 21-year-old Jimmy Ray Payne and 17-year-old William Barrett were dead.

Then, finally, the police got a break in the case.

In the early morning hours of Friday, May 22, 1981, a police officer was staking out the Jackson Parkway Bridge, when he heard a loud splash. Moments later, the officer saw a car's headlights turn on. Then the vehicle drove off. The officer radioed his colleague at the other end of the bridge, who pulled the white Chevrolet station wagon over.

The driver was 23-year-old Wayne Williams. Asked about his presence on the bridge, Williams offered a story that later proved to be a lie. However, at the time, the police had no reason to detain Williams, so they let him go.

The next day, officers did some checking into Williams' background. He was known locally as a braggart and a liar, passing himself off as a big-time music producer. He was also known to have a morbid interest in road accidents, often scanning police frequencies, then racing to the scene to take photographs and shoot video, which he'd later sell to local news networks.

None of this, of course, made Williams a murderer, but he was nonetheless the number one suspect when the body of 27-year-old Nathaniel Cater was fished from the Chattahoochee River two days later.

Williams was put under surveillance while investigators waited on warrants to search his house and car. When the FBI brought Williams in for questioning, he stuck to his reason for being on the bridge, claiming he was on his way to audition a singer named Cheryl Johnson. Once traced, Johnson disputed this claim.

Williams told other lies too, specifically about his whereabouts earlier in the evening. Three polygraphs were administered. Williams failed each one.

On June 21, police arrived at Williams' home with an arrest warrant for the murder of two adult victims, Jimmy Payne and Nathaniel Cater. Williams would eventually be found guilty of the murders, the case relying heavily on forensic evidence that linked fibers found on the victims to Williams' house and car. He was sentenced to two terms of life imprisonment.

Although Williams was never charged with any of the other murders, evidence from those crimes was presented at his trial in order to illustrate a "pattern." Soon after his incarceration, police closed the book on the Atlanta child murders.

27. Juan Corona

Country: United States

Confirmed Victims: 25

Suspected Victims: 25+

Goro Kagehiro's peach farm sat on the banks of the Feather River, five miles north of Yuba City, in Sutter County, California. On May 19, 1971, Kagehiro was making a tour of his orchards when he noticed a freshly dug hole between the trees. He could not understand why someone had dug the hole and asked a nearby picking crew. They too had no idea who might be responsible.

Kagehiro decided to let it go, but the episode perplexed him, so he returned to the orchard that evening to view the hole again. To his surprise, it had been filled in. Concerned about trespassers on his property, the farmer decided to report the matter to the police.

The following morning, a couple of deputies arrived to view the hole. They began digging in the disturbed earth and before long uncovered the body of a slim white man. He'd been stabbed several times in the chest, struck on the head and slashed across the skull with a thin bladed weapon. In addition, there were deep cuts to his hands, which looked like defensive wounds.

Four days later, on May 24, workers driving a tractor on an adjoining farm came across a subsidence in the earth. Aware that a body had recently been recovered from a shallow grave nearby, their foreman called the police. The subsidence turned out to be another grave, in it the body of a drifter named Charles Fleming.

A search of the area turned up no further clues. However, one of the searchers picked out a path leading through some weeds down to the riverbank. There, police officers spotted more disturbed earth and soon found another corpse. Like the other two, the man was white and middle-aged. He'd been bludgeoned about the head and slashed with a thin-bladed implement, possibly a machete. There was another clue, a receipt from a local market made out in the name of Juan V. Corona.

Local law officers were familiar with Corona. He'd been implicated in a vicious assault on a gay man in Marysville and was known to have issues with homosexuals. He definitely warranted a closer look, but that would have to wait, more graves had been discovered.

The dig continued through the night with the fire department setting up floodlights and several off-duty cops lending a hand. Meanwhile, detectives started questioning fruit pickers working on local farms and a pattern soon emerged. Several of the murdered men had been seen with Juan Corona shortly before they disappeared. It wasn't enough to support a murder charge, but it was enough to obtain a search warrant for Corona's home, office and vehicles.

On May 26, sheriff's deputies arrived at Corona's home and took him into custody while they carried out a search. Among the items retrieved were a stained wooden club, a machete, a hatchet and a meat cleaver. Police also found bundles of clothing that did not belong to Corona or any of his family. Then there were bloodstains in his van and in his Chevrolet Impala. Most incriminating of all, was a ledger with the names of 34 men, including several of the victims. At Corona's office, they found a loaded pistol, a long dagger and a number of receipts similar to those found in the grave.

Meanwhile, the search for victims had concluded, with 25 mutilated corpses pulled from shallow graves. Juan Corona was duly charged with 25 murders, at the time the highest number attributed to a single killer in the US.

Initially assigned a public defender, Corona soon fired his counsel when an attorney named Richard Hawk came forward and offered to represent him. Hawk made it clear that he was going to tackle the prosecution's evidence head on, describing it as 'circumstantial and contaminated.'

He had a point. The Sutter County Sheriff's office had made numerous evidence handling mistakes. Much of the "blood evidence" turned out to be either paint or animal blood. Blood in one of Corona's vehicles had originated from an injured worker whom he had transported. There was no blood on the machete or any of the weapons retrieved from Corona's home. The machete believed to be the murder weapon could not be conclusively matched to wounds on any of the victims. The tire tracks did not match any of Corona's vehicles, and the bullet removed from one of the victims was not fired from Corona's gun. No fingerprints were taken from the receipts found at the crime scenes, leaving the defense to conjecture that they might have been planted to deliberately incriminate Corona.

In addition, Corona had an alibi. During the time when most of the victims were murdered, he had been on crutches due to a leg injury.

The matter eventually came to trial on September 11, 1972, in Solano County. Three months and 113 witnesses later, the prosecution rested its case. Then the defense attorney rose to ask for a dismissal. When this was denied, he dumbfounded all present by resting his case, insisting that the prosecution had failed to prove Corona guilty beyond a reasonable doubt.

It was a high-risk strategy and it backfired badly when the jury found Corona guilty on all 25 counts of first-degree murder. He received 25 life sentences.

Corona was incarcerated at the California Medical Facility in Vacaville, because of a heart condition. During his first year in prison, he was attacked by four other inmates and suffered 32 slash and stab wounds resulting in the loss of an eye. While he was recovering he reportedly confessed the murders to a priest. He also confessed to a Mexican consular official and later in a letter to Judge Patton, although Corona later recanted both confessions.

Five years after his first court appearance, the California appeals court granted Corona a new trial, citing the incompetence of his trial attorney. The result, though, was the same. Corona was returned to prison to serve his time. He is currently held at Corcoran State Prison's Security Housing Unit.

26. Marcel Petiot

Country: France

Confirmed Victims: 27

Suspected Victims: 60+

On the morning of March 6, 1944, residents of the upper-class Rue le Sueur, Paris, phoned the police to complain about foul smoke issuing from the chimney at number 21. It had been going on for days they protested. When they'd gone to complain to the owner, Dr. Marcel Petiot, they'd found he wasn't home. A note pinned to the door of the luxury three-story villa informed them that he'd be away for the rest of the month.

The police officers soon learned that Petiot maintained another home, two miles away at 66 Rue Caumartin. When they made a telephone call to that residence they found the doctor at home. "Don't do anything," he cautioned. "I'll be there in 15 minutes."

Half an hour later, Petiot still hadn't shown, and with the smoke worsening and the street filling with onlookers, the gendarmes decided it was time to call the fire brigade.

There was still no sign of Petiot by the time the firefighters arrived. Entering the building through a second-story window, two firemen began searching for the source of the conflagration. A short while later they emerged, wide-eyed, one of them stopping to throw up in the garden.

Three police officers then entered the building. Following the firefighters' instructions, they headed directly for the basement. The first thing they noticed was the stench of seared flesh. Its source was soon obvious. A coal-fed stove blazed away in one corner, a human arm dangling from its open door. Nearby, stood a pile of coal and beside it a stack of dismembered human corpses.

Stunned by the grisly display, the officers staggered from the basement just as Dr. Petiot arrived on his bicycle. Petiot immediately called them into a huddle and dropped his voice. "This is serious," he whispered. "My head could be at stake."

After questioning each of the cops to ascertain that he was a "loyal Frenchman," Petiot explained that he was the leader of a Resistance cell and that the bodies in his cellar were of Germans and collaborators. He insisted that he had over 300 confidential files at his home that needed to be destroyed, lest they fall into the hands of the Gestapo. Convinced by Petiot's apparent sincerity, the gendarmes let him go. It would be seven months before they eventually caught up with him again.

Marcel André Henri Félix Petiot was born January 17, 1897, in Auxerre, France. As a child, he displayed many of the traits of the fledgling serial killer, including animal cruelty, bed-wetting and a precocious interest in sex. He was also a disruptive student who was expelled from school several times. At age 17, he was diagnosed as mentally ill.

During World War I, Petiot served in the French infantry and was wounded in action. He was also diagnosed with various mental ailments and eventually discharged with a full disability pension.

At the conclusion of the war, Petiot entered the accelerated education program available to war veterans, completing a medical degree in just eight months. He then served a two-year internship at Evreux Mental Hospital receiving his medical degree in December 1921.

Petiot moved next to the small town of Villeneuve-sur-Yonne, where he set up a practice and quickly gained an unsavory reputation for performing illegal abortions and supplying narcotics to drug addicts.

In 1926, Petiot began an affair with Louise Delaveau, the daughter of an elderly patient. Delaveau disappeared in May 1926. Despite evidence that Petiot might have been involved in her death, she was listed as a runaway. That same year, Petiot was elected mayor of Villeneuve-sur-Yonne, a position he held until 1931, when he was ousted for embezzling town funds.

Undeterred by this setback, Petiot stood as a councilor for the Yonne district. Here too he was accused of embezzlement, eventually being dismissed for the theft of electricity. By then, he had already moved to Paris, where he quickly built up a roster of loyal patients.

World War II arrived two years later, bringing disaster to all of Europe. To a man like Marcel Petiot, though, it presented nothing but opportunity. In 1941, he recruited three accomplices and began putting the word out that he was operating an escape route. For a price of 25,000 Francs, Petiot promised that he could smuggle anyone out of the country to South America, via Portugal.

It was, of course, a scam. Desperate people, most of them from wealthy Jewish families, would pay the 25,000 Franc fee and arrive at his premises at 21 Rue le Sueur laden with cash, jewelry, furs and other valuables, ready to flee the country. Petiot would inform them that the Argentinean government insisted that they receive inoculations before being allowed into the country. He himself would deliver the shots. But the "inoculations," he administered were usually cyanide, sending his victims to a swift and unceremonious death.

Petiot would then take possession of their valuables and dispose of the bodies. At first, he simply dumped them in the Seine. But when the number of corpses being pulling from the water aroused suspicion, he changed his disposal method to submersion in quicklime and later to incineration.

In April 1943, the Gestapo became aware of Petiot's operation and sent a Jewish prisoner named Yvan Dreyfus to approach the escape network. He promptly disappeared. Undeterred, the Gestapo tried again and this time succeeded in arresting Petiot's three confederates. Under torture, they quickly gave up Petiot. He'd remain a prisoner of the Gestapo for eight months. Ironically, this would later convince many people of his Resistance credentials and help him to escape.

***

After the police allowed Petiot to leave the house at 21 Rue le Sueur, he disappeared. A subsequent search of the property produced ample evidence of mass murder, with enough body parts discovered to make "at least ten complete bodies." But still the police wavered, uncertain whether Petiot was, in fact, a murderer, or the hero of the Resistance he claimed to be.

Petiot, meanwhile, had gone to ground with the assistance of friends and loyal former patients. He re-emerged seven months later, having grown a beard and adopted the alias Henri Valeri. He even joined the French Forces of the Interior, gaining the rank of captain and at one stage assisting in the hunt for the elusive Dr. Petiot.

Valeri was eventually outed when someone spotted him at a Paris Metro station on October 31, 1944, and recognized him as Petiot. Committed for trial on March 19, 1946, he was found guilty of 26 murders and sentenced to death.

Marcel Petiot went to the guillotine on May 25, 1946. To his credit, he walked unflinching to his death, even joking with his jailers in the moments before the blade fell.

25. Cedric Maake

Country: South Africa

Confirmed Victims: 27

Suspected Victims: 35+

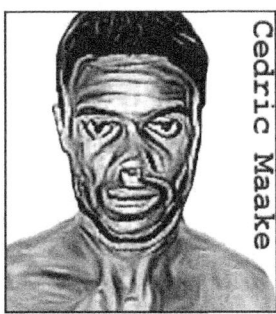

Wemmer Pan is a small, man-made lake situated in the southern Johannesburg suburb of La Rochelle. By day, it is a popular picnic spot for families and courting couples, but at night the area is isolated and poorly lit, the perfect hunting ground for a predator. Between April 1996 and December 1997, a particularly deadly predator, named Cedric Maake, turned the area into his private killing field.

Maake is a most unusual serial killer. Whereas most murderers of this type have a preference for a certain type of weapon, Maake killed with guns, knives, rocks and hammers. Whereas most serial killers target a particular victim type, he murdered young women, couples, taxi drivers and shop owners. Young or old, black or white, didn't matter to him. If ever a murderer fit the profile of a "killing machine," it was Maake.

The first killing attributed to Maake occurred in April 1996 when he raped and murdered a still unidentified woman at Wemmer Pan. Over the next eight months, ten more people were murdered at the lake (four bludgeoned to death, six shot) and the case was allocated to renowned serial killer expert, Captain Piet Byleveld of the Brixton Murder and Robbery Squad.

But even as that investigation was ongoing, another serial killer began operating in Johannesburg. This man targeted a very specific type of victim, Indian tailors operating their small businesses in the city's Central Business District. Eleven men lost their lives between December 1996 and April 1997, all of them bludgeoned to death with a hammer. The only clue that the police had was an invoice signed by a man named Cedric Maake.

In May and June, two minibus taxi operators were lured to isolated spots, shot to death and robbed. All of this while the Wemmer Pan killings continued unabated, nine couples and a woman attacked during June and July alone.

Even in a jurisdiction as beset by violent crime as Johannesburg, this spate of attacks caused alarm. It was as though a plague of serial killers had descended on South Africa's largest city. Little could the police have imagined that a single perpetrator was responsible.

By December 1997, thirteen more shop owners had been assaulted, while the killer had moved the nexus of his attacks away from the now heavily patrolled Wemmer Pan, onto the streets of the surrounding suburbs. One man had been bludgeoned to death on the street, three families had been brutalized in their homes.

Then, finally, a break in the case. In December 1997, Captain Byleveld announced the arrest of Cedric Maake, the man they'd been hunting for the Hammer Murders. Maake was a married father of four, originally from Pietersburg in South Africa's rural Limpopo province. He'd moved to Johannesburg in the mid-eighties and had been working as a self-employed handyman at the time of his arrest. He admitted freely to the 'Hammer Murders,' then gave investigators an unexpected bonus when he confessed that he was also the 'Wemmer Pan Killer.'

Maake was initially keen to assist with the investigation, even leading investigators to the sites of the various attacks. However, by the time the matter came to court in October 1999, he'd changed his tune and was now insisting that he was innocent.

The trial would last eleven months during which the true depravity of the killer would be revealed. Survivors of the attacks recounted how Maake screamed obscenities as he struck and kicked them; forensic experts described the horrendous extent of the injuries inflicted on victims, some of their skulls so badly pulverized that brain matter spilled through the cracks.

Maake, meanwhile, ranted and raved, threatened to kill the judge and the prosecutor, banged his head against the frame of the dock. On one occasion, when the judge ordered his removal from the courtroom, it took six burly police officers to subdue him.

On September 6, 2000, Cedric Maake was found guilty of 27 murders as well as a raft of other charges including rape, robbery, and attempted murder. He was sentenced to 27 life terms, effectively 1,340 years in prison. He is currently serving that term at the maximum security C-Max prison in Pretoria.

Investigators who worked the case believe that Maake is responsible for at least 60 deaths.

24. Dean Corll

Country: United States

Confirmed Victims: 28

Suspected Victims: 40+

Dean Corll was born on December 24, 1939, in Fort Wayne, Indiana. His father, Arnold, was a strict disciplinarian, his mother, Mary, tended to be overprotective. Their marriage was not a happy one and, in 1946, the couple divorced. An attempted reconciliation, in 1950, also ended in divorce, three years later.

Dean went to stay with his mother, who later married a traveling salesman named Jake West and moved the family to the town of Vidor, Texas. Not long after, Mary started a small candy business, which flourished and was soon providing the family with a full-time income.

Corll's mother divorced Jake West in 1963, the same year that Dean was drafted into the US Army. He served just 10 months before receiving a hardship discharge, on the grounds that he was needed in the family business.

In 1965, the Corll's candy business relocated to new premises, across the street from Helms Elementary School. Corll was soon luring young boys to the shop with offers of free candy. One of the boys, 12-year-old David Brooks became a regular. Three years later, he and Corll would become lovers.

In 1970, Corll's mother closed the candy business and moved to Colorado. Corll stayed behind and found work as an electrician with the Houston Lighting and Power Company. Not long after, he committed his first murder.

The victim was an 18-year-old college freshman, named Jeffrey Konen, who disappeared while hitchhiking on September 25, 1970. He'd be found, three years later, in a shallow grave at High Island Beach.

At around this time, Brooks walked in on Corll while he was sexually assaulting two teenaged boys. Corll promised Brooks a car in return for his silence. He also made a standing offer of $200 for any youths Brooks was able to lure to Corll's apartment. Brooks accepted both proposals, receiving a green Corvette from Corll, and soon after, bringing two 14-year-olds, James Glass and Danny Yates, to Corll. The boys were raped and tortured before being strangled to death and buried beneath a boatshed Corll had recently rented.

Six weeks after the murder of Glass and Yates, Corll and Brooks abducted brothers Donald and Jerry Waldrop. The boys were raped and tortured, before being strangled. They were later buried beneath the boatshed.

Three more victims followed between March and May 1971 – 15-year-old Randell Harvey, 16-year-old Gregory Winkle and David Hilligiest, 13. Winkle and Hilligiest were friends who were abducted and murdered together on May 29, 1971.

On August 17, 1971, Brooks helped Corll abduct a friend of his. 17-year-old Ruben Haney was invited to attend a party at Corll's apartment. Once there, he was strangled. He too ended up under the boatshed.

The next teenager that Brooks procured for Corll was Elmer Wayne Henley. However, for some unexplained reason, Corll decided not to kill Henley. Instead, he made Henley the same offer he'd made David Brooks – $200 for any boy he could lure to Corll's apartment. Henley soon complied, bringing 17-year-old Willard Branch to Corll on February 9, 1972.

One month later, 18-year-old Frank Aguirre was murdered, a month after that, 17-year-old Mark Scott. But Henley wasn't just a procurer for Corll. By now he was an active and willing participant in the murders. According to Brooks later testimony, Henley strangled at least two of the victims, Billy Baulch and Johnny Delone.

Between July and August 1972, two more young men – 17-year-old Steven Sickman and 19-year-old Roy Bunton – met a horrible fate at Corll's hands. Less than two months later, Wally Jay

Simoneaux and Richard Hembree were murdered, a month later, it was Richard Kepner.

In March 1973, Corll moved to 2020 Lamar Drive, in Pasadena, a suburb of Houston. On June 4, 15-year-old William Ray Lawrence was brought back to this address, where he suffered three days of horrendous abuse before being strangled. He was later buried at Lake Sam Rayburn. Less than two weeks later, 20-year-old Raymond Blackburn was abducted, strangled, and buried at the same location.

Corll's bloodlust was up now and he was accelerating, claiming five victims during the month of July 1973. In August, he claimed his last and youngest victim. James Dreymala was just 13 years old when he was snatched from his bicycle and taken back to Corll's house. There he was raped, tortured and strangled before being buried in the boat shed. Four days later, Dean Corll would be dead, shot during an altercation with one of his own accomplices.

On the evening of August 7, 1973, a tearful phone call from Elmer Henley summoned Pasadena police to Corll's residence. They found Dean Corll shot to death, six bullet holes in his shoulder and back. Henley claimed full responsibility for the shooting but said that he'd acted in self-defense. Corll, he said, had gone crazy after Henley had arrived at his house with a girl. He'd threatened Henley with a gun, but Henley had managed to turn the weapon on him. The girl who'd been the cause of the altercation was 15-year-old Rhonda Williams, and she backed up Henley's story, as did her boyfriend, Timothy Kerley.

But just as the cops were beginning to think that they might be dealing with a case of justifiable homicide, Henley stunned them by admitting to more murders.

That afternoon, Henley led police officers to Corll's boat shed, where over the next two days they would recover 19 bodies. Henley meanwhile had given a full statement, implicating David Brooks who, despite his protestations of innocence, was taken into custody. Two bodies were later recovered from Lake Sam Rayburn and six from High Island Beach, bringing the total to twenty-seven victims – at the time the worst case of serial murder in American history.

Elmer Wayne Henley and David Owen Brooks were tried separately for their roles in the murders. Henley was brought to trial in San Antonio on July 1, 1974, charged with six murders. He was found guilty and sentenced to six consecutive 99-year terms - a total of 594 years – meaning he will never see the outside of a prison cell.

David Brooks stood trial on February 27, 1975, accused of four murders committed between December 1970 and June 1973. He was found guilty on one charge and sentenced to life imprisonment without the possibility of parole.

23. David Simelane

Country: Swaziland

Confirmed Victims: 28

Suspected Victims: 45+

The tiny southern African kingdom of Swaziland seems an unlikely hunting ground for one of the world's most deadly serial killers. Yet between October 1999 and April 2001, just such a man had the entire Swazi nation living in fear. His name was David Simelane and his case closely mirrors that of another African serial killer, Moses Sithole of South Africa.

Simelane was born in Luyengo, Swaziland, in 1956. Little is known about his early life, but he grew up to become a habitual criminal, acquiring a lengthy rap sheet for offenses ranging from rape to robbery. By the time he embarked on his murder spree he had acquired 18 convictions, the last of these earning him a 20-year sentence for a rape he insists he did not commit. Simelane would serve 15 years of that sentence, most of it simmering at the injustice perpetrated against him, and plotting vengeance.

Simelane wasted little time in exacting that revenge. Shortly after his release from prison in 1998, the woman who had laid the charge against him was found dead. Simelane was immediately suspected, but the police were unable to find him. He'd adopted the alias David Albert Mhlanga and gone on the run, spending much of his time hiding out in the Usuthu forest, an area he knew very well. But he wasn't just hiding out. Far from sating his anger, the murder of his accuser had whetted his appetite for more carnage. Soon he'd turn his deadly attentions on the women and children of Swaziland.

The next murder attributed to Simelane occurred in October 1999. On that occasion, he lured Thandi Dlamini to the Bhunya Forest with the promise of work. Dlamini had her one-year-old son with her. Simelane strangled both mother and child and buried them in a shallow grave.

Over the 16 months that followed, Simelane traveled far and wide trawling for victims. He adopted a simple but highly efficient M.O., posing as an employment agent and luring his victims with promises of work. In a country like Swaziland, where paid employment is hard to come by, such offers are almost irresistible.

Victim after victim fell for Simelane's glib line of talk and ended up raped, strangled and buried beneath a shallow layer of earth and pine needles. Some he knew, like his long-time girlfriend, Vosho Dlamini, and another lover, Zanele Thwala, but most were complete strangers. Sometimes the women had babies or young children with them but that did nothing to deter the killer. He showed the children no more mercy than he'd shown their mothers.

And the dire unemployment situation in the country actually helped conceal Simelane's murder spree. Swazis often range far from home to earn a living and are not always in contact with their families. Many of the murdered women were never reported as missing.

In the end, it took the suspicions of a jealous boyfriend to bring Simelane to justice. The man's fiancée had been missing for several days when someone told him that she had been seen in the company of an unnamed "employment agent." The man began searching for Simelane, eventually tracking him down and passing on his whereabouts to the police. Simelane was arrested at a supermarket in the southern Swaziland town of Nhlangano.

Once in custody, Simelane quickly confessed, although he'd later retract and claim that the confession had been beaten out of him. Nonetheless, there can be little doubt that he was the serial killer the police were looking for, as he led them to his various burial sites. There, the police uncovered the ravaged corpses of 41 women and four children – a nine-month-old baby and toddlers aged two, three and four. Some of the victims had been buried, others carelessly discarded in the undergrowth. Some had their breasts hacked off, others their vaginas cut out. Still others had been decapitated. Most had been strangled. In the more recent victims, there was clear evidence of rape.

David Simelane went on trial at the High Court in Manzini, Swaziland, in 2004. In a trial that would be delayed and postponed several times, he was eventually found guilty of murder and sentenced to death on April 1, 2011, sparking mass celebrations across the country. However, as Swaziland has not carried out an execution since 1983, it remains to be seen whether Simelane will pay the ultimate price for his heinous crimes.

22. Stephan Letter

Country: Germany

Confirmed Victims: 29

Suspected Victims: 42+

An unmarked van rolls to a stop outside the cemetery gates in the picturesque Alpine town of Sonthofen. Six hooded figures emerge, all dressed in white biological suits. Their job is to exhume 42 bodies, all of them suspected victims of Stephan Letter, Germany's worst serial killer since the war.

As a boy, Stephan Letter was always interested in pursuing a medical career. His first ambition was to become an ER doctor, but mediocre academic results meant that he had to settle for nursing instead. Yet, so keen was Letter to begin helping those in need that he volunteered at the Red Cross while he attended nursing college in Ludwigsburg.

One of his jobs at the Red Cross was to drive elderly patients from their homes to a clinic for treatment. Those who worked with Letter would later testify that he would become extremely distressed by the sickly condition of his frail charges. In January 2003, having graduated from Ludwigsburg, he finally had the chance to start doing something to help.

Letter's first posting was to the Sonthofen Clinic, a hospital in the idyllic mountainside village of Sonthofen, Bavaria. He started working there shortly after his graduation, pulling the night shift. Within a month, there was an upswing in the number of deaths at the hospital. Yet, as the deceased patients were mainly over 75 years of age, the deaths caused little alarm. Two of the younger victims, aged 40 and 47 respectively, had been gravely ill and their deaths also, were not entirely unexpected.

But there were other deaths that should have raised a red flag. Beata Giehl, 79, was taken to the Sonthofen Clinic on April 30, 2003, having suffered a suspected heart attack. She responded well to treatment and by that afternoon was sitting up in bed, laughing and chatting with her daughters. By 10 o'clock that evening she had passed away.

Pilar Del Rio Peinador, a 73-year-old Spanish national, had been admitted to the clinic with breathing problems but was recovering well and had been talking to hospital staff about a planned holiday to her homeland. Then one morning, having shown no deterioration in her condition, she was dead.

These cases might well have alerted the authorities, but when the case eventually broke it was not a suspicious death, but missing drugs, that pointed to the presence of a serial killer.

In July 2004, hospital administrators called the police to report that stocks of a muscle-relaxing drug were missing. The medicines did not come under the dangerous drugs law and were therefore freely available for medical personnel to use as required. However, given in sufficient quantities they could potentially be lethal.

Tracking down the culprit was a relatively easy matter. Detectives compared the clinic's duty roster against the dates when the drugs had disappeared. The evidence pointed to one man – Stephan Letter. A subsequent search of his apartment turned up enough of the missing drug to have killed ten people.

Thus far, Letter was suspected of nothing more that theft of hospital property, but as the police began pressing him on why he'd taken the tranquilizers, he suddenly blurted out that he had killed at least 16 patients, adding that, "there may be more."

Letter then went on to explain his motive. He said that the deaths were mercy killings, designed to release the patients from their suffering, to "release their souls," as he put it. He said that he would listen in as doctors discussed a patient's condition and determine whether they were likely to recover. If not, he'd administer a cocktail of tranquilizers and muscle relaxants during the night, to stop their breathing. Later, he'd alert a doctor to the patient's death. Often, he'd console grieving relatives.

The only problem with Letter's story was that many of his victims were recent admissions whose conditions had not even been properly diagnosed at the time he sent them to oblivion.

Stephan Letter went on trial at the Bavarian state court in Kempten in December 2006. His mercy-killing defense exposed as a lie, he was convicted of 12 counts of murder, 15 of manslaughter, and one count of killing on demand. He was also found guilty of attempted manslaughter and of causing grievous bodily harm.

Letter was sentenced to life in prison. In a highly unusual move for Germany, the judge ruled that no upper limit should be placed on the life sentence, ensuring that Letter could not be released for good behavior after 15 years.

21. Karl Denke

Country: Germany

Confirmed Victims: 30

Suspected Victims: 40+

At around 1 p.m. on the afternoon of Sunday, December 21, 1924, a man named Vincenz Olivier staggered into the police station at Munsterberg, Lower Silesia, (now Ziębice, Poland). He was covered in blood that emanated from a nasty head wound. According to Olivier, a local man named Karl Denke had attacked him with a pickaxe.

At first, the police officers refused to believe Olivier's story. The man he'd named as his attacker was an upstanding citizen, a man who neither drank nor smoked nor dallied with women; a man who played the organ in church and carried the cross at funeral processions; a man so universally loved that people called him "Papa" or "Father Denke." Surely there must be some mistake.

Olivier, though, was sticking to his story, and after a doctor examined the wound and verified that it had indeed been inflicted by a pickaxe, the police decided to bring Denke in for questioning.

Denke was only too willing to cooperate. He readily admitted to striking Olivier. However, in his version of events, he'd acted in self-defense, after Olivier had tried to rob him. It sounded to the police officers like a more viable version of events but with neither accused nor accuser prepared to give any ground, the police made the call to lock up both men, while they decided how to proceed.

Denke was placed in a holding cell and told that he'd be spending the night. At around 11:30 that evening, a police sergeant looked in on him and found him dead. He'd asphyxiated himself with a noose fashioned from a handkerchief.

The question was why? Why would a respectable man commit suicide over such a minor charge?

Karl Denke was born in Oberkunzendorf, Silesia (now Kalinowice, Poland) on August 10, 1870. His parents were wealthy farmers but from an early age it was clear that something was not quite right with Karl. He wasn't retarded exactly, just slow and somewhat dim-witted, lacking the ability to learn or even to speak (he was six years old before he uttered his first words).

In other ways too, Denke was unlike other children. He was said to be fearless for one thing, and not at all squeamish. In addition, he was known to be a glutton, once polishing off two pounds of meat at a single sitting.

At age 12 he quit school and went to work as an apprentice to a gardener, a trade he continued to work at until 1895. That was the year his father died and Denke inherited enough money to buy a piece of land and set himself up as a farmer.

The farm, however, was an abject failure and Denke soon sold the land and bought himself a two-story house in Munsterberg. Then came World War I and in its wake a period of hyperinflation that led to Denke having to sell his property. Eventually, he was left with just a small apartment and the once well-to-do landowner was forced to support himself by selling leather trinkets, shoelaces and, occasionally, pieces of pickled pork.

Fortune had not been kind to Karl Denke, but it had done nothing to dampen his spirits. Although somewhat reclusive, he enjoyed a good reputation in the town of some 8,000. He was well known for his generosity, often helping those in need and even allowing vagrants to spend the night at his apartment. Now, one of those vagrants had accused him of attempted murder and Denke had responded by taking his own life.

Following Denke's death, the police turned over his corpse to his relatives for burial. Three days later, on Christmas Eve, 1924, a contingent of officers went to his apartment to do an inventory of his belongings and to secure the property.

The officers had barely begun their search when several of them had to leave the small apartment to throw up in the bushes outside. Three medium-sized pots stood on the stove, filled with chunks of flesh in a congealed cream sauce, skin still intact, some pieces with hairs protruding from the dermis. One pot was only half full, suggesting that Denke had eaten the remainder before his arrest. A pathologist would later verify that the cuts were from the buttocks.

That was only the first of the horrors.

Pickling in brine, in a wooden barrel, were bones and chunks of meat. The flesh was reddish brown in color, but the pale (and sometimes hairy) skin, still in place, left the officers in no doubt as to its origin. On one cut, a navel was clearly visible, on another, a nipple.

More human remains were found in the shed, chunks of pickled flesh and a barrel full of bones, including 16 femurs, eight elbows, one-hundred-and-fifty ribs, and over 200 toe and finger bones. In addition, there was a collection of teeth, totaling over 150 pieces. All in all, the pathologist estimated that the bones were from at least eight individuals. Remains later found buried in the yard, and in a nearby municipal park, would point to over 40.

There were other indicators of Denke's carnage too, trunks filled with bloodstained clothing, piles of identity documents and the implements of murder and dissection, three axes; a large wood saw; a pickaxe and three long-bladed knives.

And then there were the bizarre artifacts of Denke's leather tannery and soap making efforts, belts and suspenders of tanned human skin, shoe laces plaited from human hair and crude bars of soap made from human fat. Denke, it seemed, was not a wasteful man.

Yet even as the horrific truth of Denke's activities came to light, the police were left with one bothersome question. How was it that a man could carry out wholesale slaughter in such a small town without anyone noticing?

The answer was two-fold. On the one hand, Denke had been exceedingly clever in his choice of victims, targeting only vagrants and iterant journeymen who he picked up from the railway station, just a few blocks from his house. On the other hand, there was public indifference. It seemed that Denke's activities had not gone unnoticed after all.

As word leaked out of the horrific finds in Denke's apartment, several of his neighbors came forward to report on the suspicious goings-on they'd witnessed. On one occasion a man had been seen running from the house covered in blood. On another, a vagrant complained to one of Denke's neighbors that Denke had looped a chain around his neck, but that he'd managed to fight him off. Neither of these incidents was reported to the police.

Denke's neighbors also spoke of the horrendous smells coming from his home and the late night hammering and sawing noises. One man had seen Denke pouring out buckets of blood in the courtyard, others had seen him leaving his apartment in the middle of the night, lugging heavy suitcases only to return later empty handed. It also seemed suspicious that, with the country under near famine conditions, Denke was always well supplied with meat. They assumed it was dog meat, but no one thought to question him about it or alert the authorities.

In the end, Denke avoided justice by taking his own life. However, he is not forgotten. These days the museum in his hometown boasts a display commemorating the infamous cannibal.

20. Jane Toppan

Country: United States

Confirmed Victims: 31

Suspected Victims: 31+

With the recent high-profile trials of medical serial killers like Dr. Harold Shipman and Dr. Michael Swano, you might be forgiven for assuming that such killers are a fairly modern phenomenon. Not so. For as long as doctors and nurses have tended the sick and ailing, there have been those who have used their positions to harm rather than heal.

One such individual was Jane Toppan, a jovial, buxom woman whose reputation for competence earned her positions with many of New England's most prominent families. Little did they know that 'Jolly Jane,' the woman to whom they'd entrusted the lives of their loved ones, was one of the most heinous murderers in the annals of American crime.

Like most serial killers, Jane Toppan (born Honora Kelley in Boston in 1857) had an insalubrious start to life. Her parents were poor, Irish immigrants, her father a violent drunk prone to eccentric behavior that earned him the nickname 'Kelley the Crackpot.'

Neither was that the worst of young Honora's problems. Her mother, Bridget Kelley, died of tuberculosis while Nora was still a child. Not long after, she and her older sister Delia were placed in the Boston Female Asylum, an institution for orphaned and needy children.

Then, in 1865, she was placed in the care of Mr. Abner Toppan and his wife Ann, of Lowell, Massachusetts. Some accounts have it that Nora was adopted by the Toppans, but this arrangement was never formalized. What the placement meant was that she was effectively a live-in servant. Abner Toppan did, however, give her his last name and also changed her name from Honora to Jane.

Her time in the Toppan household was probably the happiest of Jane's life, although it must also have left her confused and humiliated. On the one hand, she was treated as a member of the family, on the other, she was left in no doubt as to her lowly background and her position as a servant. Nonetheless, she appeared normal. Indeed, she excelled at school and displayed such a sunny disposition that she was known to all as 'Jolly Jane.'

That was the face Jane Toppan showed to the world. Below the surface, though, a more sinister persona lurked. She became a compulsive liar who enjoyed spreading malicious rumors about people she disliked. Like many fledgling serial killers, she also became a pyromaniac, deriving sexual pleasure from the fires she set.

In 1885, Toppan enrolled as a student nurse at the Cambridge Hospital in Massachusetts. She once again excelled at her studies, even if her classmates and instructors were somewhat disturbed by her obsession with autopsies.

According to Toppan's later confession, it was during her tenure at Cambridge that she first began drugging patients with morphine and atropine. This was no casual undertaking. Toppan took to poisoning like a mad scientist, conducting a whole series of sick experiments. She began altering the prescribed dosage, first withholding medication and then overdosing the patient to see how they'd react. Eventually, she perfected the skill of prolonging a patient's suffering by doping them into unconsciousness and then reviving them before making the kill. In their last moments, she'd get into the deathbed and hold them while they breathed their last. She said that this gave her the ultimate sexual thrill.

Despite the high number of patients that died under Jane Toppan's care, no suspicion seems to have accrued to her. In 1889, she was offered a position at the prestigious Massachusetts General Hospital and remained there for a year, during which time she claimed several more victims. This time, though, her activities did not go unnoticed. She was hauled before a disciplinary board and fired, although the matter was not reported to the authorities.

Toppan returned to her prior position at Cambridge. But her second term was short-lived before she was fired due to the 'reckless prescription of opiates.' Unperturbed by the latest setback, she advertised her services as a private nurse and over the years that followed developed a reputation as a competent, charming, and sympathetic caregiver, even if few of her clients survived her ministrations.

In the summer of 1901, Toppan was vacationing at a cottage in Cataumet, owned by an old friend, Alden Davis. Within a matter of weeks, Davis and two of his daughters were dead. Toppan then moved back to Boston and began a relationship with her late foster sister's husband. As before, death soon followed. The man's sister died under mysterious circumstances and then he himself became ill, with Toppan insisting on taking personal responsibility for his care. She even poisoned herself to avoid suspicion. Fortunately, the man saw through the ruse and ordered Jane to leave his house, even though he declined to take the matter up with the police.

Toppan had once again escaped prosecution. But her luck was about to run out. The Davis family was deeply suspicious of the sudden deaths of Alden and his daughters. They ordered an autopsy on the youngest girl, the toxicology exam providing conclusive evidence that she'd been poisoned. It didn't take a genius to figure out who was responsible and on October 26, 1901, Jane Toppan was arrested and charged with murder.

Toppan had no hesitation in confessing to the charges brought against her. In fact, she seemed to derive genuine pleasure from describing her crimes. The motive she said was the "irresistible sexual impulse" she derived from holding her victims in her arms as they died. She also claimed that her ambition was "to have killed more people – helpless people – than any other man or woman who ever lived."

Placed on trial at the Barnstable County Courthouse in June 1902, Toppan was found to be "morally insane," in other words, a criminal psychopath. She was committed to the Taunton Insane Hospital, with the stipulation that she should never be released. She died there on August 17, 1938, at the age of 84.

19. Vasili Komaroff

Country: Russia

Confirmed Victims: 33

Suspected Victims: 33+

The early 1920's were desperate times in Russia, the country having just emerged from a bloody revolution and in the midst of a genocidal civil war. The royal family was dead, the eventual Bolshevik victory still lay in the future. Meanwhile, in the nation's capital, a populace hardened by war hunkered down against a new threat, a fearsome serial killer known as "The Wolf of Moscow."

Russia has produced more than its fair share of serial killers over the years, but this is one of the first documented cases. Over a period of some 16 months, from late 1921 to early 1923, 21 brutalized male corpses had been discovered in and around Moscow's Shabolovki district. The corpses were trussed "liked chickens for roasting," and shoved into sacks, their bodies carrying signs of bludgeoning and strangulation.

Very little physical evidence was found at the dumpsites, but eventually, investigators began to pick up a pattern to the killings. The freshly slain corpses always seemed to turn up on a Thursday or Saturday. Trying to make sense of this anomaly, detectives came to believe that the murders were linked somehow to the Shabolovki horse market, which took place every Wednesday and Friday.

Could it be that the killer was working the crowds at the market, waylaying victims and killing them, then dumping their bodies? It seemed a lead worth pursuing.

Uniformed and plain-clothes officers were dispatched to the area and began questioning the locals. Had they seen anything unusual, anyone acting suspiciously? Soon one name began to emerge, that of Vasili Komaroff, a local horse trader.

Other traders reported that although Komaroff seldom brought his horses to market these days, he was often seen haggling with customers on market days. On a number of occasions, he'd left the market with a potential customer in tow, only to return later on, alone.

It didn't seem like much to go on, but with no other clues in the case, detectives decided to look into it. From Komaroff's neighbors they heard that he was a friendly man, always quick with a smile and a greeting and by all accounts devoted to his family. Yet others of his acquaintance spoke of his quick temper and propensity for violence. One man related a story of how Vasili had strung up his own 8-year-old son. The boy had only survived because Komaroff's wife had intervened and cut him down.

None of this, of course, amounted to evidence of murder. But by now the police were desperate and prepared to follow any thread. They put together a contingent of officers and converged on Komaroff's stable to carry out a search. The police said they were there to search for bootleg liquor, but a panicked Komaroff climbed through a window and fled. It was soon apparent why he'd run. A search of the property turned up his latest victim, trussed and bagged under a pile of hay in the stable. Komaroff was captured soon after.

Once in custody, Komaroff confessed to the murders and readily explained his M.O. to investigators. He'd work the crowds on market day, touting his stock at a significant discount to that being offered at auction. Once he'd hooked a prospective buyer he'd lead the man back to his stables. While the buyer was inspecting the horses, Komaroff would creep up behind him and strike him on the head with a hammer. He'd then strangle the man. The motive was robbery, he said, although he'd only netted on average eighty cents from each of the killings, a paltry $26.40 for the 33 murders he admitted to. Komaroff subsequently led investigators to five undiscovered bodies. The other corpses had been thrown into the Moskva River, he said. They were never found.

Vasili Komaroff went on trial for murder on June 7, 1923, his wife Sofia beside him in the dock as an accomplice. Such was the interest in the case that it was decided to move the proceedings from the courthouse to Moscow's massive Polytechnic Museum, in order to accommodate spectators.

After a trial lasting just one day, the judge delivered a guilty verdict and sentence of death on June 8. Komaroff took the verdict in his stride, declaring that he had led a good life and was ready to die. As he was being led from the courtroom, the Wolf of Moscow was heard to remark, "Well, it's my turn to be put in the sack now."

The execution was set for three days hence, but in an apparent change of heart, Komaroff decided to launch an appeal. It was swiftly dealt with, delaying the inevitable by just 10 days.

Vasili and Sofia Komaroff were executed by firing squad on June 18, 1923.

18. John Wayne Gacy

Country: United States

Confirmed Victims: 33

Suspected Victims: 33+

John Wayne Gacy was born in Chicago, Illinois, on March 17, 1942. An overweight and clumsy child, he had a difficult relationship with his alcoholic father. Despite this, Gacy seems to have had a relatively happy childhood, albeit one peppered with traumatic experiences. At age nine, he was sexually molested; at 11, he was struck on the head by a swing, leaving a blood clot that caused him to suffer blackouts; at 17, he was diagnosed with a heart ailment that would cause him problems at various times during his life.

Gacy failed to graduate high school, dropping out instead to move to Las Vegas, where he found work as a janitor in a funeral parlor. Returning to Chicago, he got a job with Nunn-Bush Shoe Company and was enrolled in their management trainee program in Springfield, Illinois.

In September 1964, Gacy married a co-worker, Marlynn Myers, whose father owned a string of Kentucky Fried Chicken outlets in Waterloo, Iowa. When he was offered the opportunity to manage the restaurants, Gacy leapt at the chance.

The Gacys settled in Iowa and began raising a family. Their son, Michael, was born in March 1967; a daughter, Christine, would follow in October 1968. But by then, the marriage already lay in tatters. In May 1968, Gacy was arrested for sexually assaulting a 15-year-old named Donald Voorhees. Tried and found guilty he got ten years at Iowa State Reformatory. Shortly after, his wife divorced him. He'd never see her or his children again.

On June 18, 1970, Gacy walked free from prison, having served just 18 months of his 10-year sentence. He returned to Chicago, where he worked for a time as a short order cook. Later, he started a contracting business called PDM Contractors. In the interim, he married Carole Hoff, a recently divorced mother of two.

The first murder attributed to John Wayne Gacy occurred on January 2, 1972, when he stabbed 15-year-old Timothy McCoy to death. McCoy was buried in the crawlspace under Gacy's house, to be joined in 1974 by another, unidentified, youth. In May 1975, he murdered one of his PDM employees, 17-year-old John Butkovitch. A year later, in April 1976, he killed Darrell Sampson.

After the Sampson murder, Gacy's killing spree gained momentum. Just five weeks later, 15-year-old Randall Reffett disappeared while walking home from school on May 14. That same day, Gacy abducted and murdered 14-year-old Samuel Stapleton. Reffett and

Stapelton ended up in the same shallow grave in Gacy's
crawlspace.

On June 3, 1976, Gacy killed 17-year-old Michael Bonnin,
strangling him with a ligature and burying him in the crawl space.
Ten days later, 16-year-old William Carroll was murdered and
buried directly beneath Gacy's kitchen. Two unidentified youths
were killed between June 13 and August 6 and buried in the same
grave as Bonnin. They were joined by two more "John Doe"
victims, killed between August and October 1976.

On October 24, Gacy abducted and killed two teenage friends
named Kenneth Parker and Michael Marino. Both boys were
strangled before being buried in the same grave in the crawl space.
Two days later, 19-year-old PDM employee, William Bundy,
disappeared. He ended up in the crawlspace directly beneath
Gacy's master bedroom.

PDM employee, Gregory Godzik, 17, went missing in December
1976. A month later, on January 20, 1977, another PDM employee
John Szyc, vanished. Gacy would later be found in possession of a
TV set and a class ring belonging to Szyc. For now, though, no one
suspected him.

By March 1977, Gacy had murdered another unidentified victim
and also taken the life of 20-year-old Jon Prestidge, a Michigan
native visiting friends in Chicago. Yet another unidentified victim
followed Prestidge into the crawlspace.

In July 1977, Gacy abducted and killed Matthew Bowman, burying him in the crawl space with a tourniquet still knotted around his neck. By the end of the year, another six young men, aged between 16 and 21, had ended up under Gacy's house.

On December 30, 1977, Robert Donnelly, was abducted at gunpoint and driven to Gacy's home where he was raped, tortured and sodomized with various objects. Inexplicably, Gacy didn't kill Donnelly, but drove him back to the spot where he'd abducted him and released him. Gacy was questioned about the assault on January 6, 1978. He admitted to having sex with Donnelly but insisted that it had been consensual. The police believed him and no charges were filed. The following month, Gacy killed a 19-year-old youth named William Kindred.

In March 1978, another victim survived the deadly attentions of John Gacy. 26-year-old Jeffrey Rignall was abducted, raped and tortured, before being chloroformed. When he later regained consciousness, he was lying on the grass in Lincoln Park.

Rignall reported the assault. When the police failed to take action, he began staking out an exit on the Kennedy Expressway that he remembered Gacy taking. After several weeks of surveillance, he spotted Gacy's black vehicle Oldsmobile, followed it home and the passed on Gacy's address to the police.

Gacy was arrested but soon released on bail. And not even his impending trial could stop him killing. Over the months that followed, he claimed four more victims, disposing of their bodies in the Des Plaines River.

Then came the murder that would prove Gacy's undoing. On December 11, 1978, a 15-year-old named Robert Piest went missing. Piest was an employee of a Des Plaines pharmacy where Gacy had been contracted to do a remodeling job. It soon emerged that Gacy had been seen talking to Piest on the day before his disappearance.

Gacy, however, denied ever talking to the boy, raising the suspicions of the detective assigned to the case. He began looking into Gacy's background and discovered that he had an outstanding battery charge against him in Chicago and had served time in Iowa for sodomy. It elevated Gacy to the head of the suspect list.

On December 13, the police carried out a search of Gacy's home and turned up a wealth of suspicious (although not incriminating) evidence. This included a number of driver's licenses, a high school class ring, handcuffs, a two-by-four with holes drilled in the ends, a syringe, and lots of clothing items that were way too small for Gacy. It was not enough to arrest Gacy, but he was placed under surveillance.

Gacy soon began to crack under the police attention. By December 20, he was unshaven and unkempt, drinking heavily and taking long, aimless drives. The police became concerned that he might try to kill himself. On December 22, after spotting him hand over a bag of marijuana to a gas station attendant, they moved in to arrest him. The charge was possession. It would soon be much more than that.

On the afternoon of December 22, a search warrant was served at Gacy's residence. Crime scene investigators entering the house immediately commented on the smell of decomposition. They soon found its source. As evidence technician, Daniel Genty, began digging in the southwest corner of the crawlspace, he uncovered a human arm bone. Over the days that followed, 29 corpses would be removed from under the house.

Confronted with the discovery, Gacy told officers that he wanted to "clear the air." He began making his confession in the early hours of December 22, 1978, eventually admitting to killing 30 young men. He said that he either conned his victims into his car or forced them, using a fake police badge. Back at his house, the victims would be handcuffed, then sexually assaulted, raped and tortured before being strangled to death with a tourniquet, sometimes convulsing on the floor for an "hour or two," before they died.

John Wayne Gacy went on trial for murder on February 6, 1980. Five weeks later, the jury returned a guilty verdict and Gacy was sentenced to death. He would spend fourteen years on death row before that sentence was eventually carried out on May 10, 1994.

Gacy's last words were reportedly, "Kiss my ass."

17. Ted Bundy

Country: United States

Confirmed Victims: 35

Suspected Victims: up to 100

America's most notorious serial killer, Theodore Robert Bundy, was born in Burlington, Vermont, on November 24, 1946. His mother, Louise Cowell was unmarried and Ted never knew his biological father. Instead, he was brought up in the home of his grandparents and led to believe that they were his parents and that his mother was his older sister.

At the age of four, Ted and Louise moved to Tacoma, Washington, to live with relatives. A year after the move, Louise married a military cook named Johnnie Bundy, and Ted assumed his stepfather's last name.

Ted was a shy boy, uncomfortable in the company of others. Nonetheless, he did well at school, later attending the University of Puget Sound and the University of Washington. While studying at

UW, Bundy became romantically involved with a fellow student, Stephanie Brooks. When she broke off the relationship in 1968, Ted was devastated. To make matters worse, in 1969 Bundy learned the truth about his parentage. Thereafter, he began indulging in petty thievery, escalating to shoplifting and burglary.

By 1971, Bundy was dating a divorcee named Elizabeth Kloepfer and volunteering at Seattle's Suicide Hotline. He was working on the re-election campaign of Washington Governor, Daniel J. Evans, and sending out applications to various law schools. In 1973, he met up with a former girlfriend, Stephanie Brooks, and she was amazed at his transformation. The two started dating again, even discussing marriage. But then, without warning, Bundy broke off the relationship. A few months later, young women started to disappear in the Pacific Northwest.

No one knows for certain when Bundy committed his first murder, but the first attack definitely attributed to him, occurred on January 4, 1974. At around midnight, Bundy entered the basement apartment of 18-year-old UW student Karen Sparks. He bludgeoned the sleeping woman with a metal rod, then sexually assaulted her with the same object, causing extensive internal injury. Sparks survived the attack but suffered permanent brain damage.

A month later, Bundy broke into the home of Lynda Ann Healy, a UW undergraduate. He beat her unconscious, then dressed her and carried her away with him. In March, Donna Manson, a 19-year-old student at Evergreen State College in Olympia left her dorm to attend a jazz concert on campus. She never arrived. In April, Susan Rancourt disappeared while on her way from an evening advisors' meeting at Central Washington State College in Ellensburg. On May 6, Roberta Parks left her dormitory at Oregon State University in Corvallis. Parks was meant to meet some friends for coffee but she never showed.

As detectives from the King County Sheriff's Office and the Seattle Police Department started investigating the disappearances, they began to pick up their first clues. A young man had been spotted near two of the crimes scenes. He had his arm in a sling and had asked several female students for help carrying some books to his tan Volkswagen Beetle.

On June 1, Brenda Ball, 22, disappeared after leaving a bar in Burien, near Seattle-Tacoma International Airport. In the early hours of June 11, UW student Georgeann Hawkins vanished while walking down a brightly lit alley. Witnesses reported seeing a man on crutches struggling to carry a briefcase. He'd asked several female students for help.

Six young women were now missing from student communities in Washington and Oregon. Then, on July 14, 1974, Bundy pulled off his most audacious crime yet, abducting two women from Lake Sammamish, 20 miles east of Seattle, in broad daylight.

Five female witnesses would later come forward to describe a handsome young man with his left arm in a sling, who introduced himself as "Ted." He asked for help in unloading a sailboat from his tan colored Volkswagen Beetle. Four of the women refused; one accompanied him as far as his car but fled when she saw that there was no sailboat. Three other witnesses saw the same man approach 23-year-old Janice Anne Ott, and watched her leave with him. Some four hours later, Denise Naslund, an 18-year-old student, left her friends to go to the restroom and never returned. Bundy later confessed that Ott was still alive when he returned with Naslund, and that one was forced to watch the other being murdered.

With a detailed description of the suspect and his car, the police distributed fliers throughout the Seattle area, while a composite sketch was printed in local newspapers and broadcast on TV. Four separate people reported Bundy as a possible match, but the clean-cut law student with no criminal record was not considered a high probability suspect.

On September 6, hunters found the skeletal remains of Janice Ott, Denise Naslund, and Georgeann Hawkins about two miles east of Lake Sammamish. Six months later, the skulls of Lynda Ann Healy, Susan Rancourt, Roberta Parks, and Brenda Ball were found on Taylor Mountain, just east of Issaquah. All showed extensive damage from blunt instrument trauma.

In August 1974, Bundy moved to Salt Lake City to begin his studies at the University of Utah Law School. A new series of homicides began soon after. On September 2, Bundy raped and strangled a still-unidentified hitchhiker in Idaho, disposing of her corpse in a nearby river. On October 2, he abducted 16-year-old Nancy Wilcox in Holladay, dragging her into a wooded area, raping and strangling her to death.

On October 18, Melissa Smith, the 17-year-old daughter of the Midvale police chief, vanished after leaving a pizza parlor. Her naked corpse was found in the nearby mountains nine days later. Another 17-year-old, Laura Ann Aime, went missing on October 31. Her nude body was found by hikers in American Fork Canyon on Thanksgiving Day. Both women had been beaten, raped, sodomized, and strangled with nylon stockings.

On November 8, 1974, Bundy tried to kidnap 18-year-old Carol DaRonch from a Midvale mall. DaRonch managed to escape and was able to provide police with a description of her abductor. Police had not yet been able to track him down when he abducted 17-year-old Debra Kent from an auditorium at Viewmont High School.

On January 12, 1975, Bundy showed up at the Wildwood Inn in Snowmass Village, Colorado, where he abducted Caryn Campbell. Her naked body was found a month later. On March 15, Julie Cunningham, a 26-year-old ski instructor, disappeared while walking from her apartment to meet a friend for dinner. Bundy later confessed to killing her.

The next victim was Denise Oliverson, a 25-year-old who disappeared from Grand Junction, Colorado. Oliverson's bicycle and sandals were later found under a railroad bridge. On May 6, Bundy kidnapped 12-year-old Lynette Culver from Alameda Junior High School in Pocatello, Idaho. He drowned the girl, then sexually assaulted her corpse in his hotel room. Later, he disposed of her body in the Snake River, north of Pocatello.

On June 28, Susan Curtis disappeared from the campus of Brigham Young University in Provo. Bundy confessed to this murder just before his execution. Curtis's body, like the bodies of Nancy Wilcox, Debbie Kent, Julie Cunningham, Lynette Culver, and Denise Oliverson, has never been found.

Bundy's luck, though, was about to run out. On August 16, 1975, he was pulled over in a routine traffic stop and found to be in possession of burglary tools. Although released, he was placed under surveillance and later re-arrested after hairs found in his car were matched to Caryn Campbell, Melissa Smith, and Carol DaRonch.

Picked out of a police lineup by DaRonch, Bundy was charged with aggravated kidnapping and attempted criminal assault. That earned him a 15-year term in the Utah State Prison. Worse was to follow in October 1975, when Colorado authorities charged him with Caryn Campbell's murder and began extradition proceedings.

On June 7, 1977, while attending a preliminary hearing in the Campbell case, Bundy escaped. He remained at large for six days before he was eventually recaptured.

Bundy was returned to the prison at Glenwood Springs. On December 30, while most of the jail staff were on their Christmas break, he managed to crawl into an air conditioning duct and work his way to a trapdoor that opened into the chief jailer's apartment. There, he changed into street clothes and then simply walked out of the front door to freedom. By the time the alarm was raised, he was already in Chicago.

Bundy's next move was south. Using a combination of stolen vehicles and buses, he worked his way to Ann Arbor, Michigan, then to Atlanta, Georgia, and finally to Tallahassee, Florida, arriving on January 8.

During the early hours of January 15, 1978, Bundy broke into the Chi Omega sorority house at Florida State University. There, he bludgeoned 21-year-old Margaret Bowman with an oak log, beating her so severely that her skull was splintered and a portion of her brain was exposed. He then entered the bedroom of 20-year-old Lisa Levy, beat her unconscious, strangled her, and then viciously attacked her with his teeth, almost severing one of her nipples, and leaving deep bite marks on her buttocks. Levy was also raped and sexually assaulted with a hairspray bottle. In the adjoining room, he attacked Kathy Kleiner, breaking her jaw and causing deep lacerations to her shoulder. Then he turned his attention to Kleiner's roommate, Karen Chandler, beating her so savagely that he shattered her jaw and knocked out several of her teeth.

Bundy then left the sorority house, walking eight blocks before he broke into a basement apartment and attacked FSU student Cheryl Thomas, fracturing her skull and jaw and leaving her with permanent deafness and equilibrium damage that ended her dance career.

With police sirens blaring as they raced towards the sorority house, Bundy disappeared into the night. He showed up next on February 9, in Lake City, where he abducted 12-year-old Kimberley Leach from Lake City Junior High School. Leach's decomposing remains were found seven weeks later, discarded in a disused pig shed near Suwannee River State Park.

On February 15, at around 1:00 a.m., Pensacola police officer David Lee spotted an orange VW Beetle driving erratically near the Alabama state line. A check showed the car to be stolen, so the officer pulled it over and, after a struggle, placed the driver under arrest. Lee had no idea that he'd just captured America's most notorious serial killer.

Ted Bundy stood trial for the Chi Omega murders in June 1979. Despite having access to five court-appointed attorneys, he insisted on handling his own defense. Offered a plea bargain that would have saved him from the electric chair, Bundy turned it down, saying that he believed he could win his case. He was wrong in that belief.

Based largely on forensic evidence relating to the bite marks on Lisa Levy's body, Bundy was found guilty and sentenced to death. Six months later he received another death penalty for the murder of Kimberly Leach.

Bundy was sent to the penitentiary at Starke, Florida, to await execution. He'd remain there for nearly a decade before he eventually kept his date with the executioner on January 24, 1989. Those present say that he was so paralyzed with fear that he was unable to walk and had to be carried to 'Old Sparky.'

16. Gennady Mikhasevich

Country: Belarus

Confirmed Victims: 36

Suspected Victims: 55

The official view, the one sprouted by the Tass news agency, was
that serial killers did not exist in the Soviet Union. Who then was
killing the women of Ist? 'The murders are separate incidents,' the
police insisted, 'not connected at all.' And so off they went to arrest
a suspect, four in fact over a 14-year period, one of whom was
executed. It was an arcane and inept stance, one that allowed a
killer to massacre at least 33 young women in 14 years.

Gennady Mikhasevich was born in the village of Ist, in what is now
Belarus. In May 1971, he returned to his hometown after serving a
term in the army and found that his girlfriend had married
another man. Distraught at her desertion, Gennady drank himself
into a stupor for several days, before deciding to commit suicide.

On May 14, 1971, he bought a length of rope and started walking along the road to Polotsk. His intention was to hang himself in the woods but on the way he encountered a woman walking in the opposite direction. His anger displaced from his faithless girlfriend to this stranger, he dragged the woman into the woods and strangled her.

Mikhasevich must have found murder to his taste, because he killed again in October 1971, and twice more in 1972. In the meantime, he set about building up the façade of a normal life, graduating from Vitebsk Technical College in 1973, finding employment at a government motor works, marrying in 1976, fathering two children. He was known as a diligent worker and a good family man. He was a functionary for the local Communist Party. He was even a volunteer policeman, and in this capacity, was involved in investigating the murders that he, himself, was committing.

By now, his M.O. had evolved. With his early murders, he would wait at an isolated spot, hoping that a woman would chance along. Now he had a car, a red Zaporozhets, so he cruised the roads looking for victims. None of the women ever refused to get into his car. In a backwater like Ist, a ride in a motor vehicle was a real treat.

Mikhasevich would drive his victim to an isolated spot then turn on her, throttling her into unconsciousness. He'd then rape the woman before strangling her with a rope. Then he'd rob the victim of money and valuables, toss the body at the side of the road and drive off. In common with many serial killers, he often kept souvenirs.

Given the incompetence of local law enforcement, Mikhasevich might have gone on killing indefinitely, but in 1984, a young investigator named Nikolay Ignatovich was assigned to the case. Unlike his colleagues, Ignatovich firmly believed that the murders were the work of one man, and he approached the case accordingly.

His first move was to check on owners of red Zaporozhets, as such a vehicle had been spotted near several of the crime scenes. When local vehicle databases proved unequal to the task, Ignatovich ordered his officers to stop and question any driver of a similar vehicle.

But these measures proved ineffective. 1985 was a particularly bloody year, with the killer claiming 12 more victims and seemingly always a step ahead of the police. The reason would later become obvious. Mikhasevich, as a volunteer policeman, was privy to many aspects of the investigation. This enabled him to avoid roadblocks and focus his attentions in areas the police weren't covering. Still, he was getting nervous. Ignatovich did not seem like a man easily deflected from his goal. Mikhasevich decided to throw him some deception. It would turn out to be a bad mistake.

The ruse Mikhasevich played was this. He wrote a letter, purporting to come from an underground organization called the "Patriots of Vitebsk." In it, he claimed that the organization was responsible for the murders and would intensify their struggle to rid the country of "lewd women."

At first, the police thought the letter was a prank. But when a note drafted in a similar hand was found beside the body of the next victim, they knew they were onto something. Ignatovich immediately instructed his investigators to start comparing the sample against the handwriting of every male resident in the region.

It was a mammoth task, but handwriting experts eventually matched the 'Patriots of Vitebsk' letter to the writing on a receipt issued from the government car pool. It had been written by Gennady Mikhasevich.

Arrested on December 9, 1985, Mikhasevich initially denied involvement in the murders, but later broke down and confessed. He later led investigators to a well on the outskirts of town, where he'd hidden the keepsakes he'd taken from his victims. He was executed for his crimes in 1987.

15. Serhiy Tkach

Country: Ukraine

Confirmed Victims: 29

Suspected Victims: 100+

Serial killer cops are an unusual but by no means unheard of phenomenon. The most famous American case was that of Gerard Schaefer, a Florida deputy sheriff who used his position of authority to lure, rape and murder at least nine young women between 1969 and 1973. But Schaefer pales in comparison to Serhiy Tkach, a Russian-born sex slayer who may have claimed as many as 100 victims. Tkach had left the police department by the time he started his killing spree, but he used his detailed knowledge of forensics and investigative procedure to avoid capture for 25 years.

Serhiy Tkach was born in Kiselyovsk, Russia, on September 12, 1952. Very little is known about his early life but we do know that he spent time in the Russian military and was wounded while serving in Afghanistan. After completing his military service, he joined the police in Kemerovo, Siberia, eventually advancing to the rank of inspector. He was considered an expert in forensics.

Tkach left the force in 1982 and moved to the Ukrainian city of Dnipropetrovsk. Over the next 25 years, he'd live in Crimea, Zaporozhye and Kharkov, working at various coal mines and industrial plants, marrying three times and fathering five children. He'd also carry out one of the most brutal killing sprees in Ukrainian history, earning him the nickname, "The Pologovsky Maniac."

The first known victim of the elusive serial killer was a teenager, strangled to death and then raped postmortem in Simferopol in 1980, shortly after Tkach arrived in the Ukraine. After finishing with the corpse, Tkach phoned the police and reported the murder. Investigators would find no trace evidence at the scene or on the victim. This was to prove a recurrent pattern of the case.

Over the years that followed, Tkach continued to hunt and murder one victim after the other, all of them young girls aged between 8 and 18. He'd later claim that part of his motivation was to embarrass the police and to this extent he went to great lengths to destroy evidence and mislead investigators. Usually, he'd commit his murders in fields that stood beside highways or railway lines in order to create the impression that the killer might be a truck driver or from out of town.

He'd remove or destroy all obvious clues from the scene. The victim's clothes were taken away and burned; shoe and tire marks were scuffed over, evidence that carried DNA (like hair or semen) was obliterated or vacuumed up. He was also in the habit of spilling cheap perfume at his crime scenes in order to confuse police tracking dogs.

But for all Tkach's cleverness, he made a number of crucial mistakes. For starters, he was unable to resist the serial killers' compulsion for collecting souvenirs from his victims. When he was eventually caught the police would recover an extensive collection that included jewelry, tubes of lipstick, makeup mirrors, purses, and underwear. Tkach also broke the cardinal rule of any serial killer hoping to evade detection. He killed someone he knew.

The victim was 9-year-old Katya Marquises, the daughter of a friend. Katya's brutalized body was found in the city of Zaporozhye in July 2005. Unbeknownst to Tkach, some of the little girl's friends had seen her in his company on the day she disappeared. Those friends saw Tkach again at the funeral and pointed him out to their parents, who informed the authorities.

Tkach was arrested soon after. His response to the arresting officers: "What took you so long?"

It didn't take much persuasion to get Serhiy Tkach to confess. Indeed, he seemed eager to spill the details of his gruesome crimes. He had an incredible recall of each murder, not only remembering the victim's name but also her appearance, what she was wearing, even her height. As to his motivation, he said he'd started killing as a way of revenging the mistreatment he'd received from women, and also to show how inept the police force was. Once he got started he found he had a taste for murder and necrophilia and just couldn't stop.

Tkach was eventually convicted on 29 counts of murder and 11 of attempted murder, although he insisted that the courts were vastly underestimating the extent of his killing spree. He demanded the death penalty, but as Ukraine had recently suspended capital punishment he was sentenced to life imprisonment instead. It is highly unlikely that he will ever be released.

14. Donald Harvey

Country: United States

Confirmed Victims: 37

Suspected Victims: 87+

Unlike most serial killers, Donald Harvey was raised in a loving family environment and was by all accounts a happy, well-adjusted child. Born in Butler County, Ohio, in 1952, Harvey grew up in Booneville, Kentucky, where he was described as a quiet, well-behaved, child and a bright student. It was therefore a surprise to his teachers when he dropped out before graduating.

After leaving school, Harvey relocated to Cincinnati, Ohio, where he worked in a factory, until being laid off in 1970. A few days later Harvey's mother asked him to visit his ailing grandfather at Marymount Hospital in London, Kentucky. At a loose end after losing his job, Harvey agreed.

While Harvey was in Kentucky, he spent most of his time hanging around the hospital. He was polite and personable and before long had been offered a job at the facility as an orderly. He gladly accepted.

Although he had no medical training, some of Harvey's duties involved attending to patients – changing bedpans, inserting catheters and passing out medications. He enjoyed the work and was well liked by both staff and patients.

But then, just a couple of months into his employment at Marymount, an incident occurred that drove Harvey to commit murder. A patient hurled feces into Harvey's face, causing him to react angrily and smother the man with a pillow. Afterwards, he calmly cleaned up before reporting the death to the duty doctor.

No one suspected anything but natural causes. Harvey, exhilarated at having gotten away with murder, waited just three weeks before he killed again. This time, he disconnected an elderly woman's oxygen tank. Again, no one suspected foul play.

Over the next year, Harvey claimed twelve more victims, killing by a variety of methods – suffocation with plastic bags, morphine injections, cocktails of other drugs. Some of the murders were motivated by mercy, he'd later claim, but that was certainly not the case in all of them. Some were purely recreational, others committed out of anger. After an argument with one patient, Harvey snuck in during the night and punctured the man's catheter. Infection set in. Within a few days, the patient had died in agony.

On March 31, 1971, an inebriated Harvey was pulled in by police and questioned about a burglary. While he was being interrogated he started muttering about the murders he'd committed. Arresting officers were stunned, but when they tried to probe for more information, Harvey clammed up. With no evidence to go on, the police were forced to let the matter drop. Harvey eventually paid an admission of guilt fine on the burglary charge. A short while later, he resigned from Marymount and joined the US Air Force.

Harvey served less than a year in the Air Force before receiving a general discharge in March 1972. The grounds for the discharge were not stated, but it sent Harvey into a spiral of depression. In July 1972, he checked himself into the Veteran's Administration Medical Center in Lexington, Kentucky, where he'd spend the next six months in and out of the mental ward.

Following his discharge from the VA hospital, Harvey found part-time work as a nurse's aide at Cardinal Hill Hospital in Lexington. In June 1973, he got a second nursing gig at Lexington's Good Samaritan Hospital, working both jobs until August 1974, when he took up a clerical post at St. Luke's Hospital in Fort Thomas, Kentucky.

In September 1975, he was back to a hands-on nursing job, working the night shift at Cincinnati V.A. Medical Hospital. His duties were varied, giving him access to virtually any area of the hospital. Harvey took full advantage.

Over the next 10 years, he would murder at least 15 patients, keeping a detailed diary of his crimes. His methods were as varied as they were sickening; pressing a plastic bag over the mouth and nose; rat poison in the patient's food; adding arsenic and cyanide to beverages; injecting cyanide into an intravenous tube or into a patient's buttocks.

Eventually, as Harvey refined his knowledge of drugs and poisons, he began taking his activities outside the hospital. One of the first to suffer was Harvey's gay lover, Carl Hoeweler, although in this case, Harvey's intention wasn't to kill, but to keep Hoeweler bed-ridden and therefore reliant on him.

He also preyed on his neighbors. After an argument, he spiked one woman's milk with hepatitis serum, nearly killing her. Another neighbor was poisoned with arsenic. She died a week later.

After an argument with Hoeweler's parents in April 1983, Harvey started poisoning them too, lacing their food with arsenic. Henry Hoeweler was hospitalized as a result, whereupon Harvey finished the job by dropping arsenic into his dessert.

Harvey's murderous career was temporarily put on hold in July 1985, when he was found in possession of a .38 caliber pistol on hospital property. Giving the option of resigning or being fired, he chose the former, walking away with a clean work record. Seven months later, he was back in medical employment, this time at Cincinnati's Drake Memorial Hospital.

It wasn't long before Harvey started killing again. Within just over a year, he'd murdered another 23 patients - disconnecting life support machines, injecting air into their veins, suffocating them, injecting them with arsenic, cyanide, even drain cleaners.

In fact, so many patients died under Donald Harvey's care that he earned an ominous nickname, "Angel of Death." Still, no one suspected anything was amiss until April 1987, and the murder of John Powell.

Powell had been in a coma for several months but had been showing signs of recovery when he died suddenly. During the autopsy, the coroner detected a faint scent of almonds, a telltale sign of cyanide poisoning. Tissue sample proved that the patient had been poisoned, and an investigation was launched leading inevitably to Donald Harvey.

Harvey would eventually strike a deal with prosecutors, offering up a full confession in exchange for avoiding the death penalty. In it, he provided details of over 70 murders, committed over a 17-year period.

On August 18, 1987, Donald Harvey pled guilty to 24 counts of aggravated murder and was sentenced to four consecutive 20-years-to-life sentences. Subsequent convictions ensured that he would remain behind bars until at least 2047.

13. Moses Sithole

Country: South Africa

Confirmed Victims: 38

Suspected Victims: 38+

Moses Sithole was born in Boksburg, Gauteng Province, South Africa, on November 17, 1964. His father died when Moses was still a child and his mother then abandoned him and his two younger siblings. Shipped off to an orphanage in Kwazulu-Natal, Moses suffered systematic abuse, causing him to run away and head for Johannesburg.

Sithole grew up to be a handsome young man, who by all accounts had a string of conquests. Yet behind his glib line of talk and charming demeanor, a monster lurked, perhaps created by the anger he felt towards his mother for abandoning him. He wanted revenge and as his mother wasn't there, he directed his rage at the women around him.

No one knows when Sithole first began his campaign of terror, but the first rape that can be definitely attributed to him occurred in September 1987, when he attacked and sexually assaulted 29-year-old Patricia Khumalo. Three more rapes followed before he attacked Doris Swakamisa in February 1989. She reported the crime to police, providing a description that led directly to Sithole's arrest. Tried and found guilty, he was sentenced to six years in prison. He emerged in 1993, having served four.

Sithole had always maintained that he was innocent, and had spent four years inside seething at the injustice. To make matters worse, he'd been abused in prison, both physically and sexually, so that by the time he was released, he was angry at the world in general and women in particular.

Between January and April 1995, the bodies of four young women were discovered in Atteridgeville, west of Pretoria. All had been raped and strangled, and evidence found at the scenes suggested to police that the same man was responsible.

Unfortunately, it was only the beginning of the nightmare. Over the next few months, several more women were found raped and strangled in and around Attridgeville, all bearing the killer's macabre signature, their bodies discovered in open fields, strangled with their own underwear.

On July 17, 1995, Absalom Sangweni, a worker at a gold mine in Boksburg, east of Johannesburg, saw a man and a woman trespassing on mine property. He tried to warn them off but they ignored him and continued crossing the field, before disappearing into a grove of trees. A short while later, the man emerged alone.

Sangweni waited until the man had left before walking to the trees to see what he had been up to. He found the woman (later identified as 25-year-old Josephine Mlangeni) lying on the ground. She'd been strangled with her underwear. It appeared the Attridgeville killer had shifted his killing ground.

Facing mounting pressure in the media, the police established a special investigative unit to look into the series. A pattern quickly emerged. It appeared that many of the victims had told friends and family that they were going to see someone about a job. It looked like a promising lead, but it hardly helped to stop the carnage.

On September 16, 1995, a body was discovered at the Van Dyk Mine near Boksburg. Police units responded quickly to the call, but as crime scene experts began working the scene they made a horrific discovery. They had stumbled on a mass grave. Within the next 48 hours, 10 more bodies came out of the ground. In varying states of decomposition, some of them still wore the killer's grisly ligatures around their throats.

In the weeks that followed, the task force uncovered a promising lead. One of the victims, Amelia Rapodile, had told friends that she was going to see a man named Moses Sithole who had offered her a job. A job application form for an organization known as "Youth Against Human Abuse," was found in her possession. The police could find no official record of such an organization, but when

Sithole's name came up in connection with a second victim they knew they had a likely suspect.

The only problem was that they couldn't find Sithole. A massive manhunt was launched, but while the killer remained elusive, evidence of his handiwork kept showing up. When three more bodies were found over the next 10 days, the decision was made to release Sithole's details to the media.

With Sithole's identity now in the public domain, he must have feared mob justice (a not uncommon occurrence in South Africa) as much as he feared the police. Desperate, he contacted his brother-in-law and asked if he could provide him with a gun. A meeting was set up, whereupon the brother-in-law informed the police. They were lying in wait for Sithole when he showed up at a Benoni factory on October 18, 1995. During the scuffle that ensued, Sithole was shot in the leg and stomach.

Sithole was taken to a military hospital in Pretoria, where he remained under guard. While completing his recovery, he was interviewed by detectives and confessed to his crimes. Five days later he was charged with 29 murders.

Sithole went on trial in October 1996. Found guilty on 38 counts of murder and 40 counts of rape, he was sentenced to a total of 2,410 years. He is currently held at Pretoria's maximum security C-Max prison. Since his incarceration, he has been diagnosed HIV-positive.

12. Ahmad Suradji

Country: Indonesia

Confirmed Victims: 42

Suspected Victims: 70+

Indonesia is a country of contrasts. On the one hand, you have a burgeoning developing nation, typified by the skyscrapers of its capital city Jakarta. On the other, you have a country where old beliefs and superstitions persist, the reliance on witchdoctors for example. Such mystic advisors are commonplace in Indonesia and make a good living providing advice on matters such as money, romance, and health. And their clientele is by no means confined to uneducated, country bumpkins. Go to any shopping mall in urban Indonesia and you're likely to find a stall set up by one of these practitioners, usually several.

One such practitioner was Ahmad Suradji. Ahmad was a respected sorcerer living in Medan, the capital of the North Sumatra province. Many relied on his advice and his business flourished, so much so that he was able to buy a farm and become a cattle breeder. But like many in his profession, Ahmad was always looking for ways to increase his mystic powers. Then one night he had a dream that showed him how to do that.

In the dream, Ahmad was visited by his long dead father. The senior man told him that in order to access greater mystic powers, he'd have to kill 70 women and drink their saliva. Ahmad took the apparition at its word.

At the time, many of Ahmad Suradji's clients were women, either prostitutes seeking to make themselves more attractive to men, or ordinary women wanting him to cast spells that would make their husbands or lovers faithful. This was, of course, very convenient for the soon-to-be serial killer. He didn't have to go looking for victims. They came looking for him. Not only that, but they willingly participated in their own deaths, only realizing what Ahmad had in mind when it was too late.

Over the next decade, from 1986 to 1997, Ahmed committed at least 42 murders. His modus operandi seldom varied. He'd arrange for the client to meet him at his farm where he'd convince her to walk with him into the sugarcane fields. There, he'd have a pre-prepared hole dug and he'd ask the victim to step into it. He'd then bury her up to the waist. Don't worry, he'd say, this is all part of the ritual. However, once the woman was incapacitated, he'd loop a rope around her neck and strangle her to death. He'd then lick the saliva that had dribbled from her mouth during her death throes.

Once the woman was dead, Suradji would remove the body and bury it elsewhere on the farm, always close to his house with the head facing towards his homestead. This, he believed, would also increase his magical powers.

It seems incredible that 42 women could vanish after going to see Suradji and that no suspicion was attached to him. But, in this, Suradji was helped by the victims themselves. The police were not going to put in any great effort to find missing prostitutes. And as for the other women, most of them were embarrassed by the purpose of their visit to the witchdoctor and therefore kept it a secret from friends and family.

But Suradji was never going to get away with wholesale slaughter indefinitely. Eventually, the father of one of the missing women went to the police and voiced his suspicions about what had happened to her. Police officers then called on Suradji's farm and carried out a search, uncovering a recently buried, corpse. A more thorough search of the property yielded 41 more bodies, many of them mere skeletal remains.

Ahmad Suradji was arrested on May 2, 1997, along with his three wives. In custody, he confessed to murdering 42 women, ranging in age from 11 to 30 years. He seemed genuinely to believe that his motive justified the killings. He'd be proven wrong in that assumption. Both Suradji and his senior wife, Tumini, were charged with murder.

By the time the matter came to trial in April 1998, Suradji had changed his story. He now claimed that he'd killed no one and knew nothing about the bodies buried on his farm. His confession, he said, had been beaten out of him by the police.

But Suradji's mystical powers should have told him that such a defense was never going to hold up, especially as the victims' clothing and personal effects had been found in his house.

Ahmad Suradji was found guilty of murder on April 27, 1998. The sentence of the court was that he be put to death by firing squad. That sentence was eventually carried out on July 10, 2008.

11. Alexander Pichushkin

Country: Russia

Confirmed Victims: 48

Suspected Victims: 61

Russia has produced some horrendously prolific serial killers, most notably Andrei Chikatilo, a homicidal maniac who claimed 53 victims in the city of Rostov during the eighties. But in the early nineties, a killer emerged who challenged even Chikatilo's ghastly record. His name was Alexander Pichushkin and, if he is to be believed, he murdered 61 people between 1992 and 2006.

Like many serial killers, Alexander Pichushkin was a nobody. At 27, he was an alcoholic supermarket shelf packer who still lived with his mother and passed his time watching pornography and drinking vodka. He also had an unhealthy obsession with Chikatilo, plastering his bedroom with newspaper cuttings about the depraved killer.

By now, Pichushkin was already a killer himself. In 1992, he had bludgeoned a fellow student to death, a crime of which he had never been suspected.

For the next nine years, Pichushkin's murderous instincts lay dormant. No one knows why, but perhaps he found the act of murder not to his liking. Yet, who can tell what those intervening years did to his already damaged psyche, for by 2001, Alexander Pichushkin had developed a plan that was going to lift him from the drudgery of his mundane life. He was going to outdo his hero, Chikatilo.

Pichushkin scheme was diabolically simple. He was going to kill 64 people, one for each square on a chessboard. He had the perfect hunting ground too, the vast tract of forested land known as Bittsevsky Park lay right on his doorstep in southwest Moscow.

Over the next five years, 16 bodies were found bludgeoned to death in the park, in addition to the numerous people who simply vanished from the area. The police suspected a serial killer, but despite a series of massive operations, the "Bittsevsky Maniac" remained at large.

Then, in June 2006, there was finally a break in the case, when the horribly mutilated corpse of a 36-year-old woman was found lying in a stream in the park. She'd been bludgeoned to death and wooden stakes had been driven into her skull and eye sockets.

The victim's name was Marina Moskalyova, and her 15-year-old son was able to share some interesting information with the police. On the day of her death, Marina had phoned the boy to say that she was going for a walk in the park with a colleague from the supermarket where she worked. The man's name was Alexander Pichushkin.

Hauled in for questioning, Pichushkin readily admitted to killing Marina. But she wasn't the only one, he said. In fact, he'd murdered 61 people, more than Chikatilo. His only regret was that he'd fallen three short of his target before being captured.

The police were initially skeptical, but as Pichushkin talked, they began to give more and more credence to his confession. He claimed that he had killed mainly homeless men, many of whom were known to him. He'd employed a standard ruse to tempt them into the woods, telling them that he wanted to drink a toast to a favorite dog that he'd buried there. Unable to resist the promise of free vodka, the men had inevitably followed him. After they'd had a few drinks, Pichushkin would strike them from behind with a hammer, then bludgeon them to death. He'd then force sticks and shards of glass into the gaps that had appeared in the skull bone. He said that he particularly enjoyed the sound the skull made as it cracked.

Asked about the motive for the murders, Pichushkin said that killing people made him feel like God. "For me, life without killing is like life without food for you," he famously told his interrogators.

Any remaining doubt that the police had indeed captured the "Bittsevsky Maniac" was removed during the following days as

Pichushkin led them to various burial sites and revealed details of the murders that only the killer would know. He also provided an explanation as to what he'd done with the rest of the bodies. He said that he'd thrown them into the sewers, some while still alive.

This, too, had the ring of truth. One man had, in fact, been pulled out of a storm drain with severe trauma to his skull. He said that he'd been attacked by a hammer-wielding assailant.

But had Pichushkin really committed the 61 murders that he claimed? The police could only connect him to 49 and that was the number he would eventually be tried for.

Convicted on all counts in October 2007, he was sentenced to life in prison, with the first 15 years to be spent in solitary confinement. Russia had suspended capital punishment in 1996, failing which there is little doubt that Pichushkin, like his hero Chikatilo, would have been executed.

10. Gary Ridgeway

Country: United States

Confirmed Victims: 49

Suspected Victims: 70+

For almost two decades, from 1982 to 2001, an elusive killer preyed on prostitutes along the Sea-Tac Strip, between Seattle and Tacoma, Washington. The fiend first announced his presence with the murder of 16-year-old Leann Wilcox, on January 21, 1982. However, it would be six months before the police acknowledged that they had a serial killer on their streets. By then, six young women were already dead, and the killer was accelerating. By the time a fisherman discovered three bodies in the Green River on August 15 (the killer's 7th, 8th, and 9th victims) the police were already hunting the most prolific murderer in Washington's history. Little did they know, he was only just getting started.

In late August, 17-year-olds Kase Lee and Terri Milligan went missing; on September 15, it was 18-year-old Mary Meehan; five days later, 15-year-old Debra Estes. Linda Rule joined the list on September 26. Her remains would be found in January the following year.

The carnage continued into October when there was a new tweak to the killer's M.O. He was no longer confining himself to prostitutes, now he was targeting hitchhikers and runaways too.

Denise Bush, age 22, died on October 8, 1982; 17-year-old Shawnda Summers, the next day. In late October, Shirley Sherrill was gone. She was followed to the grave by Rebecca Marrero and Colleen Brockman before year's end.

After a short break, the Green River killer (as he was now being called) murdered 19-year-old Alma Smith on March 3, 1983. Then, as unlikely as it seems, he upped the pace of his killings, claiming eleven victims in just two months.

The police, meanwhile, were at a loss. A profile drawn up by famed FBI investigator, John Douglas, had gotten them no closer to their quarry (and would later prove to be largely inaccurate). They knew that the killer preferred certain dumpsites, but he always seemed one step ahead of them, switching sites whenever they got close. They knew also that there were ritualistic elements to the murders. Many of the victims had been found covered with foliage. Some had small, pyramid-shaped stones inserted into the vaginas. Other than that, the police had nothing. Not a print, not a fiber, not a sighting.

But that was soon to change. On April 30, Marie Malvar got into a dark pickup and promptly disappeared. Malvar's brother later obtained a description of the truck and went looking for it. He found the vehicle parked outside a house and passed the address on to the police. They questioned the resident, Gary Ridgeway, but he denied picking up Malvar, or any prostitute for that matter. The police believed him.

And still, the murders and disappearances continued unabated. Two women died in June, two in July, one in August. In September and October, the killer upped his pace again, claiming six victims. By the end of the year, another two women had been added to the growing death toll.

Something clearly had to be done to stop the carnage. In January 1984, a task force was belatedly assembled to look into the Green River killings. During the first few months it was in operation the force began reviewing its suspect list. By the time detectives got around to examining Gary Ridgeway's file, three more women had fallen prey to the killer.

Ridgeway was only on the list because he'd been questioned regarding the disappearance of Marie Malvar. He was not considered a high priority suspect. But investigators couldn't help noticing that he'd once been arrested for choking a prostitute. He'd also been picked up for soliciting sex from an undercover policewoman. Ridgeway was therefore asked to take a polygraph. He agreed and passed with flying colors.

In November 1984, Ridgeway again appeared on police radars after prostitute Rebecca Guay claimed that he'd tried to strangle her. The attack, Guay said, had happened two years earlier. Ridgeway was again questioned and readily admitted to the incident. In his version of events, he'd only choked Guay to subdue her, after she'd bitten him. Mindful that Ridgeway had already passed a polygraph, the police accepted his story and took no further action.

By 1986, the task force had focused most of its attention on a man named Bill McLean. Once McLean was cleared of any involvement in the murders they began to look again at Ridgeway. The Green River killings had by now slowed from their earlier fevered pace, but still Ridgeway managed to murder two women while the police ostensibly had him under surveillance.

In April 1987, task force officers carried out a raid on Ridgeway's home, vehicles, and work locker. They found nothing incriminating. Meanwhile, semen lifted from several of the victims had been sent for DNA analysis and had failed to turn up a match because the sample was too small.

In 1988, Ridgeway married his third wife. The Green River killings had in the interim come to a complete halt and the task force investigators had become convinced that their quarry had slipped the net, or had been killed, or jailed on another charge. They were wrong in that assumption. Although Ridgeway was by no means the killing machine he'd been a decade earlier, he committed at least two murders during the 1990's. 31-year-old Marta Reeves was murdered in March 1990, Patricia Yellowrobe slain on August 4, 1998.

But time and technology were about to catch up with Gary Ridgeway. In September 2001, semen samples were sent to the state lab to be tested again. DNA testing had advanced significantly over the intervening years and this time the samples produced a match – to Gary Ridgeway.

Ridgeway was arrested on four counts of murder on November 30, 2001, the charges eventually rising to 48 counts as police matched forensic evidence to their suspect. Yet despite the mounting evidence, Ridgeway continued to maintain his innocence until April 10, 2003, when he eventually broke down and confessed.

On November 5, 2003, Gary Ridgeway, then aged 54, admitted to the murders of 48 women, most of them killed between 1982 and 1984. The confession was part of a plea bargain in terms of which Ridgeway would avoid the death penalty and accept 48 life sentences without the possibility of parole.

He is currently serving those sentences at Washington State Penitentiary in Walla Walla.

9. Angel Makers of Nagyrev

Country: Hungary

Confirmed Victims: 45

Suspected Victims: 300+

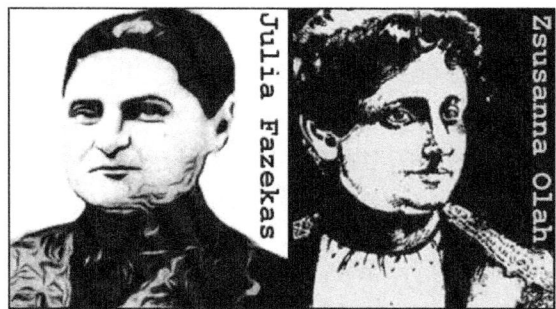

If the story of the "Angel Makers of Nagyrev" had been written as fiction, it would probably have been dismissed as fanciful nonsense. Yet, every word of this bizarre tale, of an entire village turned to wholesale slaughter, is true. It happened in a tiny rural enclave in Hungary during the early part of the 20th century. By the time it concluded at least 45 people, and possibly as many as 300, lay dead.

Nagyrev is an agricultural village on the banks of the River Tisza, about 60 miles southeast of Budapest. The people who lived there at the time of this story were of simple farming stock, deeply religious and set in their ways. Parents exerted firm control over their children, and husbands over their wives. When a young girl became of marrying age, it was her parents who chose her husband, often an older man. Once the wedding ceremony was concluded, rights of authority passed to the new spouse. He could sexually and physically abuse his young wife if he so chose, or come home falling down drunk every night of the week. And many did.

All of that was to change with the outbreak of World War I in July 1914. Hungary (at the time part of the Austrian-Hungarian Empire) sided with Germany and the Central Powers. Soon all able-bodied men were being shipped to the front, leaving Nagyrev denuded of its male population. Not for long, however, as the military powers decided that the village would be an ideal place to house Allied prisoners of war.

Security at the Nagyrev POW camp must have been particularly lax, because it appears that the prisoners had the virtual run of the village. It wasn't long before affairs had sprung up between village women and foreign prisoners. Spoilt for choice, many of the women took two or more lovers.

But then the war ended, the foreign soldiers were shipped off, and the men of Nagyrev came marching home. War had taken its toll on those who returned, some carried the scars and injuries of battle, others psychological trauma.

Most sought to find solace in the bottle. If they were aware of their wives' wartime shenanigans, they were prepared to let bygones be bygones. All they wanted was to return to the old ways, where a man worked the land, and his wife abided by his authority and submitted to his demands.

The wives they'd returned to, though, were not the same women they'd left behind. They'd had a taste of freedom and were not about to return to servitude. It was a clash of ideologies. Something had to give.

Enter Julia Fazekas, the unlikely protagonist of the story. Fazekas was a middle-aged midwife who had arrived in Nagyrev in 1911 bringing with her a daughter but, tellingly, no husband. Although an outsider, she quickly became an influential member of the community. Nagyrev had no resident doctor, so Fazekas became the town's de facto medical practitioner. She was also the go-to person for an illegal abortion. She had, in fact, been arrested on two occasions for performing such procedures, although sympathetic judges had let her off.

Now a stream of unhappy women was arriving at Fazekas' door, looking for birth control remedies and complaining about the rough attentions of their husbands. Fazekas listened sympathetically, then offered a solution. A problematic husband could be gotten rid of, she said, just like a problematic pregnancy.

Over the weeks and months that followed, Fazekas' humble cottage saw a steady flow of visitors. There, she and an associate, Zsusanna Olah, dispensed a deadly arsenic potion distilled by boiling flypaper and skimming off the lethal residue. They also provided advice on the correct dosage to ensure a swift death.

It was murder on an installment plan. Fazekas and Olah took 120 penges (about $20) as a down payment, 120 penges when the troublesome spouse breathed his last, and a final installment of

120 penges when the estate was settled. And there was no shortage of takers. It has been estimated that, at the height of the poisoning mania, there were no fewer than 50 poisoners operating in Nagyrev and the nearby town of Tiszakurt.

Soon it wasn't just inconvenient spouses that were being treated to the flypaper potion. Any annoying relative or neighbor might find themselves dispatched to an early grave. One woman, Marie Kardos, murdered her husband, her lover, and her 23-year-old son. Another, Maria Varga killed seven members of her family. She later testified that the death of her husband had been a Christmas present to herself.

With so many unexplained deaths in such a confined area, you might have thought that there would have been some kind of reaction from the authorities, but Fazekas had that covered. Her cousin was responsible for issuing death certificates in the town, so each of the deaths was recorded as "natural causes" or "accidental." It was good enough to keep nosy officials at bay for 15 years.

But a conspiracy this big was never going to stay under wraps forever. There are different versions about what eventually brought about the downfall of Fazekas and her brood of lethal women, the most popular being that the wife of a local official exposed the plot after trying unsuccessfully to murder her husband.

Whatever the case, in 1929, police officers from Budapest arrived in Nagyrev to question Fazekas and Olah. They, of course, denied any wrongdoing, but after the interrogation, the officers only had to sit back and watch as the women scurried from house to house warning their cohorts not to answer any questions. In doing so, they conveniently and unintentionally pointed out all of the poisoners to the police.

Thirty-eight arrest warrants were served the next day, with more over the weeks that followed. In the end, 26 women were put on trial for murder and eight were sentenced to death. All but two of those sentences were later commuted to life in prison.

The two women who eventually went to the gallows were Zsusanna Olah and one other. Some versions of events say that the second woman was Julia Fazekas. Others say that the poison priestess avoided the hangman by imbibing some of her own deadly concoction.

8. Anatoly Onoprienko

Country: Ukraine

Confirmed Victims: 52

Suspected Victims: 52+

They called him "The Terminator," an apt name for a killer who wiped out whole families with the efficiency of a Nazi death squad and left entire villages quaking in fear.

Anatoly Onoprienko was born in Laski, in the Zhitomirskaya district of Ukraine, on July 25, 1959. When he was just one year old, his mother died, and his father handed him over to relatives who cared for him for the next three years. At age four, he was placed in an orphanage, an abandonment that would later fuel his pathological hatred of families and impel him to commit serial murder.

At 17, Onoprienko joined the navy, serving a number of years. After his discharge, he enrolled as a forestry student at a local university. During this time he was also diagnosed with schizophrenia, but for the most part, his life appeared unremarkable.

All of that was to change in 1989.

Onoprienko was 30 before he claimed his first victim, relatively old by the standards of most serial killers. He and a friend, Sergei Rogozin, had formed a criminal partnership and begun robbing homes in the area. However, during one of these burglaries, they were surprised by the householders. Rather than risk arrest, they murdered the entire family, shooting to death two adults and six children.

A few months later, Onoprienko, now acting alone, killed five people who he found sleeping in a car, later burning their bodies. Among the victims was an 11-year-old boy.

Shortly after these latest murders, Onoprienko fled Ukraine and spent the next five years traveling around Europe. Not much is known about his movements during this time, but by his own admission he worked mainly as a manual laborer and supplemented his income by petty thefts.

He claimed not to have killed during this period, but experts consider it unlikely that his murderous urges would have lain dormant for so long. Nonetheless, there are no murders that have been definitely linked to him outside his home country.

By late 1995, Onoprienko was back in Ukraine, and about to embark on his bloodiest spree yet. On December 12, 1995, he broke into the Gamarnya home of a university lecturer named Zaichenko, killing the man, his wife, and two infant sons. Nine days later, he massacred four members of the Kryuchkov family, shooting them to death and setting their home alight. A man who saw him fleeing the scene was also shot and killed.

On January 5, 1996, two businessmen named Odintsov and Dolinin were gunned down while sitting in a car just outside Energodar. That same night a pedestrian and a police officer were shot to death in the nearby village of Vasilyevka-Dnelprorudny. The following day, three men were executed in their car, as they stood stalled on the Berdyansk-Dnieprovskaya highway.

The killer was in Bratkovichi again on January 17, where he murdered all five members of the Pilat family, before torching their home. Two witnesses to the crime were shot dead as he made his escape.

Four more victims, including a 28-year-old nurse and her two young sons, died at Onoprienko's hands on January 30, this time in Fastova. On February 19, he massacred the Dubchak family at their home in Olevsk. Father and son died from bullet wounds to the back of the head; mother and daughter were bludgeoned to death with a hammer.

Eight days later, in Malina, four members of the Bodnarchuk family met a similar fate, adults shot, children hacked to death with an axe. A neighbor of the Bodnarchuks died the same day, shot and mutilated in his home.

And still, the carnage continued. On March 22, Onoprienko showed up again in the village of Bratkovichi where he shot four members of the Novosad family before setting their house alight.

With villagers throughout the region in an uproar, the authorities eventually responded, dispatching a National Guard Unit and putting 2,000 police officers on the ground in an effort to catch the killer.

There was little doubt that the killings were connected. The killer always followed the same M.O., targeting isolated homes during the predawn hours, shooting or bludgeoning everyone present (even sleeping babies) then looting the home before setting it alight. Frequently, police would find family photos scattered on the floor, as though such mementos infuriated the killer.

A massive manhunt was now underway. But despite the numbers on the ground, the police were making very little headway. It seemed like only a matter of time before the killer reappeared to commit yet another atrocity. Then, on April 7, 1996, there was finally a break in the case.

At around noon on that day, a small town cop named Igor Khuney received an unusual call from a man named Pyotr Onoprienko, an officer at the Bratkovichi military base. Pyotr said that a long-lost cousin, named Anatoly, had been staying with him and his family for a few weeks but had been asked to leave after Pyotr had found him in possession of a stash of weapons. Angered by his eviction, Anatoly had made a veiled threat, saying that Pyotr and his family would, "pay by Easter." He'd then left, but Pyotr was concerned about his family's safety.

A less vigilant cop might have written it off as a family quarrel, but Khuney was interested to hear that Pyotr had spotted among his cousin's stash a 12-gauge, Russian-made Tos-34 hunting rifle. Such a weapon had been used in one of the recent massacres.

After obtaining an address for Anatoly in the nearby town of Zhitomirskaya, Khuney put together a squad of 20 men and set off for the apartment that Onoprienko shared with his girlfriend and her two young children. He immediately knew that he had his man when a tape deck found in the apartment was linked to one of the murder victims.

Once in custody, Onoprienko insisted that he would only speak to a general. He then gave a rambling confession, admitting to 52 murders, claiming that he had killed under instruction from "another world," and declaring himself, "the world's best killer."

Onoprienko's trial was much delayed. When he was eventually prosecuted in 1999, he was convicted of murder and condemned to death. The sentence would later be commuted to life in prison, but in Onoprienko's case that amounted to just 14 years. He died at Zhytomyr prison on August 27, 2013, having suffered a heart attack.

7. Andrei Chikatilo

Country: Russia / Ukraine

Confirmed Victims: 53

Suspected Victims: 56+

Andrei Romanovich Chikatilo entered the world in the village of Yablochnoye, Ukraine, on October 6, 1936. Born in the midst of Stalin's ill-fated land reform policies, he was familiar with hardship from an early age. It was an era when many desperate people resorted to cannibalism in order to survive. In fact, according to Chikatilo's mother, his older brother Stephan had been waylaid by some of their neighbors, killed and eaten. Whether the story was true or not it had a profound effect on young Andrei.

Chikatilo was an intelligent boy who preferred reading books to playing with friends. His effeminate demeanor made him an easy target for bullies. He was also a chronic bed-wetter, a habit that earned him regular beatings by his mother.

By the time he reached his teens, Chikatilo was a tall, gangly individual who was editor of the school newspaper and the student body's "political information officer." Those positions earned him some kudos from his fellow students, but he was still painfully shy, especially around girls.

At 18, Chikatilo applied to Moscow University to study law but failed the entrance exam. By then, he'd attempted a number of sexual liaisons with women, all of them ending in humiliation when he failed to maintain an erection. During his compulsory military service, he tried to force himself on a woman who had spurned his advances. The woman fought back and while Chikatilo struggled to subdue her, he became aroused and ejaculated. Afterwards, he reflected that the violence of the struggle had been more exciting to him than the sexual act.

After completing his national service, Chikatilo moved to the small town of Rodionovo-Nesvetayevsky, just north of Rostov, where he found work as a telephone engineer. While living here, Chikatilo's sister introduced him to a woman named Fayina, who became his wife. The couple would later have two children.

Not long after he married, Chikatilo enrolled in a correspondence course with Rostov Liberal Arts University. In 1971, he gained a degree in Russian Literature, a qualification that enabled him to find a position as a teacher at Vocational school No. 32 in Novoshakhtinsk.

Chikatilo was poor at his new job, lacking the necessary authority to control his students. He did, however, acquire a reputation for sexual harassment. In one notable instance, he was put in charge of a boys' dormitory, but was beaten up by a group of students after he was found fondling a sleeping child.

That incident led to Chikatilo being fired. Over the years that followed, he flitted from one teaching job to another, moving on whenever a new scandal arose.

In 1978, Chikatilo moved his family to Shakhty. Shortly after, he committed his first murder, luring a 9-year-old named Lena Zakotnova to a shack, where he raped and murdered her, later discarding her body in the Grushevka River. Chikatilo was questioned about the murder but released after his wife provided him with an alibi. Another man, Alexsandr Kravchenko, would eventually be tried, found guilty, and executed.

In 1981, Chikatilo was made redundant from his teaching job. Unable to find similar employment, he eventually accepted a position as a supply clerk at a local industrial complex, a job that involved regular travel. On September 3, 1981, almost three years since he'd killed Lena Zakotnova, Chikatilo claimed a second victim.

Larisa Tkachenko was 17 years old when she met Andrei Chikatilo at a bus stop outside the Rostov library. Chikatilo offered to buy her a meal and some drinks in exchange for sex and Larisa agreed. Once in the woods, he beat her into submission and then suffocated her by forcing dirt and leaves down her throat. He then bit off one of her nipples and ejaculated over her corpse before covering the body with branches. She was found the next day.

Over the next year, Chikatilo claimed seven more victims, five females and two young males. He then went to ground for six months, before re-emerging on June 18, 1983, to slaughter 15-year-old Laura Sarkisyan. Before the summer was over he'd claimed three more victims. Lyuda Kutsyuba, 24, an unidentified woman aged between 18 and 25 and a seven-year-old boy, Igor Gudkov.

By September 1983, with the victim count at 14, the Moscow militia, therefore, assigned one of their best investigators, Major Mikhail Fetisov, to the case. Fetisov quickly established that the murders had their epicenter around Rostov, and decided to base his team there, assigning operational command to the brilliant forensic analyst Victor Burakov.

Burakov's first move was to question every known sex offender in the area, particularly those of blood type AB, the type lifted from semen found at the crime scenes. Andrei Chikatilo was one of the men interviewed. But he was not considered a strong suspect, as his blood type was A.

In September 1984, a police inspector named Aleksandr Zanosovsky was patrolling the Rostov tram station when he spotted a middle-aged man wandering through the crowd. The man seemed to be paying particular attention to young girls, so Zanosovsky approached him and asked for his papers. The documents identified the man as Andrei Chikatilo. With no reason to detain him, Zanosovsky let Chikatilo go.

Several weeks later, Zanosovsky was patrolling the bus station when he spotted Chikatilo again. He pointed the man out to his partner and the two of them decided to keep him under surveillance. Over the next several hours, the detectives followed Chikatilo on and off trams and buses to various locations. At each place, Chikatilo approached random females and tried to strike up a conversation. At one point, an intoxicated young woman allowed him to fondle her breasts. Then the girl stood up and started shouting at him before stalking off.

After that incident, Zanosovsky approached Chikatilo and ordered him to open his briefcase. Inside was a length of rope, a jar of Vaseline, and a long-bladed knife.

Chikatilo was arrested and charged with harassment. While he was detained, the police began looking into his past, discovering his numerous sexual attacks on children, his ownership of the shack close to where Lena Zakotnova had been killed, his resemblance to the man in the initial police identikit. Zanosovsky was certain they had their man, but there was a problem. Chikatilo's blood type was A; the killer's was AB.

If only the authorities had taken samples of Chikatilo's hair and saliva, they'd have discovered that Chikatilo was, in fact, blood type AB. He fell into the small percentage of the population that are non-secretors. This means that his blood tested as type A, due to the low levels of antigens.

In 1985, Chikatilo started a new job, at a locomotive factory in Novocherkassk. This job too involved travel, but his close shave with the law seems to have shaken him up. It was August before he killed again, coaxing a mentally retarded girl from a train and hacking her to death in the woods near Shakhty.

In May 1987, he stabbed a 13-year-old boy to death in the town of Revda in the Ural Mountains. In July, he killed another youth in Zaporozhye in the Ukraine, and in September another young boy perished at his hands, this time in Leningrad.

Nine more victims died in 1988, most of them while Chikatilo was on his travels. A notable exception was the murder of 16-year-old Tatyana Ryzhova, murdered in Chikatilo's hometown of Shakhty.

By now, the police were noticing ever more extreme mutilations to the corpses they recovered. Several were missing body parts, usually the uterus and nipples in females, the genitalia in males. In addition, noses and tips of tongues were often sliced or chewed off. The victim profile was also changing. Chikatilo's early victims had been mainly female, seven of the last nine were boys aged between seven and sixteen.

One of those victims was 16-year-old Vadim Tishchenko, killed October 30, near Rostov's Leskhoz train station. After Tishchenko's body was discovered a ticket seller told police that he'd seen the boy in the company of a tall, older man, with glasses. The man was a regular traveler, the ticket seller said, and he'd often seen him on the station trying to engage young people in conversation.

The police net was closing on Andrei Chikatilo, but unfortunately it didn't close fast enough to save his final victim. 22-year-old Svetlana Korostik was lured into the woods near Leskhoz station, where she was beaten, stabbed and mutilated. Chikatilo cut off the tip of her tongue and both nipples and ate them at the scene. He then covered the body with leaves and branches before walking back to the station. As Chikatilo approached, a police sergeant spotted him and asked for his papers before letting him go. After Svetlana's body was found, Chikatilo was placed under surveillance and elevated to the top of the suspect list.

On November 20, officers saw him try to pick up two young boys and decided to make their move. They placed Chikatilo under arrest. The briefcase he was carrying contained a length of rope, a jar of Vaseline, and a knife with a long blade.

But Chikatilo wasn't about to be cowered or beaten into a confession. He maintained a stoic silence for nine days, only opening up after Dr. Bukhanovsky, a psychiatrist who had prepared a profile of the killer, won his confidence. Then, he stunned investigators by admitting to 56 murders, describing in chilling detail how he'd raped, brutalized and killed his victims, sometimes devouring their body parts and drinking their blood.

Andrei Chikatilo's trial began on April 14, 1992, and lasted three months, the proceedings frequently interrupted by the defendant's bizarre outbursts.   Eventually, on October 15, 1992, he was found guilty and sentenced to death.

Chikatilo was executed by a bullet to the back of the head on February 14, 1994, a much kinder fate than he'd given any of his victims.

6. Yang Xinhai

Country: China

Confirmed Victims: 67

Suspected Victims: 67+

China has produced a number of horrendous serial killers over the past few decades. None, however, is as prolific as Yang Xinhai, a demented psychopath who annihilated 67 victims over a four-year killing spree, hacking and bludgeoning with hammers, meat cleavers, axes, shovels, anything he could lay his hands on.

Yang Xinhai was born on July 17, 1968. As a boy, he was described as sensitive and intelligent, with a love of books. This went beyond reading. Yang also authored his own stories, filling every exercise book and scrap of paper with his meanderings, although he would allow no one to read them. When a relative sneaked a peak at the stories the boy was creating, he was shocked at its content. Yang had invented a fictional place that he called "Plato Heights," using it as a setting for stories of murder, mutilation, and mayhem.

There were other signs too that all was not right with Yang. He was prone to rambling to himself and to flying off the handle at the slightest provocation. A promising student when he was younger, Yang lost interest in his studies once he entered high school, eventually dropping out in 1985 and finding work as a laborer.

Out on his own, Yang hit the road, traveling between towns on foot or by bicycle, stopping wherever he found work, moving on whenever the mood took him. He also fell into a life of crime graduating from petty theft to burglary to rape. Inevitably, the law caught up with him. He was sent to labor camps on two occasions, in 1988 and 1991. Then, in 1996, he earned a five-year prison term for a rape committed in Zhumadian, Henan Province.

Yang emerged from prison in 2000, with a seething hatred against society. However, his anger was assuaged somewhat when he met a young woman and fell in love. The young lady appeared equally smitten at first, but when she found out that Yang had served prison time for rape, she dumped him. It was the tipping point, the spark that ignited Yang's homicidal fury.

Over the next four years Yang traveled constantly between the Chinese provinces of Henan, Anhui, Shandong and Hebei, leaving behind a trail of bloody destruction. His victims were usually farming folk whose homes he entered while they slept. He is known to have carried out 26 such attacks, claiming 67 victims, many of them women and children. On at least two occasions he wiped out entire families.

A typical attack occurred on December 6, 2002. The Liu family, Liu Zhanwei, 30, his wife, son, daughter, mother and father, were farmers from Liuzhuang Village in Henan's Xiping County. At the time of the attack they were in the process of moving to a new home and Liu Zhanwei's 68-year-old father, Liu Zhongyuan, had spent the night at the new residence, which he was readying for the family's arrival.

He returned to the family home the following morning and walked in on a scene of utter carnage. There was blood everywhere. His young granddaughter lay on the ground, a gaping hole in her head that exposed her brain matter. In another room, Zhongyuan found his son, daughter-in-law and grandson, all of them brutally bludgeoned to death. Only Zhongyuan's wife was still alive, but she'd been so severely beaten that she could only blink her eyes. She died in the hospital 10 days later. Police later found a pair of bloody white gloves at the scene, a signature of the "Monster Killer."

The police, of course, knew by now that a serial killer was rampaging through the provinces. But in common with other serial murder cases in China, the investigation was pitifully inadequate. The police appeared more concerned with protecting the image of the Chinese state than with catching the killer. The media was also prevented from reporting on the case. This too is common practice in China when dealing with serial murder cases.

Yang Xinhai might never have been caught but for a chance raid on a nightclub in Canzhou, Heibei Province, on November 3, 2003. One of the police officers thought Yang was behaving suspiciously and therefore took him into custody. Back at the station, Yang's prints were run, turning up a match to murder enquiries in Anhui, Shandong and Henan. It was only once DNA testing was carried out that the police realized they'd captured the elusive "Monster Killer."

On February 1, 2004, Yang appeared before the Intermediate People's Court in Luohe City and was found guilty after a trial that lasted less than an hour. He was sentenced to death, the sentence carried out by a bullet to the back of the head on February 14.

5. Daniel Camargo Barbosa

Country: Colombia / Ecuador

Confirmed victims: 72

Suspected Victims: 150+

Colombia has the highest per capita murder rate of any nation on earth, much of it politically and/or drug related. It has also produced three of the world's most savage child murderers. Pedro Lopez, the so-called, "Monster of the Andes," claimed the lives of over 300 young girls. Luis Garavito, dubbed "La Bestia" (The Beast), murdered a reported 400 victims during a seven-year rampage. And then there's Daniel Camargo, slightly less prolific than the other two, he nonetheless managed a staggering toll of 150 kills.

Daniel Camargo Barbosa was born in Bogota, Colombia on January 22, 1930. His mother died when he was still a young boy and his father delegated his upbringing to an abusive stepmother, who beat him regularly and often dressed him in girl's clothing. Unsurprisingly, given this mistreatment, the boy spend much of his time away from the family home and soon fell into a life of street crime.

In his early twenties, Camargo began a relationship with a woman named Alcira and had two children with her. At age 28, he fell in love with another woman, Esperanza, who he planned to marry. However, after discovering that Esperanza was not the virginal bride he wanted, he announced that he was leaving her and returning to Alcira. Esperanza begged him to stay and the two soon hit on a sickening compromise. He would stay with her, provided she helped him in procuring young virgins to have sex with.

The depraved couple soon developed an efficient but horrific M.O. Esperanza would lure the girls to her apartment with promises of work or food. Once there, the victim would be drugged with sleeping tablets and Camargo would then rape her, later releasing the bewildered and disorientated child onto the streets in another part of town. At least six victims were sexually assaulted in this way before one of them remembered enough to lead police back to Camargo's apartment. Both Camargo and Esperanza were arrested, with Camargo eventually convicted of sexual assault on April 10, 1964.

Camargo would serve his full term before being released in 1973. He showed up next in Brazil, but was deported after he was found to be without valid documentation. Back in his home country, he moved to the town of Barranquilla, where he set up a small business, repairing televisions. Soon after, the police began to notice a marked increase in the number of missing persons reports involving young girls.

In May 1974, Camargo was returning a television to one of his
customers when he spotted a 9-year-old girl walking along a
street. Luring the girl to a deserted building, he raped and then
strangled her before fleeing. It was only later that he realized he'd
left behind the TV he'd been carrying. Camargo returned to the
murder scene to retrieve the set and was arrested by the police.

Despite being a suspect in multiple homicides, Camargo was tried
with the rape and murder of only one victim. Found guilty, he was
sentenced to 30 years at the notorious Gorgona Island prison.

However, Camargo had no intention of rotting in jail for the next
three decades. In November 1984, he escaped, launched a crude
raft into the waves and made for the mainland. The breakout was
widely reported at the time, with authorities confidently
announcing that Camargo had either drowned or been eaten by
sharks. They were wrong. Camargo had spent years studying the
ocean currents from his cell window and had used this knowledge
to safely navigate to the coast of Ecuador.

Camargo made his way to Quito, then to the town of Guayaquil,
arriving there on December 6, 1984. Soon after, he set himself up
as a street vendor, selling ballpoint pens.

On December 18, he abducted a nine-year-old girl from the nearby
city of Quevedo. The following day, a 10-year-old disappeared
from the same area. Soon the pattern of disappearances that had
plagued Barranquilla would be repeated across Ecuador's Los Rios

province, the frequency so prolific that police at first believed that a criminal gang was responsible.

Camargo's M.O. was simple, yet effective. He targeted young, underprivileged girls, approaching them for directions to a church and promising a reward if they would show him the way. Usually, he'd flash a roll of bank notes in order to provide extra motivation. Once the girl agreed to guide him, he'd follow her until they reached a wooded area, then lure her into the woods on the pretense of looking for a short-cut, offering candy as an incentive. He'd then turn on the girl and rape her, then strangle her to death, sometimes hacking up the body postmortem. He'd usually leave the corpse where it lay, relying on scavengers to disperse the evidence.

Over a period of just fourteen months, Camargo was able to lure, rape and murder over 70 young victims in this way. And he might have continued indefinitely had it not been for a chance stop by police on February 26, 1986.

Unbeknownst to the officers, Camargo had killed a nine-year-old girl named Gloria Andino just minutes before they spotted him walking along the Avenue Los Granados. His actions appeared suspicious, so the officers stopped him and asked to check his bag. Inside, they found a bloody dress belonging to his latest victim, and a copy of Dostoyevsky's "Crime and Punishment."

Taken into custody, Camargo claimed that his name was Manuel Bulgarin Solis, and denied any wrongdoing. He impressed his inquisitors with his intelligence, quoting freely from Hesse, Vargas Llosa, Garcia Marquez, Nietzsche, Stendhal and Freud.

However, once the body of Gloria Andino was discovered and found to be clutching a candy wrapper bearing his fingerprints, Camargo confessed. He then shocked his inquisitors by claiming an additional 71 murders.

Over the weeks that followed, Camargo led the police to several undiscovered bodies, many of them bearing the signs of hacking and slashing with a machete. He claimed that he killed in revenge for the "unfaithfulness of women" and said that he chose virgins because he liked to hear them cry as he raped them.

Camargo was eventually convicted in 1989 and sentenced to 16 years in prison, the maximum allowable under Ecuadorian law. He'd never see out that term. He was stabbed to death by a fellow inmate on November 13, 1994. The assassin was Luis Narvaez, the cousin of one of Camargo's young victims.

4. Javed Iqbal

Country: Pakistan

Confirmed Victims: 74

Suspected Victims: 100

In early December 1999, a letter arrived at the Daily Jang newspaper in Lahore, Pakistan. "I have sexually assaulted 100 children before killing them," it read. "All the details of the murders are contained in a diary that has been left at my home. This is my confessional statement."

A near-identical letter had arrived at Lahore's main police station earlier that same day, but the authorities had paid scant attention to it. It was only once the police heard that the newspaper had sent reporters to the address that they responded. Within minutes, units were racing through the crowded streets of Lahore, sirens wailing.

By the time the cops burst into the small apartment, the reporters were already there, standing gape-mouthed and ashen-faced among the carnage. There were blood spatters on the walls, bloody handprints on the doorjamb. On the floor lay a length of chain, also encrusted with blood. Five large plastic bags were stacked against a wall, full to overflowing with children's shoes. More bags contained over a hundred children's clothing items. Then there were the photographs, piles of them, each documenting a victim in the moment before death, some of the boys as young as nine.

Each of these displays had been carefully arranged, a neatly stenciled sign tacked to the wall explaining its significance, as though the killer had turned his home into a macabre museum.

But the worse was yet to come. In the corner of the room stood a vat of acid, in which partially dissolved human remains bobbed near the surface. "The bodies in the house have deliberately not been disposed of so that the authorities will find them," read the placard above this exhibit.

As the police began reading the journals left behind by the killer, the sheer magnitude of the crimes came to light. He was claiming to have murdered 100 young boys, aged between nine and fifteen years old. What is more, he'd carried out his killing spree in just five months.

Now the hunt was on to find the killer. He'd identified himself in his letters as Javed Iqbal.

Javed Iqbal was born in Lahore, Pakistan in 1956, the pampered child of a wealthy merchant. From his teenage years, he began surrounding himself with a small army of young boys, as well as writing letters to hundreds of adolescent pen pals.

In 1980, Iqbal was arrested for sodomizing a teenager, although the charges were later dropped. Thereafter, his family began pressuring him to get married. He eventually did (in 1983) but the union lasted only two months. Iqbal was more interested in young boys.

Over the next decade, Iqbal started a number of businesses, a video games store, a tropical fish emporium, a gymnasium, all of them aimed at attracting adolescent boys.

Iqbal's father died in 1993, leaving him a hefty inheritance. He splurged on a large house and several cars. He also opened another video games store, this one bigger than any he'd owned before.

In September 1998, Iqbal was attacked by two boys who he'd previously assaulted. Severely beaten, he was rushed to Lahore General Hospital where he remained in a coma for 22 days. Upon his eventual discharge, he laid a complaint of robbery, claiming that the boys had stolen 8,000 rupees from him. The police dismissed his complaint. To add insult to injury, they then charged Iqbal with sodomizing the two youths.

Worse was to come. The cost of his medical treatment was expensive. Iqbal was forced to sell his house, cars and businesses to pay for it. In the midst of all this, his mother died, which Iqbal claimed was due to the stress surrounding his hospitalization and subsequent arrest.

Bitter and angry, Iqbal swore vengeance. He would kill 100 young boys, he decided, revenge for the perceived injustices dealt to him by society.

Working with four young accomplices – Sajid Ahmad, 17, Mamad Nadeem, 15, Mamad Sabir, 13, and another youth known only as Billa – Iqbal began luring young victims from Lahore's Mina-i-Pakistan Square in May 1999.

Convincing them to come back to his apartment was easy. The streets of Lahore literally teem with street children, willing to do almost anything to earn a few rupees.

Iqbal would drug them, sodomize them and strangle them with a length of chain. He and his accomplices would then cut up the body and dissolve it in a vat of acid, before dumping the residue in a local river. One hundred boys had met their fate this way and the authorities were not even aware that they were missing.

Now, though, the case was causing a huge uproar, with the public directing most of its anger at the corrupt and incompetent Lahore police department. Spurred into action, the cops launched the biggest manhunt in Pakistani history.

Iqbal had stated in his letter that he intended committing suicide by throwing himself into the Ravi River. The police dragged the waters without finding a body.

Meanwhile, Iqbal's four young accomplices had been picked up in Sohawa and subjected to a brutal interrogation, during which one of them died. Still, they failed to give up Iqbal's whereabouts. It appeared they genuinely didn't know where he was.

Iqbal might have remained at large indefinitely had he not decided to give himself up. On December 30, 1999, with police across the country hunting him, he walked into the offices of the Daily Jang and calmly surrendered.

Iqbal and his three surviving accomplices were tried for murder in early 2000. During the grueling trial, he changed his story, now claiming that it was all an elaborate hoax and that he hadn't killed anyone.

The court wasn't buying it. On March 16, 2000, Judge Allah Bakhsh Ranja handed down a sentence of death, ordering that Iqbal be strangled with the same chain he'd used to kill his victims. His body was then to be cut into 100 pieces and dissolved in acid. This barbaric sentence would never be carried out.

On October 8, 2001, Iqbal and his accomplice, Sajid, were found dead in their adjacent cells. Apparently, they had hanged themselves with bed sheets, although an autopsy would later reveal that they'd been severely beaten prior to death.

3. Pedro Lopez

Country: Colombia / Ecuador / Peru

Confirmed Victims: 57

Suspected Victims: 300 +

Pedro Alonzo Lopez, considered by many experts to be the most prolific serial killer of all time, was born in Tolmia, Colombia, in 1949, the seventh of thirteen children. His mother was a sadistic prostitute who beat her children at the slightest infraction. She eventually threw Pedro out onto the streets when he was just 8 years old, after catching him having sex with his younger sister.

Alone on the mean streets of Tolmia, fortune seemed to smile on the boy when an older man bought him a meal and offered him a place to stay. But the man was a pedophile. He lured Pedro to an abandoned building where he was beaten and repeatedly sodomized.

The attack, brutal though it was, probably saved Pedro's life. Over the months that followed, he remained wary of strangers, hiding in abandoned buildings by day, emerging at night to forage in dumpsters. Eventually, as his confidence grew, he took to the road and made his way to Bogotá, Columbia's capital and largest city.

Again luck was with him, within days of his arrival, a resident American couple found him scrounging on the streets and took him home with them. Over the next three years, they provided him with a home and enrolled him in school.

But in 1963, Pedro's faith in humanity was shattered again, when a male teacher sexually molested him. His trust in his newfound stability destroyed, Pedro decided to return to the streets, leaving without a word to his surrogate parents. He survived by begging and petty thievery. Eventually, he became a skilled car thief, with a steady clientele of chop shops.

But, as with most habitual criminals, Pedro's luck eventually ran out. Arrested in 1969, he was sentenced to seven years in prison.

Arriving as a naïve, 18-year-old, Lopez was soon initiated into the harsh reality of prison life. Two days after beginning his sentence, he was savagely beaten and gang raped by a gang of four inmates.

Lopez immediately began plotting his revenge. He stole a spoon from the prison mess and honed it into a razor-sharp shank. Within two weeks he'd knifed each of his assailants to death, four murders for which a meager two years was added to his sentence.

The murders had done something to Pedro Lopez. All of his life he'd been abused by other people. Now he'd finally struck back and it felt good. Combine that with the other issues gnawing at his psyche, his fear of women, his inability to connect with other people, his simmering hatred, his addiction to pornography, and it is perhaps easier to understand the monster that he would become.

Released from prison in 1978, Lopez took to the road, traveling widely throughout Columbia, Ecuador, and Peru. It was during this time that he began his killing spree, targeting young girls from the various indigenous tribes.

In northern Peru, he was caught trying to kidnap a nine-year-old Ayacucho girl, and might well have been killed but for the intervention of a local missionary.

Lopez was handed over to the Peruvian authorities, who sent him back to Ecuador. Within months the Ecuadorian police began to notice an increasing number of missing young girls. However, as the girls were mainly from peasant families, they failed to take action. It was widely suspected that the children had been kidnapped by sex slavers.

Then in April 1980, flooding near Ambato, Ecuador, caused the authorities to reassess that theory when rising waters unearthed the corpses of four missing girls.

Days after the flood, a woman was shopping at a market in Ambato when a stranger attempted to abduct her 12-year-old daughter. The woman's cries brought local merchants to her assistance and the man, Pedro Lopez, was apprehended.

By the time local police arrived at the scene, Lopez was babbling and incoherent, leading them to conclude that he was a madman. Back at police headquarters he clammed up and refused to speak.

Investigators tried a different track, putting a local priest, disguised as a prisoner, into a cell with Lopez. Under gentle probing from the padre, Lopez began to talk, his revelations so horrendous that the priest opted out after just one day.

Lopez said that he had murdered 110 girls in Ecuador, 100 in Colombia, and more than 100 in Peru.

"I went after my victims by walking among the markets," he said, "searching for a girl with a certain look on her face - a look of innocence and beauty. She would be a good girl, working with her mother. I followed them sometimes for two or three days, waiting for when she was left alone. I would give her a trinket like a hand mirror, then take her to the edge of town where I would promise a trinket for her mother.

"I would take her to a secret hideaway where prepared graves waited. Sometimes there were bodies of earlier victims there. I cuddled them and then raped them at sunrise. At the first sign of light, I would get excited. I forced the girl into sex and put my hands around her throat. When the sun rose I would strangle her.

"It was only good if I could see her eyes. It would have been wasted in the dark. I had to watch them by daylight. There is a divine moment when I have my hands around a young girl's throat. I look into her eyes and see a certain light, a spark, suddenly go out. The moment of death is enthralling and exciting. Only those who actually kill know what I mean.

"It took the girls five to fifteen minutes to die. I was very considerate. I would spend a long time with them making sure they were dead. I would use a mirror to check whether they were still breathing. Sometimes I had to kill them all over again.

"They never screamed because they didn't expect anything would happen. They were innocent.

"My little friends liked to have company. I often put three or four into one hole. But after a while, I got bored because they couldn't move, so I looked for more girls."

The police were initially skeptical of these admissions. But then Lopez offered to take them to one of his gravesites and all doubt was removed. In a remote area near Ambato, the remains of 53 young girls, aged eight to twelve, were uncovered. Thereafter, Lopez led investigators to various other sites and although no more bodies were found, the police surmised that the remains had been washed away by floodwaters.

Lopez was charged with 57 counts of murder. Found guilty, he was sentenced to life in prison.

On August 31, 1994, Lopez was released from his Ecuadorian sentence and handed over to the Colombian authorities. Charged with only a single murder in Columbia, he was found to be insane and sent to a psychiatric hospital.

That period of incarceration ended in 1998, whereupon Pedro Lopez was released on bail of $50 and promptly disappeared.

2. Luis Garavito

Country: Colombia / Ecuador

Confirmed Victims: 138

Suspected Victims: up to 400

Luis Alfredo Garavito was born on January 25, 1957, in the town of Genova, in the coffee growing region of Colombia. The eldest of seven sons, he endured severe abuse as a child, both from his alcoholic father and at the hands of a couple of pedophilic neighbors who regularly raped him. Unsurprisingly, given these conditions, the boy turned to substance abuse at a young age. By his teens, he was already and alcoholic. At 16, he quit school and became a drifter.

Over the decades that followed, Garavito ranged far and wide across his native land and also into Ecuador. He supported himself through menial jobs or by selling religious artifacts on the streets, blowing most of his earnings on booze. Garavito was a violent drunk, something that often got him into trouble. When that happened he'd simply hit the road to another town. Somewhere during that period he also turned his hand to murder, with devastating results.

It seems a strange quirk that three of the world's most prolific serial killers, Daniel Camargo, Pedro Lopez, and Garavito, are all Colombian. Yet, look below the surface of that South American nation and it is easy to see why. Each of these monstrous psychopaths preyed on poor, often homeless, children, many of them displaced by social upheaval and civil strife. Such children are a familiar sight on the streets of many Colombian cities. They are easy prey for a wily predator like Luis Garavito.

The disappearances of many of Garavito's victims went unreported, and those that were brought to the attention of the authorities received scant consideration. It was only once a mass grave was discovered in the province of Pereira in November 1997, that the police began to take the case seriously.

The grave contained the skeletal remains of 25 young male victims, many of them bearing clear signs of torture. Initially, the police refused to believe that the killings could be the work of one man and a number of outrageous theories –ranging from satanic cults to organ harvesters – were pursued.

But eventually, the task force began to pick up on other, similar cases. And then stories began to emerge of a dark-haired, green-eyed man with a scar on his left arm, trying to accost young boys in the areas where several of the murders had been committed.

There were other similarities too. The rope used to bind each of the victims' hands was of the same type. And most of the victims had disappeared between 10 and 12 in the morning, usually on a weekend. It appeared too much of a coincidence.

Working now on the theory that a single perpetrator might be responsible, detectives drew the next logical conclusion. Their suspect was highly mobile, therefore unlikely to have a fixed abode. Yet he must be staying somewhere. They began scanning the registries of cheap hotels and flophouses in the towns where the killings had occurred. Soon they picked up a name, Luis Garavito.

A nationwide hunt was launched for Garavito. Unbeknownst to police, their man was already in custody.

On April 22, 1999, a homeless man had observed Garavito trying to drag a boy into some bushes in the town of Villavicencio. He reported the matter to the police, who distributed Garavito's description. A couple of days later, he was picked up while walking along the road out of town.

Arrested on a charge of sexual assault, Garavito gave a false name, that of a minor politician from his hometown. When the falsehood was discovered a few weeks later, he stunned prison officials by admitting to 149 murders.

He'd begun killing in 1992, he said, and had committed murders in 54 towns and cities, using a number of different disguises to lure his young victims. At different times he'd posed as a priest, a beggar, a disabled person, a street vendor and a charity worker.

Garavito targeted boys aged between 8 and 12 years. He'd lure the victim with the offer of a job, offering inducements that included money, candy, alcohol or drugs. If the boy accepted, Garavito would take him on a long walk, ostensibly to the place where the work was to be performed. He'd wait until the child tired, then overpower him and tie him to a tree with a length of nylon rope. Then he'd sodomize the boy before slitting his throat. On several occasions, he tortured the child before dispatching him. Many of the victims were decapitated.

Luis Garavito was eventually tried for 172 murders and found guilty of 138, earning a sentence of 1,853 years. However, under Colombian law, a person may not be imprisoned for a period longer than 30 years. In addition, because Garavito had cooperated with the police in locating the bodies, he received a remission of 8 years, meaning that he'd spend just 22 years in prison.

1. Harold Shipman

Country: England

Confirmed Victims: 218

Suspected Victims: 250+

The world's most prolific serial killer, Harold Frederick Shipman, was born in Nottingham, England, on January 14, 1946, the middle of three children and his mother's favorite. As a young boy, he did exceptionally well at school, although his academic performance dropped somewhat in later years. In 1963, when Shipman was 17 years old, his beloved mother died of lung cancer. She was only 43 at the time, and Shipman nursed her through her final months. It ignited in him the desire to enter the medical profession.

In 1965, he went to study medicine at Leeds University, graduating in 1970. He then served an internship at Pontefract General Infirmary before entering work as a GP in Todmorden.

By now, Shipman was married and the father of two young children. He also proved to be an excellent GP, respected and well liked by staff and patients alike. But there was another side to

Shipman. He could be confrontational and rude. He seemed to enjoy humiliating people and had a childlike insistence on having his own way.

Shipman had been at Todmorden for two years when his career came to an abrupt halt. He began suffering blackouts, which he self-diagnosed as epilepsy. The truth was rather more sinister. He had become addicted to the morphine-like drug pethidine and had been making out fraudulent prescriptions. When this was discovered, he was fired from his job and charged with fraud and forgery. The penalty was ridiculously lenient – a £600 fine. He was also barred from working in any capacity that gave him access to drugs. When this censure expired in 1977, he re-emerged as a GP in Hyde.

As he had at Todmorden, Shipman quickly established himself as a valuable member of staff. His new colleagues at the Donnybrook Surgery respected his work, while the patients loved his friendly bedside manner. In 1992, he split from the Donnybrook practice to set up on his own.

Over the next five years, Shipman built up a steady roster of patients, many of them elderly. However, by 1997, suspicions had begun to surface. The staff at a local funeral parlor had begun to notice similarities in many of the deceased that were sent to them for burial. All of them lived alone and all were found fully dressed, sitting in a chair or lying on a couch. Perhaps more tellingly, all had been found dead by Dr. Shipman or had been visited by him shortly before they died.

At the same time doctors at the Brooke Surgery, just over the road from Shipman, were becoming concerned about the number of deaths at his surgery. Both of these parties passed on their concerns to the authorities. A subsequent covert inquiry found no evidence of wrongdoing.

Then in June 1998, a wealthy patient of Shipman's, Kathleen Grundy, died, leaving him her entire estate. The will, however, proved to be a crude forgery, casting suspicion on Shipman, who had visited Mrs. Grundy shortly before her death. An exhumation order was obtained, revealing copious amounts of morphine in the woman's body. That led the police to look more closely into the deaths of other Shipman patients. Before long, 15 bodies had been exhumed and Shipman was charged with 15 murders.

The first of these murders occurred on March 6, 1995, when Shipman injected Marie West with diamorphine. He claimed she died of a stroke.

On July 11, 1996, Shipman visited Irene Turner, administering an injection to treat a cold. The syringe, however, contained morphine and Mrs. Turner died soon after. Shipman listed cause of death as diabetes.

On February 28, 1997, Shipman attended 77-year-old Lizzie Adams at her home. When a friend of Adams' arrived during the visit, Shipman claimed that he'd found Adams dead. He attributed her death to pneumonia.

On April 25, 1997, Shipman called on Jean Lilley. A neighbor went to check on Ms. Lilley shortly after Shipman left and found her dead. Shipman said the 59-year-old had succumbed to heart failure. A pathologist later determined that she'd died of morphine poisoning.

Shipman killed Ivy Lomas, 63, at his surgery on May 29, 1997, and altered her medical records two days later to fit in with his diagnosis. Mrs. Lomas was a regular at his surgery and he often referred to her as a nuisance.

Muriel Grimshaw was found dead at her home on July 14, 1997. Shipman claimed she had died from a stroke and hypertension. He then altered her medical records to support his diagnosis.

On November 28, 1997, Shipman killed Marie Quinn with an injection of morphine. He claimed Mrs. Quinn called him saying that she'd had a stroke. He rushed to her home but she was dead when he arrived. Phone records show no calls to Shipman's surgery.

Shipman also claimed that he was summoned by Kathleen Wagstaff on December 9, 1997, although records show no such call. He said she died of heart disease, but no evidence was found of any such illness.

Bianka Pomfret died at her home on December 10, 1997, shortly after a visit from Shipman. He claimed she died of coronary thrombosis. Forensic experts later found that Shipman had altered the patient's medical records in order to create a backdated history of heart problems.

Norah Nuttall was visited by Shipman on January 26, 1998. Less than an hour later her son arrived to find his mother dead. Shipman said he had called an ambulance, then canceled it when he realized Mrs. Nuttall had died. Phone records showed that neither call was made.

Pamela Hillier, an active 68-year-old, was found dead on February 9, 1998. Shipman said she died of a massive stroke. It was later proven that he'd made 10 changes to her medical records to support this diagnosis.

Maureen Ward, 57, had been suffering from cancer but was in remission at the time of her death on February 18, 1998. Shipman recorded her cause of death as a brain tumor, then altered her medical records to suggest that the cancer had spread to her brain. A cancer specialist testified that this was not the case and that she'd died from a massive overdose of diamorphine.

Winifred Mellor, 73, was found dead on May 11, 1998, having been visited by Shipman earlier in the day. He claimed she had died of coronary thrombosis and altered her medical records to make it look like she had been complaining of chest pains.

Joan Melia, 73, visited Shipman's surgery on June 12, 1998, suffering from a chest infection. Later that same day, he called at her home and claims to have found her dead. He issued a death certificate citing pneumonia aggravated by emphysema. A pathologist later found evidence of morphine but no serious lung problems.

And finally, there was Kathleen Grundy. Shipman had visited her on the day of her death to take a blood sample, ostensibly for a study on aging. Unlike in the other murders, Shipman tried to profit from the crime with his falsified Will. It was to prove his undoing.

Harold Shipman went on trial at the Preston Crown Court on October 5, 1999. The evidence against him was overwhelming, yet he maintained his innocence to the end, offering up any number of ludicrous explanations for his actions. The jury wasn't convinced. On January 31, 2000, they found Shipman guilty of 15 counts of murder. He was sentenced to 15 life terms, with the recommendation that he never be released.

But that wasn't the full extent of Dr. Shipman's killing spree. A subsequent public inquiry put the number of victims at 215. Another investigation, conducted by University of Leicester professor Richard Baker determined that Shipman killed at least 236 of his patients. Either of those numbers easily makes Shipman the most prolific serial killer in history.

Harold Shipman died on January 13, 2004, hanging himself in his cell with a noose fashioned from a bed sheet.

For more True Crime books by Robert Keller please visit

http://bit.ly/kellerbooks

Printed by Amazon Italia Logistica S.r.l.
Torrazza Piemonte (TO), Italy

51988277R00271